West Africa
before the Colonial Era

The ancient city of Benin became famous for its artistic skills in sculpture of clay and metal. This is a rare royal head in ivory, dating from the 16th century. (Werner Forman Archive)

West Africa
before the Colonial Era
A history to 1850

Basil Davidson

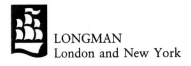

LONGMAN
London and New York

Pearson Education Limited
Edinburgh Gate
Harlow, Essex CM20 2JE
England
and Associated Companies throughout the world.

Visit us on the world wide wed at:
http://www.pearsoneduc.com

First published 1998

ISBN 0–582–31852–1 CSD
ISBN 0–582–31853–X PPR

Visit Addison Wesley Longman on the world wide web at
http://www.awl-he.com

British Library Cataloguing in Publication Data

A catalogue entry for this title is available from the British Library

Library of Congress Cataloging-in-Publication Data

Davidson, Basil, 1914–
    West Africa before the colonial era:
a history to 1850 / Basil Davidson.
        p. cm.
    Includes bibliographical references (p.   ) and index.
    ISBN 0–582–31852–1. — ISBN 0–582–31853–X (pbk.)
    1. Africa, West—History—To 1884. I. Title.
DT476.D35 1998   IN PROCESS
966′.02—dc21   97–48911
                                                  CIP

Printed and bound by Antony Rowe Ltd, Eastbourne.
Transferred to digital print on demand, 2003.

. . . .

Contents

List of Illustrations

List of Maps

Author's Note

This book is about the social and political history of the peoples of West Africa from early times until the European invasions and dispossessions of the nineteenth century: until, that is, the long period of European colonial rule which followed Africa's loss of independence. While drawing on our earlier *History of West Africa* (London, 1965 and many later editions), this is a new book, and conceived with readers outside West Africa especially in mind. But in presenting it I wish to pay tribute to many West African scholars, and above all to Professor J.F.A. Ajayi and Mr F.K. Buah, respectively of Nigeria and Ghana, whose pedagogical experience and scholarly vision did much to ensure the success of the earlier book.

Chapter 1

A Very Long History

A rock painting from Tassili n'Ajjer, Sahara, depicting a horse and two-wheeled chariot. (Werner Forman Archive and Musée Bardo, Algiers)

A Very Long History

We know from scientific evidence and calculation that Africa is among the oldest of the world's continents, and that it was there that humanity first evolved before spreading out across the world. Through countless forgotten centuries, modern Africa's remote ancestors developed all the variations of appearance, of skin colour, of ways and beliefs in everyday life. However ancient in its origins, much of this story is new in our western world of today. Up to quite recent years, the world knew little or nothing about Africa's extraordinary historical development. It has been mistakenly believed that the peoples of Africa have had no history of their own development. Therefore, it was said and widely believed that Africa's peoples must somehow be inferior in their nature and capacities to other peoples who do have that kind of history. This false belief has been one of the bases of the myths and misunderstandings of various kinds of racism.

Especially through the past half-century, the progress of modern scholarship and research has undermined all such myths, and has brought to light the realities underlying human evolution. This notable progress has been rightly hailed as one of the great liberating influences of our time. New sources of knowledge have made this progress possible. Scientific archaeology is one of these new sources. A fresh look at old books and records is another. A third, no less important, has been finding out what Africans think or remember about their past development.

This book is therefore about the political and social history, in pre-colonial times, of the vast and famous region of Africa known by historical and conventional usage as West Africa. Coined in Europe by Europeans, this old regional name has no exact geographical meaning. It is simply a handy term for all the lands (and the offshore islands) between about 20° of latitude north of the equator down to the West African coast, and eastward to about 15° of longitude.

Map 1.1 West Africa.

In another summary and familiar usage, the huge area known as West Africa is south of the Sahara Desert, although here again there is no exact meaning, for where does the Sahara begin and end? The old Arab geographers had more logic when they coined a name for the broad belt of territory where the true desert of the Sahara runs into and encloses the beginning of the grassland plains: they called it the Sahel, and this term, meaning 'shore', is still sometimes used today.

In this quite arbitrary but general way, all the lands of North Africa, meaning those bordering on the Mediterranean sea, are omitted, although these have had countless links with West Africa since desert travel first began several thousand years ago. Eastward, the old label again runs into

Map 1.2 Rainfall, vegetation, and areas affected by tse-tse flies in West Africa.

Legend:

- Total area affected by tse-tse flies
- Rain forest
- 120 cm / 240 cm / 360 cm / 480 cm Annual rainfall

**Map labels:**

N

Lake Chad

R. Benue

Kano

R. Niger

Timbuktu

Jenne

Niani

R. Senegal

Kong

Old Oyo

Ife

Benin

120 cm
240 cm
120 cm
240 cm
360 cm
480 cm

0   300   600 km

trouble, for where does West Africa end and East Africa begin? Convention disagrees with itself here, and compromise sometimes awards important countries such as Cameroun to West Africa, and sometimes not.

No doubt these definitions will continue to change as history proceeds along its way. The famous *West Africa* news magazine, now in its sixth decade of publication, still moves with the times and already does homage to relatively new pan-African loyalties and interests by allocating weekly sections to other African regions. But for our historiographical needs it will be best to stay with the old definitions of West Africa while recognizing their limitations.

While geographical definition remains fuzzy and illogical, that is not true of its temporal application. What we are concerned with in this book is not the whole of West African history but with large and important periods before about AD 1850: before, that is, the onset of the European imperialist invasions and dispossessions of the nineteenth century. For a while, after those invasions, Africans were dispossessed of the right and possibility of making their own history.

This impact of the outside world, meaning essentially Europe and North America, was profound and enduring. Intentionally or not, it carried Africans into a world greatly different from their own world of precolonial times. Yet that old African world retained its influence and value, for Africans are the children of their past as much as any other branch of humanity. In the case of West Africa, accordingly, it can make no sense to study the situation and events of today without first understanding the long and eventful centuries that came before the colonial dispossessions.

This is why the history in this book has a necessarily powerful value for understanding the history of today. Its long and wonderfully varied record opens the doors on centuries of past achievement. The story of West Africa in historical terms has formed a central part in the taming of this enormous and difficult continent for the benefit of humankind. But for the Western world in particular, the story of West Africa has a very special significance. For it was from West Africa that the ancestors of most of America's black people came across the Atlantic Ocean to settle and work in the New World.

While addressing the history of West Africa in the centuries before the European invasions and dispossessions of the nineteenth century, it will be helpful to stand back from recent centuries and consider, briefly, the distant origins and remote beginnings of humanity in this grandly productive region.

How many people, and how did they live?

Taking Africa as a whole, and summarizing a mass of more or less scientific data, we can say that the whole human population of Africa during the

Early Stone Age – up to, say, about 50,000 years ago – had managed to grow in size to perhaps 200,000 persons. No matter what the exact number may have been – and the figure here derives from various calculations or guesses as to the numbers of humans capable of self-sustainment before the times of any systematic agriculture – humanity remained rare and its stability more than fragile. The total is only an estimate, but useful.

These rare communities, spread across their vast continent, nonetheless survived and, very gradually, set about the challenge of taming their lands for human advantage. They left few or no records of their presence outside the narrow scope of archaeological remains, but our scientific linguists of today consider from their researches that these early peoples developed several distinct 'mother tongues' which, in time, became the 'distant parents' of Africa's principal language groupings, of which three – namely, Congo-Kordofanian, Nilo-Saharan and Afro-Asiatic – were to acquire dominant significance and developmental value.

But they acquired this significance and value in a very distant past. Most West African languages separated from their 'parents' an immensely long time ago. Emphasizing this 'time-depth' in a memorable lecture of 1964, the American specialist, Robert G. Armstrong, opined that 'the language ancestral to the Niger–Congo family of languages', sometimes referred to as Congo-Kordofanian, 'cannot have been spoken more recently than ten thousand years ago'.[1] This indicates just how ancient is the process of diversification in African language groups.

As these early peoples multiplied and spread across the untamed lands, they increased in numbers; and as they increased in numbers, so also did their cultures begin to vary and endlessly divide into new identities. So the scientific linguists tell us, if with due warnings against the dangers of oversimplification, that by the time Africa was entering the Late Stone Age, around 3,000 years ago (and none of these numbers must be taken too literally), there were in Africa perhaps three to four million people speaking 37 distinct African languages; and, of these, half or more inhabited West Africa south of the Sahara Desert.

All these various communities, however divided by the processes of cultural diversification, may be reasonably said to have evolved broadly common ways of life in a multitude of local variants dictated by a corresponding multitude of ecological necessities. The so-called 'ethnic' hostilities or outright conflicts of our own time (or indeed any other time) have been the product of one or other rivalry for some real or imagined local gain. That is why the majority of such conflicts have been short-lived and eventually resolved. It remains, at the same time, that territorial 'safety and possession' became factors of generally persuasive influence even if frontiers

---

[1] R.G. Armstrong, *The Study of West African Languages* (Ibadan University Press, 1964).

between communities – and eventually between organized state formations – remained in the forefront of consciousness. One needs also to bear in mind, in considering all such matters, the binding force of ecological hazards and barriers in the form of tropical forests, deserts, and the like.

And so it continued as Africans improved their skills and farming under sub-tropical and tropical conditions; and the great project of taming Africa for human benefit went forward in gradual but stubborn steps. The next great advance in the mastering of Nature came after about 600 BC, with the development and spread of the basic technologies of metal production and the forging and smithing of metal tools, notably in iron. In West Africa this crucial forward step was well installed in several localities – one, for instance, in the Benue valley (of modern Nigeria), and another in the upper regions of the Niger river – and the development of metal technology continued with the local evolution of types of forced-draught furnace and the comparable technologies of forging and smithing iron. At the same time, population numbers and their diversification into different cultural and linguistic groupings continued as before. The whole grand project of populating and inhabiting this 'empty continent' had long since become one of the outstanding successes scored by humanity in these early stages of growth.

Progress in African metallurgical skills, locally invented and locally developed, continued after about 600 BC through centuries labelled by historians as the African Iron Age; and it is this Iron Age that has given us the bulk of the historiographical record we examine in this book. The whole period of the Iron Age, continuing in one or other degree of innovation until very recent times, is immensely rich in its human drama, while the conquest of Nature moved from one stage to another, with successive generations building, against whatever setbacks and disasters, on the cultures of their ancestral forebears. And it is in this complex but nonetheless coherent and understandable process of diversification from common origins that we shall be able, with patient research, to perceive the origins of Africa's self-civilizing achievement, and come to grips with the cultural values of Africa's self-evolved historiography.

Here is where we can find the keys to elucidating otherwise opaque questions of mood and temper, or trace the source and spur of African attitudes which, for instance, have stubbornly combined a firm respect for precedent – for 'what our parents did before us' – with the restless, onward-shifting readiness for experiment that has marked all pioneers, everywhere, who have pushed 'beyond the known frontier' to where anything may become possible as long as human courage and endeavour are ready to make it so. The records of African history – of West African history in our study here – are copious and insistent on the side of custom and convention; but they are also strong on the side of new initiative. The rules for successful community life, we see, are there and are well recognized. But the changes and chances of fate may at any time overturn them; and then a person must be ready to change course or shift response, no matter what the precedents may say or the traditional customs may advise.

Ideas and beliefs

Among the keys we can use to understand the ideas of ancient peoples are those of religious or spiritual belief. Modern historiography, nourished by a vast quantity of scholarly research into the ethnography of ancient peoples, has recognized the central importance of their concepts of spiritual power. This is difficult and controversial ground to cross. But we can take, for a safe guide, the nature of these ancient and evolving communities as they grew out of the mysteries of the Stone Age, came to grips with the realities of food production (as distinct from mere food collection) in the Iron Age, and built new kinds of community.

What emerges from the records of research, centrally, is that all these peoples awarded supreme power to an idea of God as controlling everything and everyone, but doing this indirectly through subordinate spiritual powers. From this governing concept they derived – in a multitude of various ways of explanation – a ruling morality for everyday life: the power of God, they held, would always reward right behaviour and punish wrong behaviour. And from this morality they went on, again in a multitude of different elucidations, to conceive the instruments that spiritual power might use in fashioning rewards and punishments. These instruments were largely those of magical or quasi-magical power: the power of sorcery or witchcraft. Here once more is a subject of great complexity. The central fact is that the all-compelling morality of these structures of behaviour rested in its ability to reward good social behaviour and to punish the opposite; and these powers were exercised according to well-understood rules and maxims.

These ideas and beliefs, as we shall see, went together with inbuilt expectations, hopeful or otherwise, as to how people would behave in practice. When the Barotse of the Upper Zambesi valley, far into central Africa, created their rules for social behaviour they very carefully allowed for the conviction that persons with power over other people – chiefs and the like – would abuse or misuse this power unless prevented from doing so. They accordingly counterposed each power-position with another designed to limit the damage. The notion that pre-colonial society was a kind of free-for-all in which any person with power could exercise it in any way that he or she might wish is denied in our records; and the case of the Barotse, so well studied by Max Gluckman and his colleagues, affords obvious and yet by no means unique evidence of this.[2]

---

[2] Notably in M. Gluckman, *The Ideas in Barotse Jurisprudence* (Yale University Press, 1965).

We can think of pre-colonial Africa's humanity, in short, as occupying a kind of spiritual battleground between the ideas of Good and Evil. And in all this we have to make some effort to imagine the state of mind of pioneering peoples, migrating ever more distantly into unknown territories, as they met the difficult challenges of survival and development, and devised their practical and spiritual responses to them.

Climatic change and disaster

Meanwhile, through early centuries, some points of decisive change can be perceived. Early forms of civilization took shape in the spacious and well-watered grasslands and prairies of what afterwards – from about 2000 BC onwards – were to become the arid wilderness of the Sahara Desert we know today. These prairies became the focus of a New Stone Age that developed in the fifth and fourth millennia before the Christian era. The high point of this development saw the emergence, in about 3500 BC, of the splendid kingdoms of ancient Egypt.

But this whole epic of civilizing development in Egypt was accompanied by a climatic disaster which had great consequences for the wider development of Africa itself. From about 2000 BC there came a gradual change in the climate of the whole of this part of the world. From being a vast region of good rainfall and wide rivers flowing all the year round, the grassland plains of what is now the Sahara Desert plunged into a fatal and soon permanent dryness. The rains failed, the rivers dried up, the pastures turned to sand and stone. The peoples of these prairies were forced to find new homes, some to the north of the Sahara and others to the south. To the north of the desert the land of the Pharaohs, who ruled Egypt, continued to prosper and make progress. In science and arts this splendid civilization outmatched all rivals. The tragedy for Africans was that the huge, harsh deserts of the Sahara lay between Egypt and the rest of Africa.

Yet the 'cut-off' between northern Africa and the vast lands to the south of the Sahara Desert never became complete. As we shall see, nomad travellers and traders continued to find their way across the Sahara. Their chief trails became well known, even though great courage and endurance were required in order to use them. One of these chief trails, the western one, joined Morocco in North Africa to the grasslands of the western Sudan. This was not the country we know nowadays as the Sudan, in north-eastern Africa. In Arabic, ever more widely used in North Africa after the Muslim Arab conquests of the seventh century AD, the country south of the Sahara was simply the Bilad as-Sudan, 'the Southern Country'. Another famous trail, much further to the east, led from what is now Tunisia across the Hoggar mountains to the middle reaches of the River

Niger. Wells were dug along these trails; villages and towns sprang up in the oases that wells made possible. Here in these oases, once again, farming became possible, and some fruits could flourish, such as dates. Meanwhile, methods of transport improved and the horse or donkey gave way to the camel from Arabia, widely used for desert travel and transport from about 2000 years ago. Having broader feet, the camel could move better over sand, and it could walk much further without water than the horse.

Farming and the beginning of the Iron Age

Meanwhile the peoples south of the Sahara continued to develop and grow in number, as we know from archaeology. And these early peoples, very simple in their lifestyles as they may have been, possessed the keys to the future. They had already discovered how to grow food, as well as merely collecting or gathering edible plants. Now, several centuries later, came the next great discovery. And this development – or series of related discoveries – was to preside over the birth of the world we know today. As we have seen, they developed and exploited the use of metals, but above all of iron, for the making of tools and weapons. They initiated what historians, looking back on its achievements, have called the Iron Age.

The Ancient Egyptians had made bronze but not iron (save in very small quantities). Now it was found in the grassland countries south of the Sahara that iron ore was plentiful, and ways of smelting of the ore to obtain the iron from it were developed. Then new inventions or skills were used to forge the iron into tools. Gradually, archaeologists have pinpointed the places where the African metal-workers of the Iron Age developed their inventions. One of these centres of early iron-making was at Meroe on the Middle Nile river. At that time, around 500 BC, Meroe was the capital of a powerful kingdom – the kingdom of Kush. Another was in the region of the confluence of the Niger and Benue rivers, in Nigeria. Here was the centre of the Nok Culture, so named by archaeologists from its people's skill in making clay sculptures.

Other such centres of early iron-making have been traced to other parts of West Africa, but also right across the grassland belt of country to eastern and then to southern Africa. The surprising truth is that once the necessary technologies had been developed and used, these technologies passed from one Late Stone Age people to another in the course of only a few centuries. Inventing and adapting these technologies, African peoples of long ago were able to master the harsh wilderness of their continent and make it fit for human settlement and even for prosperity. This 'taming of a continent' through centuries of early human development composed, in the course of time, one of the grand achievements of early history. In that

11

Map 1.3   The Nok people lived in the area shown, and fragments of their work, in the shape of clay figures and other objects, have been found at the places marked.

period, Africans stood at the forefront of progress, and only the ancient Chinese came near them.

The revolutionary importance and value of iron – far tougher than the bronze that Ancient Egypt had made and used – were so great that the reasons for this value need some thought. A *first reason* was that it gave West Africans better weapons and tools. Iron-pointed spears were more useful than sharp sticks or stones. Iron-headed hoes, probably invented some time after iron-pointed spears, were better than stone or wooden ones. Iron-headed axes could fell trees and shape wood much better than stone or bronze axes.

These improvements in equipment made it possible to grow a lot more food. Having more food, people lived better than before. They became more numerous. But more people needed more farming land. Here lay a *second reason* why iron was important, and why its use marked the opening of a new stage of development. With iron spears and iron tools, Africans

12

could attack some of the great natural barriers of their continent. They could penetrate the deep forests, open new trails, defend themselves against wild animals, and generally move about with more safety. There are grounds for thinking that the Early Iron Age people of West Africa sent out many groups of wanderers, of migrants who moved from one homeland to a new one, through the forests of the Congo Basin and other distant lands.

Iron also brought, from about 600 BC onwards, *a new source of military power*. Those who first learnt to use it were able to rule their neighbours, especially if they also succeeded in keeping the secrets of its making to themselves. Stronger peoples began to rule weaker peoples.

And as people grew more numerous, there came a need to find new ways of ensuring law and order. Little by little, many peoples in West Africa began forming themselves into *states*. Men began to feel the need for organized *government*, and in this respect the great Egyptian precedent was again of new importance.

There were various reasons for this. With iron tools there could be more and better farming. With more farming there began to be enough food to maintain specialists who worked at making tools, weapons and other hand-made things. This *division of labour* encouraged trade, at first local and then long-distance, by producing a wide range of goods. All this, together with the growing size of populations, required more complex forms of political organization.

Early states were simple in their government compared with those we know today. Some were ruled by a single chief or king and his counsellors. Others were governed by a council of chiefs or elders. Others again were formed by several neighbouring peoples whose chiefs were bound in loyalty to one another. Elsewhere, at the same time, there were people who found it better to get along without any chiefs. Traditional groups such as clans, families descended from common ancestors, or age-sets of people born at about the same time, had influence in these early states, as in later times, because they could underpin a system of law and order. Of course it is important to remember that no one kind of state or community is more to be admired than another. A people with a strong central government was not necessarily more intelligent than another people who had no such government. The reason why there were different kinds of states, some with kings and some without, was that people lived under different conditions and faced different problems. They had to solve these problems in different ways.

The possibilities of *trade* were important in deciding what kind of states were formed. Most peoples who lived on the main routes of developing trade tended to form themselves into states with a central king or government. One important reason for this was that taking part in long-distance trade called for the kind of united decisions, especially on conditions of purchase and sale of goods, that a king or central government could

13

best take. But other peoples who lived far off these routes, and so had little interest in trade, tended to accept much looser forms of rule. They carried on living by the old family and clan customs of earlier times. All this belongs to the history of Africa's Iron Age, beginning in about 600 BC and continuing down to the threshold of modern times.

At this point the records of archaeology and of surviving tradition become sufficient to enable outlines of history to be written; and we see the gradual unfolding of early West African social structures. The general frameworks of that society become ever more clear. West Africans are seen to have been living, from some 2,000–3,000 years before the present, in recognizably distinct cultural groupings. They evolved forms and ideas of self-government that are clearly ancestral to those of later historical times, and even to those of today. As we shall see from the records that historians have been able to refine and assemble, West African life has long ceased to be predominantly rural. Early settlements developed networks of neighbouring villages or hamlets, while in some naturally advantaged regions, such as the confines of the broad valley of the great Niger river, village settlements grew into towns. There is plenty of evidence that these early towns had strong, coherent intercommunication, but the crucially developmental arts of writing, and thus of non-oral interchange, would appear only in later centuries, and then outside the influence of Ancient Egypt, through borrowing from Arabic-speaking neighbours.

All this has composed a rich and complex record. Our book here attempts to portray and explain some of the principal and decisive phases or stages of this West African history, concentrating on its main features while conveying some of its centrally decisive initiatives.

The Emergence of Trading States and Empires

The Emergence of Trading States and Empires

As we leave the beginnings of our history, sources of historical information steadily improve and widen, partly from the recording work and skills of the archaeologists of the past 100 years, and partly from the uneven but important records of Arab or Arabic-writing scholars since about the eighth century AD (the second century of the Islamic era). The pace of human development can be seen to quicken. A vivid picture of development over a long period of time begins to be available.

What has to be held centrally in mind is that this gradual mastering of a huge and often naturally hostile continent was a notable success. By the early centuries of the first millennium AD, African farmers had developed their techniques of tropical agriculture with repeated success and innovation, including important advances in ferrous technology. They had also developed a correspondingly appropriate range of cultural concepts that could and did reinforce the self-confidence and sense of corporate survival among these pioneering peoples in lands never yet occupied by humanity. All this enabled them, often with success, to meet new challenges from Nature and from the problems of living in community.

Between about AD 800 and 1600, or thereabouts, West African communities grew more numerous, developed new and more effective ways of enforcing law and order, and evolved new ways of self-government. Emerging cities grew in size and number, and in the wealth they could use and command. Specialized skills evolved with new kinds of craftspeople, politicians, priests, writers and men of learning. With their export and import trades servicing wider areas, trading cities and states grew into a valuable and much admired network of commerce that reached across the whole of western Africa and crossed the Mediterranean to southern Europe. The wider world began to hear about West Africa and its peoples.

These peoples were the forebears of those that live there today. Differing among themselves in languages, customs and beliefs, they nonetheless

17

all shared the same kind of history because they also shared the same kind of country: rolling plains or prairies dotted here and there with great baobab trees or shoulder-high thorn bushes, and watered by several big rivers, the greatest of which is the Niger, and their tributaries.

The names of these peoples remain well known in West Africa today, if otherwise much forgotten: the lordly Soninke along the banks of the Senegal river, the ingenious Malinke and their *dyula* specialists in the arts of trade, the devoutly independent Dogon on their hillside cliffs, the warrior Akan and their Yoruba and Igbo and other neighbours of the coastal forests, and, still famous, the Wolof of the far western lands of Takrur, who, later on, first had to outface and out-manoeuvre the incoming Portuguese and other seafaring Europeans bringing, as these did after about AD 1500, the perils and brutalities of an entirely new Atlantic trade in the export of African captives forced to serve as slaves.

All are present on our journey through this history of half a continent: priests and farmers, singers of heroic ballads, nameless men and women grappling with the demands and dangers of building new societies where none had existed before. Much of their hopes and deeds cannot be told here, for the story would be too long. As the Imam Ibn Fartua said of the deeds and hopes of the unforgotten Mai Idris Alooma, sultan of the famous kingdom of Kanem four centuries ago: 'We have mentioned very little, passing over much from fear of being lengthy and verbose. But the sensible reader will understand that beyond the stream there is the sea.'[1]

These peoples had their own names for their countries. The word 'Sudan' came initially from the Arab or Egyptian traders in these lands. It came into general use when the Berber-speaking peoples of North Africa began to adopt Arabic after the Muslim conquests in the eighth century AD. For them the grasslands south of the great desert became the *Bilad as-Sudan*, the Country of the Blacks; we call them the Western Sudan. These trading Berbers were intensely interested in the unknown country beyond the empty plains of the Sahara. They sent down trading expeditions and went into partnership with peoples of the west. In the course of time, leading peoples beyond the Sahara became strong enough to form large states and even empires.

Little was known or understood in Europe about this process of African state-formation. It was believed by European historians that nothing new was done in distant Africa unless it was brought by Europeans and their inventions. So it was thought that the big empires of the Western Sudan owed their origins to the traders of North Africa, who in turn had taken their progress from the traders of Europe. Modern archaeology has shown these ideas to have been wrong. In 1977 excavations by the US

---

[1] Ahmad ibn Fartua, *History of the First Twelve Years of Mai Idris Alooma* (about AD 1575), trans. and ed. by H.R. Palmer (Lagos, Nigeria, 1926).

archaeologists Susan and Roderick McIntosh at the site of an ancient city called Jenne (now within the new republic of Mali) showed that this city, today a humble town on a tributary of the great River Niger, had become a settlement of iron-making and iron-using people as early as the third century BC, long before any such activity and enterprise was thought to have existed there. This settlement at Jenne grew and prospered across ten centuries; above all, as the evidence of the McIntosh excavations amply demonstrated, as a centre of inter-regional trade across these wide grasslands. It evolved its own internal dynamic of civilizing development, in other words, long before the traders from North Africa had brought their influence. Jenne reached its greatest early development after AD 750, by which time the housing within its walls covered more than 33 hectares, a considerable size for an urban settlement of those times.[2]

At about the same period, notably in the 1960s, archaeologists were able to show that metal-making peoples of the Lower Niger region had also developed stable and important trades in bronze and copper, and then in iron, much earlier than Europeans had previously thought possible. This was confirmed by startling results from excavations undertaken by the British archaeologist, Thurstan Shaw, and published by him in 1970.[3] Bronze vessels of a wonderful ingenuity and technical skill were found to date from as early as the ninth century AD, showing once again that these trades, and their many consequences, were the product of unknown early cultures dependent on the regional stimulus of strongly local development.

From these early times, gold and ivory had been the West African products most in demand by the Berber traders who were still able to cross the Sahara after its desertification became severe. Trans-Saharan trade in these items helped to build the comfort and splendour of Phoenician and Roman cities on the Mediterranean coast, such as Carthage, Leptis and Sabratha. But the big and continuous expansion in the trans-Saharan long-distance trade came after the Muslim conquests of North Africa which took place in the eighth century AD.

This was a trade to everyone's advantage. The peoples of West Africa, for example, had one great need which the peoples of the Sahara, or those beyond the Sahara, could help to supply. This was salt. It is probably true that salt was no less valued by the peoples of West Africa than gold was by the peoples who lived to the north of the desert.

So the basis of trade between West Africa and the Berbers of the Sahara oases lay in the exchange of salt for gold. But this was only the basis of trade. The whole system became, with time, much wider, for the Saharan Berbers sold the goods they bought from West Africans to the Arab traders

---

[2] R.J. and S.K. McIntosh, 'The inland Niger delta before the empire of Mali', *Journal of African History* 22 (1981), p. 1.
[3] Thurstan Shaw, *Igbo-Ukwu* (Eastern Nigeria) (London, 1970).

of North Africa, and the traders of North Africa in due course sold them again to Europeans and Asians. European and Asian goods eventually came down into West Africa by the same methods of exchange.

Many other items were traded besides gold and salt. West Africa, for example, also needed copper, silks, and more metalware (such as pots and pans and swords) than West Africans could make themselves. West Africa also supplied ivory and kola nuts. Both sides bought a few slaves.

All this trade helped in the founding of cities. Most of these cities were especially concerned with the trade across the Sahara. They began as small trading settlements, but grew bigger as more traders came and went. They became centres for craftsmen who worked in leather, wood, ivory and metals. Then city governments were needed, as well as men trained to be put in charge of keeping accounts, of maintaining law and order, of looking after the safety of citizens. Then the rulers of these cities began to extend their power to ever wider regions of the neighbouring countryside. Gradually the cities grew into states, and the states grew into empires.

This long historical process, from trading settlements to trading empires, also occurred to the north and east of the Sahara. Trading settlements and cities also appeared in the stony lands of the Sahara itself. These were Berber cities. Some of them are alive to this day: Agadès, Ghat and Murzuk, for example. Others, like Walata and Tichitt, still exist but have lost their wealth and importance. Others again, such as Audaghost and Sijilmasa, have entirely disappeared.

The same process of city-founding and empire-building went on in the grasslands to the south of the Sahara. Here, too, some of the old cities of the Western and Central Sudan have disappeared, while others, like Timbuktu, Gao and Jenne, are still there. And the main business of these old cities of the Sudan was also to conduct the trade that came and went across the Sahara and was fed by the wealth of West Africa.

Perils of the Sahara

It was always hard and dangerous to conduct this trade. The Moroccan traveller Ibn Batuta has left a vivid description of how he crossed the desert in 1352. He tells how he travelled down from Fez to Sijilmasa, then one of the greatest of the market-centres on the northern side of the Sahara. There in Sijilmasa he purchased four months' supply of food for his camels. Together with a company of Moroccan merchants who were also travelling to the Western Sudan, Ibn Batuta journeyed on to Taghaza, a principal salt-producing centre of the great desert. At Taghaza, he tells us, 'We passed ten days of discomfort, because the water there is bitter and the place is plagued with flies. And there, at Taghaza, water supplies are laid on (by the caravan captains) for the crossing of the desert that lies beyond it, which is a ten nights' journey with no water on the way except on rare occasions.' Ibn Batuta continues:

> We indeed had the good fortune to find water in plenty, in pools left by the rain. One day we found a pool of fresh water between two rocky hills. We quenched our thirst at it, and washed our clothes.
>
> At that time we used to go ahead of the caravan, and when we found a place suitable for pasturage we would graze our beasts. We went on doing this until one of our party was lost in the desert; after that I neither went ahead nor lagged behind. We passed a caravan on the way, and they told us that some of their party had become separated from them. We found one of them dead under a shrub, of the sort that grows on the sand, with his clothes on and a whip in his hand ...

Many brave men died on those harsh trading journeys.

The trade continued in spite of all the dangers and difficulties. It brought many changes to all the peoples who had a part in it. This was the trade that shaped the growth of states and empires in the Western Sudan, foremost among which was Ancient Ghana.

Pioneers in Ancient Ghana

Pioneers in Ancient Ghana

As the McIntosh excavations at Jenne have revealed, West Africa's trading states in early times arose from a long and slow unfolding of farming and business development. But the origins of that development are lost to us in the mists of time. Only with the advent of written records can we begin to see through these mists that hide the distant past.

Written records of detailed value begin, for West Africa, with the work of highly educated scholars and travellers who were mostly of Muslim Spanish origin. Of these, the most useful for our subject here was a writer and researcher of Cordoba in the old Muslim Spanish kingdom of al-Andalus (nowadays Andalusia). This was Abu Ubayd al-Bakri. For much of his long life, this remarkable man worked and wrote in the wealthy and comfortable city of Cordoba and its near neighbour Almeria. He seems never to have travelled very far himself, but with great determination was always collecting and checking information from others who did.

What al-Bakri especially wanted to know was how people lived in the then hidden lands of the Western Sudan beyond the wastes of the Sahara Desert, information always difficult to get and then almost entirely unknown to Europeans. Happily for us, what al-Bakri learned about the Western Sudan and its peoples was set forth by him in a book of prime historical value, *The Book of the Routes and Realms* (in Arabic, al-Bakri's language, *Kitab al-Masalik wa'l Mamalik*), which was completed by him in Cordoba in AD 1068. Historians will not fail to note that this was just two years after the invasion of Saxon England by the Normans of France. So the written history of England, substantially, can be said to have begun around the same time as the written history of the Western Sudan.

The land of gold

The earliest of West Africa's big states was named Wagadu, known to the Berber traders of the Saharan market centres as Aoukar. But the world came to know it by the title of its king, which was Ghana. North African and other writers in Arabic began to mention this important state of Ghana during the eighth century AD. Soon after 770, al-Fazari wrote of it as 'the land of gold'. In about 830 al-Kwarizmi marked it on a map. And with al-Bakri, writing two centuries later, the picture becomes brilliantly clear.

The heart of this old and famous kingdom lay in its market centres. Their position, commercially, was a strong one. They stood at the *southern end* of important caravan routes from North Africa across the Sahara. But they also stood at the *northern end* of other trading routes which came, northward, from the gold-producing region of the Western Sudan. Their businessmen could obtain gold and ivory from their southern neighbours, and sell these goods to trans-Saharan and North African business partners. Being powerful in trade, they needed to be powerful in government as well. Their kings succeeded in this.

Other, although smaller, trading states arose alongside Ghana, which we shall call Ancient Ghana to distinguish it from the quite different modern republic of Ghana. By this time generally, many peoples in West Africa had advanced through early stages of civic development. They and their neighbours built the trading systems of West Africa, whether here in the grassland country or, southward, in the kingdoms of the West African forest belt near and along the coast. These forest kingdoms we shall visit a little later. Meanwhile, Ancient Ghana grew in wealth and strength.

The people who built Ancient Ghana were the Soninke, whose far descendants live in the modern republic of Senegal. The Soninke certainly built an effective state before AD 773, the date of the first North African reference to it. It is possible that they were traders in this region in very distant times. A tradition recorded in the *Tarikh as-Sudan*, an important history book that was written in Timbuktu in about AD 1650, says that there were 22 kings of Ghana before the beginning of the Muslim era (AD 622) and 22 kings after that. If this were true, it might place the origins of the Ghana kingdom in about AD 300.

By 800, in any case, Ghana had become a powerful trading state. Called Wagadu by its rulers, the name of Ghana came into general use because of one of the king's titles, *ghana* or war chief.[1] Each succeeding king was known by his own name, and also by the title of *ghana*. Another

---

[1] There are various reasons why the modern state of Ghana, though situated far away from Ancient Ghana, has the same name. The most important is that the modern founders of Ghana wished to celebrate the independence of their country – formerly the British colony of the Gold Coast – by linking their new freedom to the glorious traditions of the past.

of his titles was *kaya maghan*. This means 'lord of the gold', because the king controlled the export of that precious metal.

Nothing is known about the political methods or history of Ghana under its early kings. What probably happened was that heads of large families or descent-lines[2] among the Soninke, encouraged by the needs and opportunities of the trade in gold and other goods with Berber merchants of the Sahara, saw an advantage in having a single ruler, so they elected a king from among themselves. This king's duty was to organize the trade and keep good relations with the Saharan traders, as well as acting as senior religious leader and as representative on earth of the 'founding ancestors' of the Soninke people. In this way the king gathered power. He controlled the trade within Soninke territory. He made gifts and gave rewards to all who served him.

Next came an expansion of Soninke power over neighbouring peoples who were also busy with trade: the wider the territory the Soninke could control, the more prosperous they would be. By 800, the king of Ghana was able to make lesser kings or chiefs obey his laws and pay him taxes. And so the king's wealth increased. With more wealth, he also had more power. He could command the services of many descent-lines. He could raise big armies. He could employ large numbers of messengers and other servants. He could pay for the needs of a growing empire. All this we know from al-Bakri's careful account.

The achievement of Ghana

With the Arab conquests from Arabia in the seventh and eighth centuries, North African rulers and peoples began to accept conversion to the new religion of Islam, putting behind them the memory and many of the religious beliefs of their aboriginal cultures, including the Coptic Christian beliefs that had come to them, initially, from Byzantium. Whether by forced or voluntary conversion, Islam now increasingly held sway, although it would still be many centuries before Islam would become a majority religion.

Becoming Muslims in the ninth and tenth centuries, many of the Saharan long-distance businessmen began to be made welcome at the capital town of the reigning emperor of Ghana. But here there was no forced

---

[2] This term will be used often in these pages. A descent-line or lineage means just what it says: a line of family descent, through fathers or through mothers, which links one generation to another, and goes on for several or for many generations. This means that all the successive members of a descent-line look back to the same 'founding ancestors'. Nearly always, they revered these ancestors as persons of great authority and power in the world of the spirits.

conversion to Islam. There began instead a long, slow process of cultural adjustment to new realities, with the growing influence of Islam being of course among these. This emperor held fast to his ancestral beliefs, drawn from the ancient culture of the Soninke and their neighbours; but the advantages of the long-distance and trans-Saharan trade easily persuaded him to allow the Muslim visitors to build and inhabit a town of their own.

The 'town of the Muslim traders' was 10 kilometres away from the emperor's own town with its surrounding settlements. While the latter were built in the traditional materials of West Africa – hardened clay, thatch, and wooden beams – the most successful Muslim traders preferred to build their houses in stone, according to their own customs in North Africa. It is not known exactly where the capital was when al-Bakri wrote his book. In the course of Ghana's long history, the king's capital was undoubtedly moved from one place to another. But we can add a good deal to al-Bakri's picture by studying the remains of Ghana's last capital, which lay at Kumbi Saleh about 320 kilometres north of modern Bamako. Here too there was a town where the king of Ghana lived, and another town nearby where the Muslim traders had their houses and stables. At the height of its prosperity, before AD 1240, this city of Kumbi was evidently the biggest West African city of its day, and had as many as 15,000 inhabitants or even more.

So long as they obeyed the laws of Ghana and paid their taxes, the traders from the north were sure of safety and hospitality. This was a partnership in long-distance trade that went on for a very long time. Its safety depended on the strength of the emperor and his government. Al-Bakri has left us a description of all that. King Tunka Manin, he wrote, 'is the master of a large empire and of a formidable power'. So powerful was this king that he could put over '200,000 warriors in the field, more than 40,000 of them being armed with bow and arrow'. This was surely an exaggeration: the real strength of the Ghana armies, as we know from other North African sources, came from their power in iron-pointed spears.

Working from eyewitness accounts which he had received from Muslim travellers, al-Bakri described the pomp and majesty of King Tunka Manin:

> When the king gives audience to his people, to listen to their complaints and to set them to rights, he sits in a pavilion around which stand ten pages holding shields and gold-mounted swords. On his right hand are the sons of the princes of his empire, splendidly clad and with gold plaited in their hair.
>
> The governor of the city is seated on the ground in front of the king, and all around him are his counsellors in the same position. The gate of the chamber is guarded by dogs of an excellent breed. These dogs never leave their place of duty. They wear collars of gold and silver, ornamented with metals.

The beginning of a royal meeting is announced by the beating of a kind of drum they call *deba*. This drum is made of a long piece of hollowed wood. The people gather when they hear its sound . . .

These old splendours were long remembered among the peoples of the Western Sudan. As many as 600 years after al-Bakri, a writer from Timbuktu called Mahmud Kati entertained his readers with the stories of those ancient days. In his valuable history book, the *Tarikh al-Fattash*, he tells how a certain king of Ghana of the seventh century, called Kanissa'ai, possessed 1,000 horses, and how each of these horses 'slept only on a carpet, with a silken rope for halter', and had three personal attendants, and was looked after as though it were itself a king.

These old legends, magnified and embroidered with the passing of the years, also tell how the kings of Ghana used to give great banquets to their subjects, feeding 10,000 people at a time, and dispensing gifts and justice to all who came. Such stories give an idea of the greatness of Ghana's reputation in the years of its power.

Government of the empire

With the growth of Ghana, and of other states like Ghana, the peoples of West Africa were inventing new methods of living together, of governing themselves, of raising money to pay for government, and of producing wealth. These ways needed a single strong authority or government which could rule over many lesser authorities or governments. This central authority or government could only, in the thought and customs of the times, be a king.[3]

In states like Ancient Ghana, the power of government increased still further. Important kings became kings over lesser kings. They became what are called emperors. At the heart of the explanation of why this happened there was the growth of international trade. Occupying the lands to the north of the upper waters of the Niger, the old Ghana rulers and their people enjoyed a position of great power and value. Their towns and trading settlements became the middlemen between the Berber and Arab traders of the north and the gold and ivory producers of the south.

It was this *middleman position* which made Ghana strong and prosperous. It was this that gave its rulers gold and glory. It was this that paid

---

[3] Today, of course, a central government can be many things besides a king. In fact, kings have almost disappeared from the modern world. They have disappeared because *the stage of social organization*, which required kings in the old days, requires them no longer. People have invented better ways of self-government.

for its armies, and made its civilization shine with a light whose dazzling brilliance we can still glimpse in the writings of al-Bakri. Little by little, the people of Ghana and their rulers felt the need for a strong government not only over themselves, but also over their neighbours, so that they could ensure peace and order throughout a wide region of the Western Sudan. Only in this way could they make the best use of their middleman position. And at the same time as they felt this need, they also had the chance of realizing it. They were skilled workers in iron. They were able to use iron weapons against neighbours who generally did not have any.

Their system of government expanded with their success in trade. As it expanded, it became more complicated. A king and his counsellors could rule over a small country. They could not rule over a large one unless they could also rule through lesser kings and counsellors. Even with the swift horses of the Western Sudan, a king's orders would have gone too slowly through the land, and would not have been obeyed. So the king of Ghana needed governors whom he could place in charge of distant provinces.

In this way there grew up a number of lesser governments, under lesser kings or governors. These gave loyalty and paid taxes to a central government. Compared with what we have today, all this was a simple and crude sort of government. Ordinary folk ran many dangers. They were often bullied or plundered. But the growth and conduct of trade over a wide region meant peace and security over this region; and many people could benefit from this. The formation of Ghana and its growth into a large empire marked an important stage in social development.

Revenue and wealth of Ghana

Before leaving this subject we should look a little more closely at how the emperors ruled, maintained their public services, and met the expenses of keeping law and order. For they established ways of government which appeared again and again, afterwards, in the grassland countries of West Africa.

Where did King Tunka Manin and the kings who ruled before him find the wealth to pay many soldiers, and to feed and arm them? Where did they get the means to make rich gifts to strangers from other lands? Questions like these take us back to the economic system of the Ghana empire. And it is al-Bakri, once again, who gives us answers. He explains how the rulers of Ghana used their control of the long-distance trade.

The ruler of Ghana, al-Bakri tells us, had two main sources of revenue,[4] of wealth with which to pay for government. These were taxes of two

---

[4] 'Revenue' means the money or other kinds of wealth that governments get from taxes.

kinds. The first of these was what we should today call an *import and export tax*. This tax consisted of sums of money (or more probably their equal in goods) which traders had to pay for the right to bring goods into Ghana, or to take other goods out of the empire. 'The king of Ghana', wrote al-Bakri, 'places a tax of one dinar of gold on each donkey-load of salt that comes into his country'. But he also 'places a tax of two dinars of gold on each load of salt that goes out'. Similar taxes, higher or lower in value as the case might be, were applied to loads of copper and other goods.[5]

The second kind of tax was what we should call a *production tax*. It was applied to gold, the most valuable of all the products of the country. 'All pieces of gold that are found in the empire', says al-Bakri on this point, 'belong to the emperor'. But this regulation was more than a means of collecting royal wealth. It was also a way of keeping up the price of gold. For if the emperor had not insisted on taking possession of all pieces of gold, al-Bakri explains, then 'gold would become so abundant as practically to lose its value'.

Ancient Ghana, in short, adopted the monopoly system that is employed to this day for another precious commodity, diamonds. Most of the diamonds of the world are mined by a handful of big companies. These companies work hand-in-hand with each other. They have agreed among themselves not to put all the diamonds they mine on the market. If they did, they would drive down the price, for diamonds would then cease to be scarce; and what is not scarce is not expensive. Instead, the diamond companies sell their diamonds in small quantities, according to the demand for them, so their price stays high. The old emperors of Ghana did much the same with their pieces or nuggets of gold.

They were able to do this because of Ghana's strong trading position. West African gold was important to Europe as well as to North Africa and the Near East. In earlier times Europeans had obtained the gold they needed, whether for money, ornaments, or the display of personal wealth, from mines in Europe or in western Asia. These mines were becoming worked out at about the time of the rise of Ghana. Where else could Europeans and North Africans obtain gold? Only, as history shows, from West Africa.

And so it came about that the gold used in North Africa and Europe was largely supplied, century after century, by the producers of West Africa. Even kings in distant England had to buy West African gold before they could order their craftsmen to make coins in this precious metal. It was on this steady demand for gold that the states and empires of the Western Sudan founded their prosperity.

---

[5] The dinar was a gold coin of North Africa.

Ghana began the trade in gold. As time went by, other peoples began to copy Ghana's success. When Ghana disappeared in the thirteenth century AD, its place was eventually taken by another great empire built on the same foundations and by much the same methods. This new empire was called Mali. It carried the progress made under Ghana to a new level of development.

The fall of Ghana: the Almoravids

But a long period of confusion came between the fall of Ghana and the triumph of Mali.

After about 1050, Ghana began to be invaded by Berber warriors from the north-west, from the Mauretanian Sahara. These Berbers were driven by troubles of their own, mainly poverty, into striving for a share in the wealth of more prosperous neighbours. Soon after AD 1000 they began to look for a new means of livelihood.

The solution they found, as so often in history, took a religious form. There arose among them a devout and very strict Muslim leader called Abdullah Ibn Yasin. He established a centre of religious teaching, called a hermitage. He and those who followed him became known as the people of the hermitage, al-Murabethin, or the Almoravids. Gradually, Ibn Yasin brought the Berber communities of the far western lands under his influence. At the same time his missionaries set about the task of converting the rulers of those states in far western Africa whom they could reach, especially in Takrur (or Futa Toro), and in this they had some success. In 1056, moving northwards into Morocco, the Almoravids captured the great city of Sijilmasa, the main northern trading centre for West African gold. From there they went further to the north, conquering the rest of Morocco. Then they crossed the Straits of Gibraltar and took over al-Andalus, or Muslim Spain.

A southern section of the Almoravid movement meanwhile moved against Ghana. Its leader, Abu Bakr, put himself at the head of a Berber confederation, made an alliance with the people of Takrur, whom we shall discuss in a moment, and waged a long war against Ghana. In 1054 he took the city of Audaghost. In 1076, after many battles, the Almoravids seized the capital of the empire.

But these invaders, like others after them, could not hold the West African lands they had taken. There was much resistance. There were many revolts. Abu Bakr was killed while attempting to suppress one of these in 1087. By this time, however, the Ghana empire had fallen apart. Its last kings had authority over only a few of its former provinces, and we know almost nothing about them. Great changes were on the way.

Map 3.1 The Almoravid invasions.

The states that succeeded Ghana

In this time of confusion, set in motion by the Almoravid Berbers but soon bringing other peoples into action, the Ghana empire broke up, and some smaller states tried to build small empires of their own. One was the state of Takrur. Another was Diara. A third was Kaniaga. In some of these, a new name now enters on the scene, that of the Peul (or Pullo in the singular) whom in English we call Fulani (or Fulah in the singular).

These Fulani were to make several big contributions to West African history. The biggest of these will be described later on. Meanwhile we should note that the Fulani were and are a West African people of a somewhat different physical stock from most of their neighbours, but who spoke (and speak) a language related to the languages of Senegal.

They seem to have originated in the lands that lie near the upper waters of the Niger and Senegal rivers, and to have shared these lands with peoples like the Soninke who played a leading part in the formation of Ghana. They appear to have begun as cattle-keeping farmers, which is what many of them remain to this day.

When Ghana suffered the blows of Abu Bakr and his armies, the Fulani of Takrur (in the northern part of modern Senegal) became independent.

33

They in turn set out upon the road of conquest. After about AD 1200 they took control of the kingdom of Diara, once a province of Ghana. Their most successful leader, whose name was Sumanguru, seized Kumbi Saleh, then the capital of Ghana, in about 1203. Meanwhile other Fulani and allied peoples became powerful in another old Ghana province, the kingdom of Kaniaga.

But this new attempt at building an empire out of the ruins of Ghana met with no better fortune than the Berber efforts led by Abu Bakr. Two developments brought Sumanguru's enterprise to defeat. The first was that the Muslim traders of Kumbi Saleh, Ghana's last capital, rejected Sumanguru's overlordship. For reasons that were no doubt partly religious and partly commercial, they left Kumbi Saleh and travelled northward, to form a new trading centre at Walata, far beyond the reach of Sumanguru's soldiers. Secondly, and more important, in about 1240, Sumanguru was challenged by the Mandinka people of the little state of Kangaba, near the headwaters of the River Niger. The two armies fought each other at a famous battle, which is still remembered. Sumanguru was defeated and killed. His chiefs and generals retreated to Takrur.

Sumanguru's defeat opened a new chapter in history. For the little state of Kangaba was the heart and core of the future empire of Mali. It was to be the Mandinka people who would now bring peace and order to wide regions of the Western Sudan.

Summary of Ghana dates

Some time after AD 300	Origins of Ghana.
Soon after 700	New trade begins with Muslims of North Africa and Sahara.
About 1050	Ghana at height of its power. Al-Bakri describes King Tunka Manin (in 1067).
1054	Beginning of Almoravid invasion. Almoravids capture Audaghost, one of Ghana's important trading towns.
1076	Almoravids capture Ghana capital (probably Kumbi Saleh).
About 1203	Sumanguru takes Kumbi Saleh.
About 1240	End of Ghana empire.

The Majesty of Mali

Overleaf

The celebrated Cresques Atlas, made in Majorca in 1375 for the king of Portugal, showing caravan traders riding to the court of the emperor of Mali, with a stylised drawing of the emperor himself. (Bibliothèque Nationale)

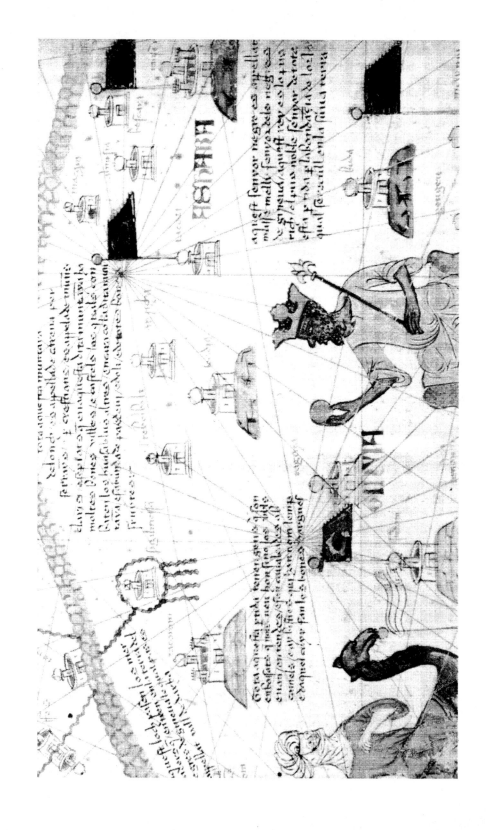

The Majesty of Mali

During all the centuries of the growth and development of Ancient Ghana, and continuing for a long time after the decline of Ghana in the thirteenth century AD, the peoples of West Africa were left to themselves: no external invasions or interruptions came to disturb their development or upset their ways of life. Neither Asia nor Europe could exercise any influence.

This would change after the Portuguese, followed rapidly by other European powers, found out how to sail across the ocean, and, with newly developed shipping and navigational skills, became able to reach the peoples who lived a long way south of the Mediterranean Sea. This, as we shall see, happened in the fifteenth century AD.

Before that time of revolutionary change, the life of West Africa was touched by no great external influence. The great magnet of external attraction for West Africa lay in North Africa and in its Muslim extension in al-Andalus, the Spanish country we call Andalusia. But it lay above all in the splendid city of Cairo, capital of Egypt and, far more importantly, fashion-setter and model of everything that civilization could at that time promise or provide.

This may sound to us, today, like something of a simplification, but it remains essentially true. The evidence for its truth is to be found in the books written at that time, and first and foremost in the great Arabic texts of the Middle Ages, composed chiefly by the scholars of al-Andalus.

Among these old records, the most impressive and in some ways the most complete in its scholarship and scholarly vision is the work of Ibn Khaldun (1332–1406). He was in a real sense the successor of the al-Bakri who had written centuries earlier about Ancient Ghana. Like al-Bakri, Ibn Khaldun never travelled south of the Sahara, a forbidding and perilous natural barricade in those days as it is today; but his history books remain a precious and often wonderfully detailed guide to the life of northern and western Africa in his time.

Ibn Khaldun took his standpoint in the greatest African city of his period. This was Cairo, a city he admired immensely and knew at first hand, as, in his own words, 'the metropolis of the universe and the garden of the world, the throne of castles and palaces adorned with monasteries and colleges', all these being 'lit by the moons and stars of erudition'. If this is not at all the Cairo of today, it is certainly the Cairo in whose prestigious streets the echo of Ibn Khaldun's words, if you will listen patiently, can still be heard upon the winds of history.

This being so, we can confidently take our stand also in that distant Cairo, and look out southward to what was then continuing to unfold in the lands beyond the Sahara and across the wide savannahs of the Western Sudan. Ibn Khaldun and his colleagues of long ago have given us reliable information. Their guidance will take us through one of the great periods of West African development.

Following Ancient Ghana's lead, great systems of imperial power took their rise over the whole period from AD 1200, with the decline of Ancient Ghana, until 1700 and even later. Their record of civic achievement, with all the contradictions of freedom and oppression that have always gone together with imperialist systems of power, remains a central feature of all that happened here.

With the decline of Ancient Ghana came the upsurge and development of the empire of Mali.

Kangaba and the origins of Mali

The old traditions of the Western Sudan suggest that Kangaba, the little state that was to grow into the mighty empire of Mali, was founded some time before AD 1000. What is certain is that the Mandinka people of Kangaba were also middlemen in the gold trade during the later period of Ancient Ghana. They were important among those who carried the gold of Wangara, the gold-bearing country that is now the northern part of the republic of Guinea, to the market centres of Ghana. It was through these gold-traders of Kangaba that the rulers of Ghana and their agents were able to secure their main supplies of gold.

In later times the traders of Mali, the Dyula or Wangara as they are still called, would become famous for their skill and enterprise. There is reason to think that they were similarly active in the days of Ancient Ghana as well. It is likely that while Kangaba was a subject country of the Ghana empire, perhaps sending yearly gifts to its ruler in exchange for friendly protection against enemies and rivals, the traders of Kangaba enjoyed positions of privilege within the empire.

There was a two-sided interest here. The government of Ghana needed gold, and it was largely from Wangara that Ghana's gold must come. But the traders who dealt in the gold of Wangara also needed a market, and it was only in Ghana that they could find this market.

When the empire of Ghana was split into pieces by attacks from without and revolts from within, this peaceful system of two-way interest was destroyed. All was then in the melting-pot for new rivalries for power. Eventually, as we have seen, Sumanguru prevailed. Once Sumanguru had mastered Kumbi Saleh and the main caravan routes, it was with him and his agents that the Mandinka of Kangaba had to conduct their business.

Yet Sumanguru, as we have also noted, was never able to set up a firm and lasting system of law and order over the lands he had conquered. Others challenged his power. The caravan routes ceased to be safe and peaceful. And no doubt the people of Kangaba, whose livelihood was thus threatened and who were increasingly oppressed by Sumanguru, were troubled by all this. In about 1240, at any rate, they decided to enter the struggle themselves. They made a bid for their own independence, and they won.

Growth of Mali

The legends tell the story in more colourful and one-sided terms. They speak of Sumanguru's harsh taxation, of his bad government, of his seizure of Mandinka women. These abuses caused the Mandinka to revolt. Fearing reprisals by Sumanguru, who had a frightening reputation as a dangerous magician, the ruler of Kangaba fled. But the situation was saved for him by a brother whom he had exiled. This brother was Sundiata Keita. Returning from exile with an army, Sundiata gathered friends and allies, increased his forces, gave them fresh heart and courage, and marched boldly against the dreaded Sumanguru.

'As Sundiata advanced with his army to meet Sumanguru', say the old legends that are still remembered,

> he learned that Sumanguru was also coming against him with an army prepared for battle. They met in a place called Kirina [not far from the modern Kulikoro]. When Sundiata turned his eyes on the army of Sumanguru, he believed they were a cloud and he said: 'What is this cloud on the eastern side?' They told him it was the army of Sumanguru. As for Sumanguru, when he saw the army of Sundiata, he exclaimed: 'What is that mountain of stone?' For he thought it was a mountain. And they told him: 'It is the army of Sundiata, which lies to the west of us.'

39

Map 4.1 The expansion of the empire of Mali (very approximate frontiers).

Then the two columns came together and fought a terrible battle. In the thick of the fight, Sundiata uttered a great shout in the face of the warriors of Sumanguru, and at once these ran to get behind Sumanguru. The latter, in his turn, uttered a great shout in the face of the warriors of Sundiata, all of whom fled to get behind Sundiata. Usually, when Sumanguru shouted, eight heads would rise above his own head.

But Sumanguru's witchcraft, the legends say, proved less powerful than the witchcraft of Sundiata. Sumanguru was struck with an arrow bearing the spur of a white cock, fatal to his power, and 'Sumanguru vanished and was seen no more . . .' After this victory, Sundiata became the master of a new empire, governing through powerful and able men who were the heads of leading Mandinka descent-lines, each with a province under his control.

The capital of Kangaba at this time was at a place called Niani, a city that has long since disappeared but was located near the River Niger, not far from the frontier of modern Guinea and modern Mali. And from about this time the name 'Mali', which meant 'where the king resides', absorbed the name Kangaba, and the empire of Mali was born.

40

The rulers of Mali

Sundiata was the founder of the empire of Mali, but not the first of Mali's kings. This was Barmandana, who is said to have ruled in about 1050. He became a Muslim, and made the pilgrimage to Mecca that all Muslims are supposed to make at least once in their lives. He was followed by other kings of whom we know nothing but their names.

Sundiata, sometimes called Mari-Diata, came to the throne in about 1245. He ruled for about 25 years, doing great deeds.

Next came his son Uli, who also took the royal title of *mansa* (lord in the Mandinka language), and followed in the conquering path of his more famous father. He ruled from about 1260 to about 1277. Like other Mali kings, he made the pilgrimage.

Then came two of Uli's brothers, Wati and Khalifa, but we do not know the dates of their reigns. They were said to be weak kings who ruled badly. Khalifa's subjects revolted against him and killed him. Power then passed to Abu Bakr who ruled until 1298.

In 1298 the throne was seized by a freed 'slave of the court'. This was Sakuru who proved one of Mali's strongest rulers. He held power till 1308. After him came *Mansa* Qu and *Mansa* Muhammad.

In 1312 another great ruler came to power, *Mansa* Kankan Musa. He ruled till 1337,[1] and was followed by *Mansa* Magha, who ruled for about four years, and then by *Mansa* Suleyman, who ruled with much success till about 1360. Then came another Mari-Diata who ruled for about thirteen years, and was followed by other kings of less importance. By about 1400 the great period of the Mali empire was drawing to a close.

The achievement of Mali

Mali repeated the achievement of Ancient Ghana on an even greater scale. Its rulers secured or regained control of the gold-producing lands of Wangara and Bambuk. They invaded most of Diara to the north-west. They pushed their power down the Niger river to the shores of Lake Deba. They formed one of the largest empires in any part of the world of that time.

Three periods of success occurred:

1 Under Sundiata (about 1235–60). He founded the empire.
2 Under *Mansa* Sakuru (about 1298–1308). He extended the
  empire. 'Under his powerful government', wrote the great North

---

[1] The year of Musa's death is often given as 1332. But Ibn Khaldun, whose writings are our best source of information on the dates of the rulers of Mali, recorded that Musa was still alive in 1337.

African historian, Ibn Khaldun, in about 1400, 'the power of Mali became mighty. All the nations of the Sudan stood in awe of Mali, and the merchants of North Africa travelled to his country.'

3 Under *Mansa* Kankan Musa (about 1312–37). He again extended the empire. His success was maintained by *Mansa* Suleyman (about 1340–60).

Mansa Kankan Musa

When *Mansa* Musa came to power, Mali already had firm control of the trade routes to the southern lands of gold and the northern lands of salt. Now Musa brought the lands of the Middle Niger under Mali's rule. He enclosed the cities of Timbuktu and Gao within his empire. He imposed his rule on trans-desert trading towns such as Walata. He pushed his armies northward as far as the important salt-producing place called Taghaza, on the northern side of the great desert. He sent them eastward beyond Gao to the borders of Hausaland. He sent them westward into Takrur.

So it came about that Musa enclosed a large part of the Western Sudan within a single system of law and order. He did this so successfully that the Moroccan writer Ibn Batuta, travelling through Mali about twelve years after Musa's death, found 'complete and general safety in the land'. This was a big political success, and made *Mansa* Musa one of the greatest statesmen in the history of Africa.

The Dyula (Wangara) traders were greatly helped by all this. Their trading companies began to travel in many parts of West Africa. These Dyula traders were men of skill and energy. But they also drew strength from being Muslims. Belonging to Islam gave them unity. They stuck together even when members of their trading companies came from different clans or territories.

Like the Mali kings before him, Musa was a Muslim. But most of his people were not Muslims, so he supported the religion of the Mandinka people as well as Islam. Different religious customs and ceremonies were allowed at his court.

Musa's pilgrimage to Mecca became famous. He began it in 1324. His magnificent journey through the Egyptian capital of Cairo was long remembered with admiration and surprise throughout Egypt and Arabia, for Musa took with him so much gold, and gave away so many golden gifts, that 'the people of Cairo earned very big sums' thanks to his visit. So generous was Musa with his gifts, indeed, that he upset the value of goods on the Cairo market. Gold became more plentiful and therefore worth less, and so prices rose.

The North African scholar, al-Omari, who lived in Cairo a few years after *Mansa* Musa's visit and wrote about it, declared that of all the Muslim rulers of West Africa Musa was 'the most powerful, the richest, the most fortunate, the most feared by his enemies and the most able to do good to those around him'. Behind these words of praise we can glimpse the power and reputation that Mali drew from its control of a very wide region of trade in precious goods such as gold, salt, ivory and kola nuts.

Mali was now a power of more than local or even regional significance. Under *Mansa* Musa, Mali ambassadors were established in Morocco, Egypt, and elsewhere. Mali's capital was visited by North African and Egyptian scholars. On returning from pilgrimage, Musa brought back with him a number of learned men from Egypt. These settled in Mali and Timbuktu. One of them, called as-Saheli, designed new mosques at Gao and Timbuktu, and built a palace for the emperor. The fashion of building houses in brick now began to be popular among wealthy people in the cities of the Western Sudan.

Niani, the capital of all this empire, has long since disappeared. Yet as late as the sixteenth century, the Moroccan traveller Leo Africanus (Hassan ibn Muhammad al-Wazzan az-Zayyati) could still describe it as a place of 'six thousand hearths', and its inhabitants as 'the most civilised, intelligent and respected' of all the peoples of the Western Sudan.

The spread of Islam also called for new methods of rule. *Mansa* Musa opened courts of law for Muslims, alongside the old courts of law for those who were not Muslims.

The government of Mali

Like Ghana before it, Mali was ruled by kings who were the heads of important descent-lines or leading families (see note on page 27). The kings ruled the different parts of the empire, called provinces, through governors; these governors were also the heads of local descent-lines. As well as these people from important families, who were persons of privilege because of their birth, the king had some officials who did not come from important families. Some of these came from families who 'belonged' to the king because they had lost their civic rights, usually through being captured in wars. Later on, as we shall see, such 'slave officials', or 'king's men', were to get more power.

In the capital, at Niani, there were various top officials. Most of these were noblemen: that is, they came from important families. One was the *hari-farma*, in charge of the fishing on the Niger. Another was the *sao-farma*, responsible for looking after the forests of the empire. A third was the *babili-farma*, the king's 'minister of agriculture', just as the *khalissi-farma* was the 'minister of finance'.

This was a more complicated kind of government than Ancient Ghana's. Populations had grown in size; trade was bigger than before; society had become more complicated.

Rivals and successors

But the very success of this far-reaching empire was also a reason for its decline. The spread of metal-working and of trade, the growth of the ideas of kingship and of strong central government, the pressures of wealth and trading rivalry – all these and similar influences stirred many peoples in West Africa. Some of these peoples saw that there were new advantages in being free to run their own affairs. The ruler and people of the city of Gao, for example, had to pay taxes to the emperor of Mali. Now they became determined to be rid of these taxes. They believed they could do better on their own.

The truth was that Mali had outgrown its political and military strength. Only supremely skilful leadership at the centre could hold this wide empire together. *Mansa* Musa commanded that skill; his successors, generally, did not. For a while, all remained well with the empire, especially under the rule of *Mansa* Suleyman (about 1340–60). Then the good days were over. *Mansa* Mari Diata II, who followed Suleyman, was described by Ibn Khaldun as 'a bad ruler who oppressed the people, depleted the treasury, and nearly pulled down the structure of the government'. He was followed by several other rulers who did little better than he had done.

Mali remained a powerful empire until about 1400. Then it ran into a host of troubles. Gao rebelled. The Tuareg nomads of the southern Sahara, always hoping to win control of the market cities of the Western Sudan, seized Walata and even Timbuktu. The peoples of Takrur and its neighbouring lands, notably the Wolof, threw off their subjection to Mali. Others in the south-western region of the empire, especially the Mossi in what is now the modern republic of Upper Volta, began to harass the emperor's governors and garrisons.

Yet the grand old system, now more than 200 years old if we reckon its life from the time of Sundiata Keita, still enjoyed widespread respect. Many peoples had grown accustomed to thinking of the Mali *mansa*, the Mali *koy*, as their rightful overlord. The habit of thinking this was slow to die. And so it came about that the fame and reputation of this once wide system of imperial rule lived on for a long while after it had become weak and defenceless.

Even in the time of the powerful Songhay emperor, *Askia* Muhammad (1493–1528), the traditional frontier of Songhay and Mali was still recognized as running through the region of Sibiridugu – astride of the upper

Niger, that is, in the neighbourhood of the river-city of Segu. And Niani, the capital of the old empire, was still a large and prosperous city. Commercially, too, the traders of Mali, the famous Dyula companies, were the most enterprising and successful merchants of all the western and central regions of West Africa. They travelled far and wide, across the plains and through the forests, trading even on the distant coast of central Guinea.

But the political power was mostly gone. As early as 1400 the Songhay ruler of Gao is said to have pillaged Niani itself. In 1431 the Tuareg rushed into Timbuktu. By the end of the century Mali had no power to the east of Segu. Even within his homeland, the Mali emperor could seldom do more than stand aside and let things happen. Yet he certainly tried. In 1534 he sent an ambassador to the coast for help from the Portuguese, with whom he and his predecessors had enjoyed good diplomatic and trading relations. But the king of Portugal was unable to help. The time was still far ahead when Europeans would be strong enough to have any direct influence on the affairs of West Africa.

Chapter 5 . . . .

Songhay Achievement

Songhay Achievement

As the political and military strength of the Mali imperial system gradually declined, others came forward to build a new system. These others, by about AD 1450, were a people of the Middle Niger region whose principal centre of trade and influence was the city of Gao. For a long time, in our own modern era, the circumstances in which the Songhay people became able to dominate their neighbours remained somewhat mysterious. Who were their early rulers? How did they rise to power?

The importance of Gao

Not many years ago an important archaeological discovery was made at the village of Sané, near the ancient city of Gao on the middle reaches of the Niger river. There came to light some old tombstones of Spanish marble, with Arabic characters beautifully carved on them. When they had been cleaned and read, the inscriptions showed that these were the tombstones of kings who had ruled over Gao many centuries ago.

'Here lies the tomb of the king who defended God's religion, and who rests in God, Abu Abdallah Muhammad', explains one of these inscriptions, adding that this king had died in the Muslim year 494, or AD 1100.

This was a valuable discovery. It provided the oldest examples of writing so far known in West Africa. It also provided the only certain knowledge so far available about the foundations of the state of Gao, later to become the heart of the famous empire of the Songhay people.

These tombstones reveal three interesting points. They show that:

1 Gao was strong enough by the eleventh century to have become a state ruled over by prosperous kings;
2 these kings had become Muslims;
3 they had extensive trading links with North Africa, and even had their tombstones brought from Muslim Spain.

The evidence of the early history of the ancient city of Gao, as it has come down to us through the books of seventeenth-century writers in Timbuktu, does not always agree with the evidence of the tombstones: the actual names of the kings on the tombstones are not the same as the names recorded from oral traditions. Otherwise the traditions greatly help to expand the three certain points that are proved by the tombstones. They confirm that Gao became a southern centre for trans-Saharan trade before AD 1000, and, secondly, that Gao had long since become a state on its own.

The traditions also show that the Songhay people established themselves at Gao at the beginning of the seventh century, pushing out the Sorko people who already lived there. But Gao was not yet their capital: this was at Kukya, further to the east, where their *dias* or kings ruled. These Songhay were enterprising traders and welcomed Lemtuna (Berber) travelling merchants from the Adrar oases to the north of them. Through these merchants the caravan trade across the Sahara, and with the Songhay market-centres, prospered and grew.

At the beginning of the eleventh century – and this is where the tombstones once again confirm the traditions – the ruling Songhay king, whose title and name were *Dia* Kossoi, was converted to Islam. According to tradition, this happened in 1010. Soon after this, the capital of Songhay was transferred from Kukya to Gao, and Gao entered upon its period of growth.

Just why *Dia* Kossoi accepted Islam, and with how much sincerity, there is no means of knowing. But probably he saw in his conversion a useful way of gaining more influence with the Berber traders, who were all Muslims, and upon whose caravan skills he and his people greatly relied for their trade. Like other Muslim kings in the Western Sudan, then and later, *Dia* Kossoi and his successors tried not to let their acceptance of Islam become offensive to their own people, who generally continued to believe in their local religions. *Dia* Kossoi even maintained court customs that were not Muslim: he tried, like many other rulers in the Sudan of those days, to combine his new position as a Muslim leader with his traditional position as a leader of Songhay religion.

Many *dias* ruled after Kossoi. Gao began to expand its power beyond the lands immediately round the city. One reason for this was that the value and size of the trans-Saharan trade were growing all the time. This growth increased the power and importance of Gao, whose position was very favourable for trade.

Map 5.1 The expansion of the empire of Songhay (very approximate frontiers).

Three hundred years after *Dia* Kossoi's reign, Gao was so valuable that the great Mali ruler, *Mansa* Musa, sent out his generals and armies to bring it within the Mali empire. Apart from the wealth of Gao, *Mansa* Musa had other reasons for doing this. He and his governors already commanded the southern end of all the caravan routes across the western region of the Sahara. By securing Gao as well as Timbuktu, they could now command the southern end of important routes across the whole Western Sudan. This helped to strengthen the system of tax-collecting on which the government of Mali depended.

But this system, as we have noted, was too wide for Mali's strength. It could not last. And Mali's overlordship of Gao lasted in fact only for some 50 years. In about 1335 the *dia* line of kings came to an end and gave way to a new line, whose title was *sunni* or *shi*. The second *sunni*, whose name is given in the traditions as Suleiman-Mar, won back Gao's independence from Mali in about 1375. Nearly a century of varying fortunes then followed for the people of Gao. After that they entered another period of expansion. Having defended themselves from their neighbours and rivals, they began to push far outward on the path of conquest.

This expansion was especially the work of a remarkable leader whose title and name were *Sunni* Ali. Like other great rulers before and after him, *Sunni* Ali came to power in a time of confusion and set out to build a large and unified system of law and order, central government, and peaceful trade.

51

The growth of Songhay: *Sunni* Ali

The Songhay people of today number fewer than one million, most of whom are farmers and fishermen along the banks of the Niger between the area of Timbuktu and the north-western borders of Nigeria. They play their part in the political life of the modern republics of Niger and Mali, but have long ceased to have a separate state of their own.

Yet their state in the sixteenth century was the largest in West Africa. The Songhay conquered many other peoples both north and south of the Niger; and their achievements hold a leading place in history. These achievements were to some extent due to their favourable position along the great river, which gave them good communications and chances of trade. But they were also the work of the Songhay or Songhay-controlled trading cities such as Gao, Timbuktu and Jenne. To the advantages of their position the Songhay repeatedly added vigour and intelligence in political ideas and organizational methods. *Sunni* Ali was their first outstanding leader after the *dia* line of kings of Gao.

Anyone who travels in the Songhay country today will find the name of *Sunni* Ali, better known as Ali Ber, or simply as the *Shi*, remembered still with honour and respect, although he died nearly five centuries ago. He is thought of as a great wizard, a man who understood a great deal about magic, but above all as a ruler of foresight and courage.

He became king of Gao and of the Songhay lands in about 1464. Mali was becoming weak and was in confusion. The Tuareg were raiding from the north, and Mossi from the south. The trade of leading cities, Gao among them, was threatened by the insecurity of the times.

Sunni Ali was one of those great military captains whose energy and ambition kept him always in the saddle, always fighting, always at the head of one army or another. Knowing no other means of uniting the Western Sudan except by war, he made war often and with ruthless skill. The early years of his reign read like a list of battles. He moved on swift horses from one campaign to the next, shifting his place of residence, reorganizing his armies, refashioning his plans. In his long reign of 35 years he was never once defeated.

He began by fighting off the Mossi, who were attacking Timbuktu, the second city of the Songhay lands. He pursued them far into the west, then turned swiftly on the Dogon and the Fulani, who were also raiders, in the hills of Bandiagara. By 1468, four years after becoming emperor, he had cleared the country of immediate danger and at once attacked the Tuareg, who had held Timbuktu since 1433. Unbeatable, he drove the Tuareg out of Timbuktu. Their chief fled to distant Walata, while *Sunni* Ali set about punishing the leaders of a city who had done little to defend themselves against these nomad raiders.

Religious disputes were at work in this. The leading men of Timbuktu had been strictly Muslim for a long time now, and generally followed the beliefs of their trading partners from North Africa and the Saharan oases. Their *qadi*, or chief religious leader, tended to regard himself as the independent ruler of a Muslim city within the largely non-Muslim empire of Songhay. Here, as elsewhere, the coming of Islam to the Western Sudan gave rise to conflicts not only of religious belief, but even more of customs, laws, and political loyalties.

Faced with Tuareg occupation of their city, the leading men of Timbuktu do not seem to have fought very hard against it: both they and the Tuareg, after all, were Muslims interested in the trans-Saharan trade. They did not want to be occupied by the Tuareg, but they may have tried to use this occupation as a means to reassert their independence against their Songhay overlord. *Sunni* Ali, at any rate, thought they had. He accused them of having acted disloyally to him, and treated them harshly. That is why the author of the *Tarikh as-Sudan*, himself a man of Timbuktu, afterwards described *Sunni* Ali as a tyrant and oppressor.[1]

With the recapture of Timbuktu, Ali had only begun his bold career. He now laid siege to Jenne, the vital market-centre for the trade in gold and kola and other goods from the southern forest lands. Jenne had never been taken by an invader, but Ali captured it after a siege of seven years. By 1476 he had the whole lake region of the Middle Niger, west of Timbuktu, securely in his hands.

Through all these years of struggle, and through later years, Ali found means to fight back against a host of raiders. In 1480 the Mossi of Yatenga daringly sent cavalry to raid as far as Walata on the edge of the Sahara. Ali launched his cavalry after them, drove them back, pinned them down again in their own country in the south. He did the same with others of their raiding kind, Gurmanche, Dogon, Noromba, Fulani of Gurma: in short, with all those peoples who lived along the southern margins of the Niger valley and envied the wealth of its towns and markets. Yet *Sunni* Ali was a skilful leader, as shown in Chapter 11 ('Clash of beliefs') in peace as well as in war.

New methods of government: *Askia* the Great

Sunni Ali died in November 1492 while returning from an expedition against the Gurma, and his son, *Sunni* Baru, was named ruler of Songhay two months later. *Sunni* Baru reigned for only fourteen months. He was

---

[1] See Chapter 11, 'Law and order' and 'Clash of beliefs', for more on this interesting subject.

defeated in battle and deposed by a powerful rebel. This rebel was Muhammad Turay, who became *Askia* the Great.[2]

Here, once again, religious disputes were mingled with personal ambitions. In Songhay at this time the market cities were of growing wealth and importance. The leaders of these towns were mostly Muslims, and, because of this, Islam was now making great progress among the townspeople of the empire of Songhay, as indeed in other parts of the Western Sudan as well. While largely loyal to the traditional beliefs of the countryside, *Sunni* Ali had found it wise to make a good many concessions to Islam, although, as we have just seen in the case of Timbuktu, he did not hesitate to oppress Muslim leaders who failed in their political loyalty to him. *Sunni* Ali, in other words, set out to protect both the interests of the Muslim people of the towns and the interests of the non-Muslim people of the countryside. Always a skilful politician, he succeeded in holding the balance between these often opposing sets of interests.

Unlike his father, *Sunni* Baru refused to declare himself a Muslim and at once made it clear that he was going to side entirely with the non-Muslim people of the countryside. Between the townsfolk and the country-folk – the traders and the farmers of Songhay – he chose the latter. But the people of the towns were too powerful to be treated in this way. They feared that they would lose power and influence, and that their trade would suffer. They found a rebellious leader in Muhammad Turay.

The consequences were far-reaching. With *Askia* Muhammad, the empire of Songhay entered on a new stage in its impressive political life. Becoming emperor at the age of 50, he reigned from 1493 until 1528, and carried the political and commercial power of the empire of Songhay to its greatest point of expansion. He is remembered for three main reasons.

In the first place, *Askia* Muhammad made a sharp break with the religious and family traditions of the *Sunni* line of rulers. He based his power firmly on the towns, and, in line with this, ruled as a strict Muslim. Although many traditional customs and practices were still observed at his court, his laws and methods were increasingly in accord with Muslim ideas. In this, clearly, he understood well the trend of power in Songhay. This is shown, among other things, by the fact that he could be absent on a pilgrimage to Mecca for more than two years (1494–97) without causing himself any trouble at home. During this pilgrimage the sharif of Mecca, spiritual leader of the Muslims, named *Askia* Muhammad as his deputy or caliph for the Western Sudan. Returning from Mecca, Muhammad set himself to remodel the laws and customs of his empire along more strictly Muslim lines.

Secondly, Muhammad took over the administrative changes made by *Sunni* Ali and developed them still further. He built up a machinery of

---

[2] The title of *Askia* came from a military rank in the Songhay army.

central government that was stronger and more detailed in its work than any known in the Western Sudan. He opened the way for men of talent in royal service who were not necessarily members of leading descent-lines.

Thirdly, he used his talents as a political and military leader to continue with the imperial plans of *Sunni* Ali, and to carry these plans to a point where he successfully united the whole central region of the Western Sudan and even pushed his power, as Kankan Musa of Mali had done two centuries earlier, far northward among the oasis markets of the Sahara.

No people of the Western Sudan were free from the pressure of Songhay power. Their disciplined cavalry were everywhere. Like *Sunni* Ali, *Askia* Muhammad fought the Mossi of Yatenga and their raiding neighbours. In 1505 he even tackled Borgu (in what is north-western Nigeria today), though not with much success. In 1512 he mounted a big expedition against Diara. Successful there, he sent his troops still further westward, and attacked the Denianke king of Futa Toro in distant Senegal.

Then he turned his attention eastward again. His generals invaded the Hausa states, meeting with serious resistance only at Kano. Yet the addition of Katsina and other Hausa states to the countries which paid tax and loyalty to Songhay was worth little unless Songhay could also gain possession of the principal caravan-markets to the north. There, too, lay the Tuareg, ancient enemies of Songhay and of the cities of the Niger. So Muhammad sent out his generals once more. He ordered them to march north-eastward into the hot and thirsty lands of the oases of Aïr, far north of Hausaland in the southern Sahara.

Faced with the armies of Songhay, perhaps the best-organized troops that West Africa had developed so far, the Tuareg could do nothing but turn about and retreat into their native desert. Muhammad ordered his generals to found a colony in Aïr. Many Songhay were settled around the ancient market of Agadès, where their descendants may be found to this day.

In 1528, by now over 80, Muhammad became blind. He was deposed by his eldest son, Musa, and died ten years later.

The rulers of Songhay

As with Mali, the empire of Songhay went through three chief periods of expansion:

1 under *Sunni* Ali (1464–92)
2 under *Askia* the Great (1493–1528)
3 under *Askia* Dawud (1549–82).

Altogether, there were ten *askia*s. Here are the dates of their reigns:

Askia	Muhammad the Great	1493–1528
	Musa	1528–31
	Muhammad Bunkan	1531–37
	Ismail	1537–39
	Ishaq I	1539–49
	Dawud	1549–82
	Muhammad II	1582–86
	Muhammad Bani	1586–88
	Ishaq II	1588–91
	Muhammad Gao	1591–?

Development of trade: Timbuktu and Jenne

As with other large states of this period, the strength and wealth of the Songhay government were based largely on the big trading cities. These became centres of a many-sided civilization in which the laws and learning of Islam played a notable part, not least in the cities of Timbuktu and Jenne.

Timbuktu today is a small and dusty town of no distinction. No doubt it was small and dusty when it was founded about 800 years ago. But then its importance was very great. For Timbuktu became one of the wealthiest markets of West Africa, famous far and wide for its trade and for the learning of its scholars. Rising to importance a good deal later than its western sister-cities Kumbi and Takrur, Audaghost and others, Timbuktu long outlived and outshone them.

By the fourteenth century, when *Mansa* Musa brought a skilled architect back from Mecca and ordered him to build new mosques and palaces, Timbuktu was well established as a trading city of importance. Yet Timbuktu never became the centre of an important state, much less of an empire. In this it differed from Gao. One main reason for this difference probably lay in its geographical position. Well placed for the caravan trade, it was badly situated to defend itself from the Tuareg raiders of the Sahara. These Tuareg were repeatedly hammering at the gates of Timbuktu, and often enough they burst them open, with sad results for the inhabitants. Life here was never quite safe enough to make it a good place for the centre of a big state. Even in *Mansa* Musa's time, when peace and order spread widely across the Western Sudan, Timbuktu never became a central point of government within the empire.

The political record underlines this special geographical weakness of Timbuktu. From 1325 until 1433 it was part of the Mali empire. Then the Tuareg had it for a few years. In 1458 it was enclosed within the growing

Songhay empire, where it remained until Moroccans invaded Songhay in 1591. These Moroccans, whose invasion we shall consider in its proper place, ruled over Timbuktu until about 1780, although for most of this time they were no more than a weak ruling class within the city, half-merged with the local population and often cut off from their original homeland. Then the Tuareg again had command of the city for a time, being followed in their overlordship by Fulani rulers in 1826, who in turn were followed by Tucolor chiefs (1862–63), again by the Tuareg (1863–93), and finally by French colonial invaders (1893–1960). Today, Timbuktu is part of the modern republic of Mali.

But this political record would be misleading if it suggested that Timbuktu did not also enjoy long periods of peace and peaceful trade. On the contrary, the arts of peace and scholarship, of writing and theology, and the development of law, all flourished here, and flourished greatly. We shall discuss them in later chapters.

Jenne, whose early foundation we have discussed, was another of the historical cities of the Western Sudan. It seems to have been founded, like Timbuktu, soon after the eleventh century, although there was probably a trading settlement here in still earlier times. But the history of Jenne is not the same as that of Timbuktu. There is an important difference between them.

Both were big trading centres. Timbuktu and Takrur, like Gao and ancient Kumbi, were middleman cities between the traders of the Western Sudan and those of the Sahara and North Africa. But Jenne, by contrast, was a middleman city between the traders of the Western Sudan (especially of Timbuktu) and the traders of the forest lands to the south. It was through Jenne, at least after about 1400, that the gold and other goods of the forest lands passed increasingly to the caravan-traders who were waiting for these goods in Timbuktu and other trading centres. And it was through Jenne that the goods of North Africa increasingly reached southward into the forest lands.

This special importance of Jenne was associated with the spread and activities of the Mandinka traders of Mali, the Dyula or Wangara trading companies. These pushed down into the forest lands and settled there as buying and selling agents, just as the Berber traders of the Sahara, further north, had settled in towns like Kumbi, Timbuktu and Gao.

These Dyula traders, each group or company united under its Dyula-Mansa by common language, Islam, and experience, were a vital link between the gold-producing forest lands and the whole wide trading network of the Western Sudan and North Africa. They dealt in many things besides gold, and all their trade passed back and forth through markets such as Jenne.

Unlike Timbuktu and Gao, Jenne retained its independence until taken by *Sunni* Ali in the 1470s, though without trying to become a large state or empire. One reason for its safety from conquest lay in its powerful defensive position. For much of every year, Jenne was encircled by the flood waters of the Niger river, as indeed it sometimes is today. Its inhabitants also built high protecting walls round their city, somewhat like those that may still be seen at Kano, and proved able to defend them.

The Moroccan invasion: firearms and disaster

After *Askia* Dawud, harsh times lay ahead. Troubles broke out at home. The old rivals along the southern fringe of the empire – the Mossi and their neighbours – were far from crushed. The Hausa states revolted against Songhay overlordship during the reign of Muhammad II. But in 1582, the year that Muhammad II succeeded Dawud, a new note was struck, full of menace for the future of Songhay. The sultan of Morocco sent a force of 200 soldiers to seize the vital salt deposits of Taghaza far in the north of Songhay but a part of its empire. These soldiers were armed with a weapon not seen before on the battlefields of the Western Sudan. This was the arquebus, an early form of musket. Firearms now appeared for the first time on any scale. They were to have a profound and sometimes very destructive effect on all the peoples of West Africa.

This brief skirmish in a remote part of the Sahara opened a war between Morocco and Songhay that proved disastrous for the men of Gao. Why did it happen?

Briefly, there were two reasons for this conflict, one military and the other commercial. In 1578, resisting an invasion by Portugal, the Moroccans had won a great victory at the battle of Al-Ksar al-Kabir. Historians have called this one of the decisive battles of the world. For many years it ended any idea of European conquest in North Africa. But it also encouraged the Moroccans to turn southward.

The Portuguese had invaded Morocco with an army of 25,000 men. At Al-Ksar al-Kabir they met with total defeat. It is said that only a few hundred Portuguese escaped to tell the tale of that day. The reigning sultan of Morocco died in the hour of victory and was succeeded by his younger brother, Mulay Ahmad, then aged 29. Skilfully, he made Morocco into a strong state again, both by the power of his armies and by generous gifts. But his purse was becoming empty, and soon he began to look round for new ways of filling it. Not surprisingly, he looked to the south, to the Western Sudan, as the Almoravids had done in earlier times. Under *Askia* Dawud, the riches of Songhay had acquired a great reputation throughout North Africa. Even the kings and merchants of distant Europe had begun to hear tempting tales of the wonders of the Western Sudan.

Map 5.2   The Moroccan invasion of Songhay, 1591.

Sultan Mulay began by nibbling at Songhay power. He raided Taghaza. But it brought him no good. He could seize the salt deposits, but he could not keep an army in that thirsty place. He thought again. He decided to launch an army right across the Sahara and attack Songhay in its own homeland. By this means, he believed, he could plunder the wealth of Songhay. He could vastly enrich himself with West African gold.

This army set out in December 1590. It was led by a soldier named Judar, by origin a Spanish Christian who had accepted Islam, and was composed of 4,600 picked men. Half of these were infantry armed with arquebuses, the most up-to-date weapon in the world of that time. Half of these arquebus-carriers were Spanish Muslims while the others were Portuguese or Spanish prisoners who had agreed to serve in the Moroccan armies, and accept Islam, rather than suffer death or long imprisonment.

This force of mercenaries and ex-prisoners crossed the Sahara, taking many weeks from Marrakesh to the Niger, and fell upon the lands of Songhay with the fury of men who knew there could be no retreat. Gathering his troops, *Askia* Ishaq II tried to resist, but the armies of Songhay now met soldiers at Tondibi on 12 March 1591 who were even better armed and disciplined. They retired before the firearms of Judar's men. Weakened by trouble and revolts at home, the Songhay ruler lost battle after battle, often with heavy casualties. The Moroccans pushed into Timbuktu and then into Gao, hoping to find large stores of wealth ready to be collected up. In this they were at first not altogether disappointed. Much valuable loot was taken back to Marrakesh, where fine palaces were afterwards built on the profits of this piratical war.

Although routed in battle and driven from their trading cities, the Songhay did not give in. The towns were lost, but the country folk fell back on guerilla tactics. Unable to meet the Moroccans in pitched battle, they built up little raiding parties, attacked Moroccan posts and garrisons, and harassed the Moroccans in every way they could. They were never more than partially successful.

Having lost the towns, Songhay proved unable to recover. Its central government was weakened from within and without. Songhay's own subject peoples seized the chance to revolt on behalf of their own freedom. Many succeeded. And with this collapse the power of Islam dwindled or was lost for many years ahead. Another stage in the history of the Western Sudan began, in which the non-Muslim peoples of the countryside were once again to assert their power.

Songhay's rivals: the Mossi states

The nearest to Songhay of their southern neighbours were the Mossi, who lived in a cluster of states between the great northward bend of the Niger river – the region of Jenne and Timbuktu – and the forest lands of Asante and Togo. They spoke (as most of them still do) the Mole-Dagbani languages, a 'sub-family' of the Gur group of languages.

These states were never brought within the imperial systems of Mali or Songhay. They conducted a vigorous and independent life of their own. Often they were a danger to their prosperous northern neighbours, for they raided northward and north-westward with strong forces of cavalry. After about 1400, too, they acted as intermediaries in the trade between the forest lands and the cities of the Niger.

In the course of time, five principal states were to emerge. These were the states of Wagadugu, Yatenga, Fada-n-Gurma, Mamprussi and Dagomba. They all became strong before 1500. The territory of these states now lies within the modern republics of Upper Volta and Ghana.

The Mossi were not in the Mali empire, but were a frequent peril to its wealth and safety. Their hard-riding horsemen took and looted Timbuktu in 1338, and continued such attacks until the armies of *Sunni* Ali of Songhay proved too strong for them. Even after that, the Mossi-Dagomba states (as historians usually call them) retained their independence until the French invasions of the late nineteenth century. Some of the rulers whom the French overpowered were the descendants of those who had founded these states many centuries earlier. The Mossi states were in fact outstanding

Map 5.3 The Mossi states.

examples of the *political stability* which West African peoples have often enjoyed in the past. They also illustrate the truth that West African states could enjoy stability over long periods without any dependence on Islam or on Muslim ways of thought and government. For the Mossi rejected all efforts to convert them to Islam, and remained true to their own customs and beliefs.

Chapter 6

Kanem-Bornu and the Hausa States

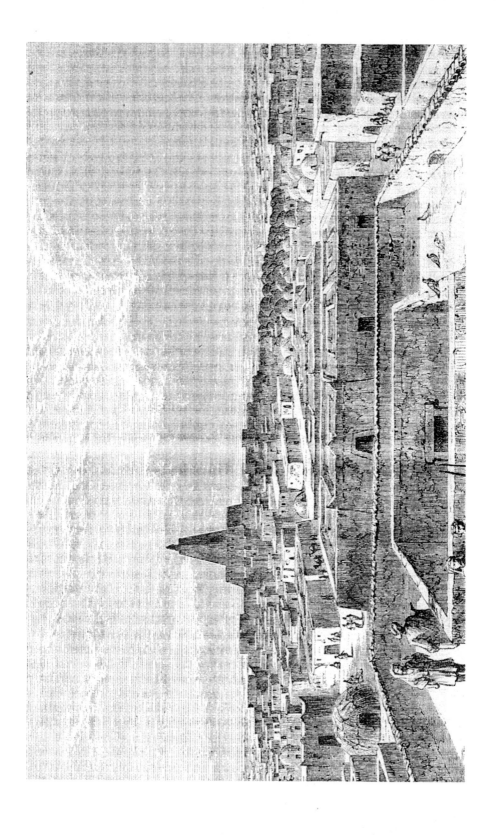

Kanem-Bornu and the Hausa States

Not all the peoples of West Africa were drawn to the same extent into new forms of social life and government. Many peoples of the grassland country, like many people of the forest lands, went on living much as they had lived before, knowing and caring little of the world beyond the reach of their pastures or farms, living as securely as they could in their villages and homesteads, content with what they had, and hoping, as we can imagine, that nobody would come and bother them.

Map 6.1 The expansion of the Kanem-Bornu empire (very approximate frontiers).

This does not mean that these untroubled peoples were any less intelligent or sensible than their state-forming and empire-building neighbours. And they, too, were influenced, as time went on, by the big changes going on around them.

The whole of West Africa, during these centuries, was moving into new types of social and political organisation.

Early Kanem-Bornu: the Sefawa

The ancient and powerful military system of Kanem-Bornu became as important for this eastern part of the Western Sudan as were the empires of Ghana and Mali for the western and central parts.

Its earliest beginnings, like those of Ghana, are little known. Probably they occurred soon after AD 800. Then it was that four or five early states, including those of the Kanuri and Zaghawa peoples, took shape in the neighbourhood of Lake Chad.

Here, as with Ghana, the trade between West Africa and North Africa was important for political as well as commercial reasons. For economics and politics always go hand in hand; and here, to the east and west of the great lake, there lay a vital crossroads of trade.

In these lands around Lake Chad were situated the southern market-centres of the trans-Saharan trade not only with Libya and Tunisia in the far north, but also with Nubia on the Middle Nile and Egypt to the far north-east. These markets were valuable exchange centres for all goods going north from the lands of eastern Guinea that lie in southern Nigeria today.

So the little states of the Chad region, like the powerful system into which they grew, faced southward towards eastern Guinea, north-eastward through the hills of Darfur to the distant Nile, and northward by way of the Bilma Oasis and the settlements of Aïr to Libya, Tunisia and Egypt. This key position did much to shape the fortunes of Kanem-Bornu. Its rulers were nearly always in touch with North Africa, with the peoples of the Nile, and with their neighbours in the south and west.

The royal traditions of Kanem-Bornu say a lot about early times. Like other royal traditions, they have two disadvantages: they are not exact, and they tell little or nothing of how ordinary folk lived and worked. All the same, they form a useful guide to the main political events.

The early state of Kanem, reaching some way to the east as well as to the west of Lake Chad, came into being under a line of kings belonging to the Sefawa family. This dynasty held power from about AD 850. Two centuries later, in 1086, there came an important change. A Sefawa king, called Hume, accepted Islam as his own religion and that of his court.

From this time onwards the Sefawa kings and emperors of Kanem-Bornu, who continued to rule for another 800 years, were always Muslims.

This happened, we may recall, at about the same time as the Almoravid Muslims were battering at the cities of non-Muslim Ghana, and not long after *Dia* Kossoi of Gao had likewise accepted Islam. So it was in the eleventh century that Islam made its first big advances in the grassland countries of West Africa, at least among their rulers and governors, and began to send trader-missionaries south into the forest lands.

Growth of Kanem-Bornu: empire and rulers

Kanuri traditions say that there were sixteen kings of Kanem-Bornu down to *Mai* (king) Dunama Dibbelemi who ruled in about 1221–59.[1] The historical record shows two main periods of early expansion.

1 Under Dunama Dibbelemi, and the kings immediately before him.

By 1250 Kanem-Bornu had become an important empire. Its rulers were known throughout the Muslim world. One reason for this was that the kings had extended the empire's control of the northern trade routes as far as the Fezzan (in southern Tunisia, on the northern side of the great desert). *Mai* Dunama Dibbelemi also gained control of Adamawa, all of Bornu, and Kano, as well as of Wadai to the east of Lake Chad.

After *Mai* Dunama Dibbelemi there followed many kings in a period when this first empire of the Kanuri went through a time of troubles. Some of these were caused by disputes between leading men and their families. Others were the result of unsuccessful wars against their neighbours.

These troubles came to a head in the reign of *Mai* Daud (1377–86). Kanem's biggest rivals east of Lake Chad, the Bulala, drove the king and his court out of the old Kanuri capital of Njimi (near Lake Chad). Another king, *Mai* Umar (1394–98), suffered worse defeats. At this time the capital of the empire was transferred to Bornu on the western side of Lake Chad. After this it is better to speak of the empire of Bornu, for that was now its permanent centre.

2 A second period of expansion began late in the fifteenth century, and especially under *Mai* Ali Gaji (1472–1504). His successful conquests were westward against some of the Hausa states, including Kano, and eastward against the Bulala, while at the same time he regained control of the northern trade routes and fought off raiders from the south (from the region of the middle Benue river).

---

[1] Note that all these dates are approximate. Not all historians agree about them.

These successes were continued under the next ruler, *Mai* Idris Katarkamabi (1504–26). He was able to liberate the old capital of Njimi from the Bulala, but the centre of the new empire stayed at the Bornu capital of Ngazargamu (founded by the king before him, *Mai* Ghaji). The Bulala once again became subjects of the empire.

Under *Mai* Muhammad (1526–45) the Bulala revolted, but without success. *Mai* Muhammad followed this victory by marching north into Aïr, then under Songhay rule; and it seems that from this time onward the country of Aïr, vital for the northern trade from Bornu and Hausaland, came under the influence of Bornu.

Under *Mai* Ali (about 1545), Bornu clashed with Kebbi in the west of Hausaland. The reason appears to have been that the kingdom of Kebbi, eager for a bigger share in the northern caravan trade, had begun raiding the Tuareg and Songhay settlers of the Aïr oases. These appealed for help to *Mai* Ali. He marched a Bornu army northward round the Hausa kingdoms (passing south of Zinder) and attacked the *Kanta* (king) of Kebbi in his fortress town of Surame, west of Katsina.

The Kebbi king pulled out of Surame, but Ali, for reasons not clear, turned back and made for home. The Kebbi army set out to chase him and his soldiers. They caught up with *Mai* Ali's soldiers near N'guru, and fought some battles. But the Kebbi men were out of luck. On the way home they were ambushed by the men of Katsina, and their king was killed.

The fortunes of Bornu now looked good, though more troubles lay immediately ahead. *Mai* Ali died in about 1546. His son, who had the right to become king, was very young, so his nephew, Dunama, took power. Dunama reigned from 1546 to 1563. He was followed by *Mai* Dala (Abdullah), who reigned from about 1546 to 1570.

Bornu suffered at this time, especially from another Bulala revolt. Dunama even took the step of fortifying the capital, Ngazargamu, a sign of weakness absent in earlier times. Raiders threatened from many sides.

A famous queen

Meanwhile the little son of *Mai* Ali was growing to manhood. This young prince, whose name was Idris, lived far away from Bornu in old Kanem, east of the lake, where the Bulala kings still ruled. No doubt he lived there because his mother was the daughter of a Bulala king, and had returned home on the death of *Mai* Ali. This woman, Queen Amsa, is said to have shown great courage in protecting the life of Idris against efforts by *Mai* Dunama and *Mai* Dala to kill him because he was the rightful heir to the imperial throne.

But Idris could not win his rights when *Mai* Dala died in 1570. Power in Bornu was seized by Dala's sister, the formidable Queen Aissa Kili; and it was only after several years of civil war that Idris at last succeeded to the throne. He reigned from about 1580 till 1617 and became one of the strongest and most successful of the kings of Kanem-Bornu. In a series of wars he revived the old empire and built a new one.

His work, like that of other great leaders, was one of political reform. This took the shape of a reinforcement of Islamic beliefs and customs, just as it had in Songhay under *Askia* Muhammad. He placed much weight on obedience to the Islamic code of law, and tried hard to raise the prestige of his magistrates, even making it a habit, so it is said, to submit his own problems to their advice and decision. In the work and policies of Idris we may see emerging, once again, the old struggle between Islam and the old religions of West Africa.

Now reunited with Kanem, east of the lake, Bornu prospered under *Mai* Idris. There was much trade with the north. There was regular contact with the rulers of Fezzan on the northern side of the Sahara. Diplomatic relations were opened with the Ottoman conquerors of Egypt. Idris even imported muskets from Tripoli and raised a company of musketeers. A Kanemi writer of those days, Ibn Fartua, has left us a description of the coming of ambassadors from the sultan of the Ottoman (Turkish) empire, and of how they were received. *Mai* Idris went out to greet the ambassadors at the head of companies of his quilt-armoured cavalry. Ibn Fartua wrote of this important occasion:

> On the next day, all the soldiers mounted their horses after equipping themselves and their horses with armour, with breastplates, shields and their best clothing. When we had all ridden a short distance we met the messengers of the lord of Stambul [the sultan of the then very powerful empire of the Ottoman Turks] . . . The troops of our lord were drawn up on the west in rank after rank, leaving enough space between their ranks for the wheeling of any restive horse. Then our troops charged [towards the Turkish messengers and their escort], and they galloped their horses towards us. This continued for a long time until the infantry were tired of standing still. After that our lord continued on his journey . . .

'O, my wise friends and companions!' continues Ibn Fartua. 'Have you ever seen a king who is equal to our lord at such a moment, when the lord of Stambul, the great Sultan of Turkey, sends messengers to him with favourable proposals?'

And so Kanem-Bornu, as in times past, stood once more at the crossroads of trade and travel between West Africa and the valley of the Middle

Nile, and between West Africa and Fezzan, Tripoli and Egypt. Strengthened and reunified by Idris Alooma, it helped to link the peoples of West Africa to the world beyond the desert.

Kanem-Bornu: methods of government

The actual size of Kanem-Bornu varied with time and fortune, as did all these imperial systems. Its central people were the Kanuri, just as the Mandinka were the central people of Mali and the Songhay the central people of the empire of that name. The Kanuri lived then, as later, around Lake Chad. But they had, of course, no frontiers in the modern sense of the word. Their kings made alliances with neighbouring rulers. When the kings were strong enough to do so, they forced these neighbouring rulers to pay tax and obey their orders.

Like other kings of those times, the rulers of Kanem-Bornu were tough and hard men. But they were not dictators. They were not all-powerful. They had to listen to the advice and opinions of their lesser kings, chiefs and counsellors. Within Kanem-Bornu itself, they generally drew their power from a central council of leaders of the Sefawa family. This council consisted of about a dozen principal governors who reigned over different parts of the empire. These men had titles which were used for many centuries. Some of the titles, like *galadima* and *chiroma*, are still used in northern Nigeria.

Firmly based in Bornu and around Lake Chad, sometimes at war and sometimes at peace with the Hausa kingdoms to the west of them, the lords of this empire usually faced their greatest difficulties in the east. Here they met with energetic peoples, notably the Bulala, who resisted their rule, and the extent of the empire shrank or expanded according to their failure or success in mastering these easterly peoples by means of diplomacy or war.

But whether large or small, according to the way things turned out, the success of the empire can be compared to that of Ancient Ghana, while it was perhaps even bigger than the empires of Mali or Songhay because it lasted longer. What the Kanuri and their allies and subjects were able to do, over a very long period and in a region of great importance, was to bring the advantages of a single system of law and order to a great many different peoples. And it was through this large system that West Africa kept in regular touch with vital centres of civilization beyond the Sahara, especially Egypt. It was through Kanem-Bornu that the goods of Egypt and other northern lands – horses and fine metalware, salt and copper – came into West Africa by way of the eastern Sahara; and it was often by the same route that the goods of West Africa, notably kola and ivory, were taken in exchange to those northern lands.

Often, of course, the Kanuri and their allies achieved their successes by invasion and conquest; and their successes were sometimes threatened, like those of other large states, with rebellion by subject peoples. These were the peoples who had to pay for the progress that Kanem achieved. And they, we may be sure, did not think that Kanem was a progressive state and empire. Can we speak, then, of progress in this connection? There is a general rule we may apply in trying to answer this difficult question. Where states and empires in the past have generally helped the expansion of production and trade, opened new ways of livelihood, found wealth for the enlargement of the arts of peace, and brought security from everyday perils and fears to large numbers of their people, then we may reasonably speak of progress in the growth of civilization.

Kanem-Bornu achieved these things. Not all the time, of course. As elsewhere, there were bad governments and foolish kings, cruel and greedy, self-seeking, oppressive. Then life became unbearable and brave men took arms and tried to change it. But there were also long periods of peace and security, when people could expand their work and develop their skills.

Origins of the Hausa states: security and trade

The traditions of the Hausa states, situated in the lands of northern Nigeria, go back to their kings of the eleventh century AD.

According to the *Kano Chronicle*, a collection of Hausa traditions written down many centuries later, and whose dates, of course, are not exact, the first *sarki*, or king, of Kano was Bogoda, who came to power as early as AD 999. Other Hausa communities, each dependent on its main settlement or *birni*, also began to turn themselves into states with kings towards the end of the thirteenth century. By about 1350 this state-forming process had gone quite a long way. The stronger Hausa states had pushed their power across the neighbouring countryside and were beginning to form frontiers between each other. Many wars followed. These did not last long or destroy much, but were designed to win this or that local advantage or to bring home plunder from neighbouring towns and markets.[2]

These Hausa states had three main reasons for existence, reasons which were to be found in their cities. Each main Hausa city or town (for these settlements were at first quite small) was a place for government and military defence. Neighbouring farmers could take refuge there when threatened by invaders or raiders. In exchange for this protection, they paid

---

[2] There were to be seven true Hausa states, or Hausa *bokwoi*: Biram, Daura, Gobir, Kano, Katsina, Rano and Zaria (Zazzau); and seven outliers, the *banza bokwoi*: Gwari, Kebbi, Kwororafa (Jukun), Nupe, Yawri, Yoruba and Zamfara.

Map 6.2 The Hausa states and their neighbours in about AD 1400.

taxes to the men who ruled the city, who in turn paid the soldiers and kept law and order. These men were in turn ruled by a *sarki* or king, a member of one or other leading family.

Secondly, each Hausa city was a market-place for the nearby countryside. Here country people could exchange their products for the goods that town craftsmen made in leather and other materials.

Thirdly, each Hausa city became gradually a centre of long-distance trade. It became a place for the exchange not only of locally produced goods but also of goods brought from North Africa and Egypt, from the rest of the Sudan, and from Guinea.

This prosperity was the result of much development. In the beginning, the Hausa states had difficult problems to solve. Before they could grow strong and wealthy, they had to build the power of their cities and extend this power over the neighbouring peoples of the countryside. Many of these peoples had their own ways, their own religious customs and beliefs. Should the new Hausa rulers impose their own customs and beliefs on the peoples of the countryside, or should they tolerantly let these people believe as they wished? The question was certainly much discussed in towns like Kano. The *Kano Chronicle* offers a vividly clear illustration of this kind of problem. According to tradition, the *sarki* in AD 1290 was a certain Shekkarau. One day Shekkarau's counsellors came to him and complained of the disloyal talk they had heard among country people coming into town.

72

Shekkarau replied that he thought such discontent could be settled without fighting. But Shekkarau's counsellors were not sure that he was right. 'If you try to make peace with these people', the counsellors argued with him, 'they will only say that you are afraid of them.' And they advised the *sarki* not to listen to the delegates of these discontented folk.

But when the delegates came to Shekkarau, and entered his palace, and stood before him, they begged him to let them keep their customs and beliefs. For 'if the lands of a ruler are wide', they argued, 'then he should be patient. But if his lands are not wide, he will certainly not be able to gain possession of the whole countryside by impatience.' And the *sarki* agreed with them. As the *Kano Chronicle* explains, 'he left them their power and their own religious customs'.

Behind this little story, nearly 700 years old, we may see how hard it was for the chiefs of the towns and the chiefs of the countryside to reach agreement and settle down together for their common benefit. We may also see that while there was warfare among these states, there was also diplomacy – the effort to end disputes by compromise and peaceful give-and-take.

There were many Hausa cities engaged in trade and politics. Daura and Gobir, Katsina, Kano and Zaria – these are only five of the better-known names. Sometimes these states cooperated for their common good. Often they quarrelled. They never had a single government that ruled them all. They did not form a Hausa empire. Yet the Hausa states, generally more friendly with each other than with their non-Hausa neighbours, had influence and commercial power over a wide area of the eastern region.

These states were in close and constant touch, sometimes by war but more often by peaceful trade, with the peoples of the forest lands along the West African coast, notably with the Yoruba and their wealthy neighbours. It was largely through Hausaland that the goods of the Yoruba country, especially kola nuts, went northward into the Western Sudan and across the Sahara to North Africa; and it was largely through Hausaland that the forest peoples could import the North African goods they needed.

The Hausa achievement

Built in a fertile land, rich in skilled farmers and determined traders, the Hausa cities and states became a strong and stable part of the West African scene.

They were deeply influenced by Muslim methods of government as practised in the neighbouring empires of Songhay and Kanem-Bornu. These methods tended to strengthen the power of kings at the cost of ordinary folk. Government taxes and tolls grew heavier. The needs of courts and armies weighed down on tax-paying citizens and the farmers of the countryside. Armouries glinted with the metal of expensive coats of chain-mail and fine helmets.

By the 1440s there were even a few muskets in Hausaland, brought in by traders from Bornu who had got them from Egypt. And now the Muslim rulers began to use slave labour on a large scale. In 1450, for instance, the then ruler of Kano, Abdullahi Burja, a tributary vassal or under-king of the empire of Kanem-Bornu, sent out soldiers on raids for captives which are said to have brought him as many as 1,000 slaves a month. He is reported to have established no fewer than twenty-one settlements of royal slaves, each with 1,000 men.

These new methods called for changes in the administration. Kings like Muhammad Rumfa, who reigned in Kano from 1465 to 1499, borrowed ideas from Kanem and Songhay. They formed troops of full-time soldiers, often from captives whom they had turned into slaves, built luxurious palaces, and owned large areas of land. As was the rule, the wealth of the privileged few had to be paid for by the labour of the many. Yet the prosperity of the cities remained impressive. Expansion of long-distance trade using currency and credit went hand-in-hand with the growth of learning, and with valuable advances in the handicraft industry.

Travellers from distant lands did not fail to notice this bustling city progress. One such visitor, the North African trade-traveller Hassan ibn Muhammad,[3] has left colourful descriptions of Hausaland as he or his friends saw it at the beginning of the sixteenth century.

Gobir in the west was rich in people and in cattle. Ibn Muhammad wrote: 'The people are in general very civilised. They have very many weavers and shoe-makers who make shoes like those that the Romans used to wear; and these they export to Timbuktu and Gao.'

Of the state of Guangara, later absorbed by Katsina, he wrote that it was 'inhabited by a great number of people who are governed by a king with more than 7,000 infantry armed with bows, and 500 foreign cavalry on call. He draws a great revenue from dealing in goods and from commercial taxes . . .'

Kano, he found, was 'encircled by a wall made of beams of wood and baked clay; and its houses are constructed of the same materials. Its inhabitants are civilised handicraft-workers and rich merchants . . .' Like some other Hausa cities, Kano was an important place for Muslim learning.

But all this prosperity, whether from trade or taxation, had its disadvantage. It attracted raiders. Thus Guangara, whose king had such great revenue from trade and taxes, was menaced by both Songhay on the west

---

[3] Captured by Christian pirates during a voyage in the Mediterranean, Hassan ibn Muhammad was taken to Rome. There he took the name of Leo Africanus, and in 1525 completed a famous book in Italian about the Western Sudan. It was first published in 1550.

and Bornu on the east. After a long siege Kano had already fallen to the armies of the Songhay emperor, *Askia* Muhammad, who obliged its ruler to pay him one-third of all the annual revenues of Kano. Other Hausa states suffered in the same way.

In the south, Zaria flourished. For much of the sixteenth century this was the strongest state in Hausaland, making vassals, or subject-states, both in the east and west. This brief though brilliant rise to supremacy is said to have been the work of a remarkable queen called Barkwa Turunda and even more of her forceful daughter, Queen Amina, who is said to have reigned for 34 years, subduing Nupe and the Jukun. Amina became famous for building Zaria's first city wall.

Little is certain about these events in Zaria; yet some points seem clear. The first is that Zaria, like Kano, held a key position in the trade between the lands of what is now southern Nigeria and the caravan markets of Hausaland and Bornu. Further to the south, so did Nupe and the Jukun, which is no doubt why these two states were often at war with Zaria. Each will have wanted to secure a greater control of the north–south trade.

Here as elsewhere in Songhay, Kanem, or the forest lands near the coast, the bare record speaks much of raids and wars, quarrels and miseries. Rulers strove with one another for power and wealth, competing for the taxes without which they could maintain neither governments nor armies, battling for the trade routes that guaranteed the taxes, struggling for the cities where the craftsmen lived and the treasuries lay.

Yet this bare record has little to say of the life of the majority of people. They suffered in the wars and raids, but less than the record suggests. The raids were painful, but they were brief. The wars were harsh, but they were small. Soldiers did not and could not occupy the land as modern armies do. Even the new firearms that were beginning to be used were harmless at a range of more than 100 metres or so. So Hausaland became rich and often peaceful. Farmers prospered; craftsmen multiplied; traders flourished; cities grew in wealth and civilization.

Hausa developments: rise of the 'king's men'

If the sixteenth century brought wealth to Hausaland, it also brought wars and raids by envious neighbours. Yet the collapse of Songhay, by invasion from Morocco, was not a disaster here. On the contrary, it relieved the western Hausa states of the danger of invasion by Songhay armies, for these were now fully occupied against the Moroccans, and in any case were far weaker than the conquering Songhay forces of the days of *Askia* Muhammad the Great (1493–1528).

Many Hausa communities prospered increasingly from their farming, handicraft industry (especially cotton weaving), and enterprise in trade. But this prosperity was also reduced by the failure of the Hausa kings and ruling groups to unite among themselves. They had never been able to unite in the past. They were not able to do so now. This failure meant that a great deal of effort went into quarrels between Hausa communities.

Generally, the Hausa states continued the political development of earlier times. Power began to be shared between people of noble families and ordinary families. The kings conceded some of their power to people of ordinary families, to 'commoners' or 'king's men', so as to lessen the power of the nobles. This helped the Hausa kings to strengthen their own positions, which were often threatened by powerful nobles. So there developed here, as we shall see, a kind of 'constitutional monarchy': of rule, that is, by kings whose power is limited by political rules.

In all the principal Hausa states – Daura, Gobir, Kano, Katsina, Zaria (Zazzau) and some others – the power of the kings was kept secure by this appointment of 'king's men', and by the increased dividing of society into different groups or classes. In the eighteenth century there were four main divisions in Hausa society. Firstly, at the top of the ladder of power and wealth, there were members of the king's own descent-line, 'big families', and of other leading descent-lines. Secondly, there were freemen who had the right to cultivate land. Thirdly, there were the special group of 'king's men', many of them eunuchs, who were recruited from certain villages and who served in the king's government, often in posts of much power. Fourthly, there were unfree men who had no political rights. As well as all these, there were the educated freemen, the *mallams*, who acted as religious leaders but were debarred from holding political jobs or from owning big farms.

Out of this structure of different groups, of 'layers', there arose a kind of constitutional monarchy. The king himself had a great deal of personal power. But he was able to act in important matters only with the agreement of his senior chiefs and officials. In securing this agreement, however, the king had one great advantage. The senior chiefs and officials were seldom if ever united against him. On the contrary, they were carefully balanced against each other in two groups. In one group were the chiefs of leading 'big families' who held their positions by right of birth, while the other group consisted of the 'king's men'. Members of the first group might plot to overturn the king and win power for themselves. But in this they were opposed by members of the second group, who could not hold power outside their appointed jobs because they were of slave origin or were eunuchs. A clever Hausa king could play off one group against the other.

This was not democracy as we know it. But nor was it dictatorship. Consider an example from Zaria in those times. Here there were two leading officials, one from each group. The *madawaki* was the minister of war, commander of the cavalry and leader of the whole army; he was drawn from one or other leading descent-lines of hereditary chiefs. Being a powerful nobleman, the *madawaki* might well be tempted to rebel against the king and seize the throne for himself. But this was where the constitutional 'checks and balances' came into action. For alongside the *madawaki* was the *galadima*, who not only looked after many civilian matters such as police, prisons and markets, but also controlled supplies to the army. So the *madawaki* could not do very much without the goodwill of the *galadima*. But the *galadima* was always drawn from the ranks of the 'king's men'. He was debarred by his origin from holding any political power except by the decision of the king, and was in any case the king's personal servant. This being so, he had no interest in helping a rebellious *madawaki*.

The king used this opposition between his leading officials to safeguard his power. Yet he too was confined by the same system of 'checks and balances'. If he wanted to go to war, it was not sufficient to persuade the *galadima* and other appointed officials of the good of what he intended to do; he also had to win the support of the *madawaki* and other hereditary chiefs. The Hausa system of government was therefore a complex and often delicate process of persuasion and rivalry between competing groups.

Rivals for trade

This useful type of government by kings of strong but limited authority was offset, as we have noted, by a failure to unite the different Hausa states for their common good. Each state continued to serve its own interests at the cost of the others. Katsina was generally the most powerful of them between 1600 and 1700, but was often on bad terms with its neighbour, Gobir. These two states were great rivals for the caravan trade of western Hausaland. Katsina also waged war against Kano. In 1649 its king won a big battle against the king of Kano, and followed this by making an alliance with raiders from Jukun in the south.

After about 1750, adding to these troubles, the western Hausa states, especially Katsina and Gobir, had to face bold raids from Tuareg who were now established near Gao on the Middle Niger. The eastern Hausa states continued, as before, to feel the pressure of Bornu. After 1804, the position was much altered by the religious and social movement of the great Fulani leader, Uthman dan Fodio, and the foundation of a new Fulani empire under his son, Muhammad Bello.

Bornu after Idris Alooma

It remains in this brief survey of political events to complete the story of Kanem-Bornu down to about 1800, after which the shadows of coming European colonial invasion began to grow and darken.

The great *Mai* Idris Alooma had come to power in about 1580. By about 1600 his rebuilding of the Kanemi empire was complete. He died in 1617, having brought its peoples many peaceful years.

Bornu traditions then speak of three reigns, those of *Mai* Muhammad (1617–32), *Mai* Ibrahim (1632–39) and *Mai* Omar (1639–57), during all of which the empire remained at peace within itself, and often with its neighbours. These rulers carried on the work of Idris Alooma, and on the whole they did it well.

This long period of security and peace, more than half a century disturbed only by occasional frontier battles or minor quarrels at home, was the ripe and smiling 'harvest time' of Kanem-Bornu civilization. While confusion and upheaval affected many other peoples of the Western Sudan, those of Kanem-Bornu had few such troubles. Farmers could work their fields in safety. Travellers and pilgrims could follow the roads without fear. Those who lived in towns and market villages could prosper with the spread of trade that came both from everyday security and from unified rule over a wide country. There was growth of learning in the towns, and of schools in the villages. There was regular traffic between Kanem-Bornu and the Egyptian and Tunisian provinces of the Turkish empire in North Africa. *Mai* Ali, who succeeded *Mai* Omar in 1657, even made three religious journeys to Arabia.

Decline of the Bornu empire

But *Mai* Ali, who reigned until 1694, had to face a different situation. It was while returning from his third pilgrimage in 1667 that the first warnings reached him of harsher times ahead.

The danger this time was not from the peoples to the east of Lake Chad, the Bulala nobles and their warriors who had rebelled so often against Kanemi rule. It came from the Tuareg of the Aïr oases in the north and, at the same time, from the Jukun in the south. Both came raiding into Bornu, just as they came raiding into Kano and other Hausa states, their common motive being to seize some of the wealth of flourishing towns. Both gave *Mai* Ali and his armies some hard defeats. Twice he was besieged by these two enemies in his capital at Ngazargamu. In the end he managed to deal with each of them separately, and drove them back. The traditions say that a great famine struck Bornu in the later years of *Mai*

Ali's reign, a disaster no doubt caused by these destructive raiding and defensive wars.

The great days of the Kanem-Bornu empire were almost over. After *Mai* Ali the traditions list seven rulers (or perhaps six, for one of them is in doubt) down to *Mai* Ahmad, who came to power in the last part of the eighteenth century, and later faced the first of Uthman dan Fodio's attacks. All these rulers saw the strength of their empire gradually decline. There occurred here the same general process as further to the west: central government found itself repeatedly weakened by revolt or independent action on the part of this or that subject people. Yet Bornu remained a powerful state whose traders continued to dominate the southern oasis trade across the routes to the Fezzan and Tripoli, playing a big part, too, along the 'gold and kola' route to Salaga in country under Asante rule.

Wadai, Darfur

Throughout the eighteenth century there were also many political changes to the east of Lake Chad. The rulers of Bagirmi and Wadai, backed partly by Fulani warrior groups settled there in earlier times, fought each other for control of Kanem, while the ancient authority of the Bulala kings and nobles vanished from the scene.

In this vast region, too, there now arose a movement for Muslim conversion and Muslim rules of government based on earlier Muslim kingdoms of the seventeenth century in Wadai and Bagirmi. In Darfur, east of Wadai, a line of kings known as the Tunjur had built a non-Muslim kingdom in the distant past. This kingdom now fell to a new line of Muslim rulers. The tall ruins of their red-brick palaces and mosques, especially those of Sultan Muhammad Teirab (reigned 1752–87), may still be seen among the foothills of Jebel Marra.

New states in the Western Sudan: disorder and revival

As in the coastal regions of West Africa, great changes occurred in the inland countries of the Western Sudan during the seventeenth and eighteenth centuries.

Firstly, there came a decline of the big market cities such as Gao and Timbuktu. This was partly the result of the Moroccan invasion of Songhay (1591). Law and order broke down across wide regions. Trade suffered. Some of the old market cities became quite unimportant, and today are almost forgotten. Timbuktu was hard hit; Gao even worse. Such was the danger from the invaders that Gao is said to have been emptied of its inhabitants. Some were killed, many fled. And as Gao fell into ruin, there was nobody to look after the farms around it. Much careful irrigation, of water-supply by canals and ditches, became useless.

Secondly, as the power of the people of the towns or cities got smaller, the power of the peoples of the countryside and villages got larger. New states were built by the peoples of the countryside. Mostly, these states were not Muslim. Sometimes they were anti-Muslim, because they were built by people who felt that the people of the Muslim cities were their enemies.

Thirdly, the seventeenth century was also a time when professional armies became bigger, and gained a marked increase in their fire-power. The new states tended to be ruled, more and more, by men whose power rested on their increasingly destructive armies.

Fourthly, the eighteenth century was generally a time of revival. Trade improved again: trade inside West Africa, but also trade across the Sahara. The disorders of the previous century began to be tackled, and at least partly ended, by new ways of government.

These new ways were part of a revival of Islam. They were invented, especially, by some Fulani groups. They led to what historians have called the Fulani reforming movement.

The destruction of Songhay

Judar Pasha and his Moroccan army of musket-carrying soldiers took control of the central area of the Songhay empire in 1591 when, having marched over the desert from Morocco, they seized the cities of Timbuktu, Gao and Jenne.

But the Songhay leaders did not give in. Defeated whenever they tried a big battle against the Moroccans, they fell back on guerrilla tactics. From their stronghold in Dendi, the southerly part of the old empire, they fought back in this way for more than half a century. In 1608, for example, the Dendi *hi koy*, or admiral of the Songhay fleet of war-canoes on the Niger, attacked Moroccan garrisons along the whole middle course of the river. A year later the Dendi *fari bar*, a leading Songhay general, carried out a very tough raiding march across the wide belt of land enclosed by the bend of the Middle Niger and attacked the Moroccans who were then in occupation of Jenne. Other Songhay units followed this surprise assault by a series of guerrilla operations against Moroccan garrisons west of Timbuktu.

Hostilities of this kind continued until about 1660. They did nothing to restore Songhay: on the contrary, they only added to the ruin of this once prosperous political structure. By about 1650, Songhay was reduced to a weak group of little states in the south-eastern part of the former empire.

It was not so much the strength of the Moroccans that prevented the restoring of Songhay as the total collapse of the empire once its central power was weakened. That system, as we have noted, had rested largely on the strength and prosperity of the cities; and this strength and prosperity of the cities had relied, in turn, largely on the subjection or enslavement of many peoples of the countryside. For them the Moroccan invasion was a chance of freedom. They seized it eagerly.

Many subject or 'slave' peoples or groups of peoples, of whom the largest were called the Doghorani, rose in revolt against their masters. They fought for their own interests, and these interests were in direct opposition to the restoring of Songhay.

With their central government destroyed and their armies smashed, the Songhay chiefs and generals faced not only the Moroccans, but many of their own subjects as well. Only a widely popular war against the invaders could have restored Songhay; but no such war was possible.

Middle Niger cities: the Tuareg

Early in the seventeenth century the rulers of Morocco began to tire of their Songhay adventure. It had brought them much wealth in gold and other goods, but not as much as they had expected; and it had cost them dear. The Moroccan ruler, Sultan Mulay Zidan, successor of Sultan Mulay the Victorious, complained that as many as 23,000 Moroccan soldiers had died in this effort at conquest. Although he had taken the title of King of Gao, Timbuktu and Jenne, the Moroccan king decided to stop reinforcing his garrisons in those cities. These had conquered the Songhay suppliers of gold, but failed to reach the Akan sources of supply. The Akan, now trading with Europeans along the coast, began reducing their deliveries to the north.

After 1621 these cities along the Middle Niger were left to the rule of locally recruited governors, called *pashas*, who offered no more than a feeble defence of the cities and nearby lands they were supposed to protect. These *pashas* and their soldiers intermarried with the local population. They gave birth to a group of Timbuktu people who were partly Moroccan in origin, and were called the *arma*. By 1700 the *arma* had little power left to them.

Timbuktu and Jenne became the target for attacks from the Bambara in the west. But they and Gao also became targets for an old enemy, the raiding warriors of the Saharan Tuareg. In about 1680 a section of the Tuareg, called the Wulliminden, seized Gao and made a camp there. From this base they turned westward up the Niger, warring continually with the defenders of Timbuktu. By 1720 the Wulliminden and Tadmekkei Tuareg had won control of much of the Middle Niger country, and in 1737 the

Wulliminden actually captured Timbuktu for a time and made the local *pashas* pay them tribute. In about 1770 they made a permanent settlement at Gao.

These Tuareg were not, of course, only raiders. They were also interested in the trans-Saharan trade. They set about trying to restore it. They were not very successful in this, partly because they were so often at war with the peoples of the Niger country, and partly because these people were so often at war with each other. But it would be wrong to think that the trans-Saharan trade disappeared. On the contrary, in spite of all the dangers and obstacles, traders found ways of carrying on their business. In 1635, for example, some English merchants in Morocco were able to tell their partners in London that they were sending many English goods by camel-caravan to Timbuktu, Gao and other parts of West Africa, and were buying in exchange a lot of West African gold. Yet the great days of the gold trade across the desert were over.

Bambara states: Segu and Kaarta

Among the country people who now began to raise their heads in the country of the Middle and Upper Niger were members of many different West African peoples who had lived here under various empires in the past. Some, like the Soninke or Sarakolle, were descendants of people who had lived in Ancient Ghana. Others, who belonged to the large and various Mande or Mandinka language-family, had been loyal to Ancient Mali. Others again, like the Dogon, had lived on the edge of these old empires. Spread among them in groups of varying size were the Fulani.

In the troubles that followed the destruction of Songhay, some of these peoples began to seek new fortunes of their own. Foremost among them were the Bambara. Under energetic leaders, the Bambara now built a small but strong state that was based on the Niger market-town of Segu and its surrounding lands. Somewhat later they built a second state that was based on the countryside of Kaarta to the north-west of Segu.

The traditions say that the Bambara state of Segu was founded by two brothers, called Barama Ngolo and Nia Ngolo, soon after 1600. These two men were possibly at first little more than leaders of a well-organized band of raiders from the countryside. They took advantage of the confusion of the times in order to enrich themselves at the expense of their neighbours, building what the merchants of the cities no doubt condemned as a robber gang. But success brought them bigger and better ideas. Under their Ngolo chiefs, these hard-riding Bambara farmers settled down and formed their own system of law and order.

We do not know exactly how they did this. Towards 1650, however, they were established in the Segu region, mainly on the south bank of the

Map 6.3 The Bambara states.

Niger. They were led by an energetic chief called Kaladian. He seems to have ruled them until about 1680, and to have extended Bambara authority over a wide region of this central country of the Western Sudan. This empire included for a while the city of Timbuktu.

Mamari Kulibali and Ngolo Diara

Kaladian's empire fell apart with his death. The next big figure in this region, the famous Mamari Kulibali – Mamari the *Tiguiton* or *Biton*, Mamari the Commander – is said to have begun his career with no more than a handful of followers. He reigned from about 1712 to 1755, and was the true founder of Segu. He defeated his rivals soon after 1712, fought off an attack by the king of Kong in about 1730, drove out another set of Bambara rivals a few years later, and left his successors with a fair-sized state.

The Bambara rivals whom Mamari drove out of the Segu region, in about 1753, moved some 300 kilometres to the north-west. There they founded a second Bambara state in Kaarta. This was the region where Kumbi, the capital of Ancient Ghana, had once flourished.

These two states dominated the country of the Middle Niger until late in the nineteenth century. Segu was always the stronger of the two. Under Mamari Kulibali it included the river country from the neighbourhood of modern Bamako all the way downstream to Timbuktu, together with the trading city of Jenne and markets along the river itself.

Mamari built his power according to the methods of the Songhay emperors after *Sunni* Ali. He relied on long-service soldiers and sailors. With these, he formed a professional army several thousand strong, and also a

83

professional 'navy' on the Niger, from war-prisoners. These prisoners, reduced to a type of slavery, became regular soldiers and canoe-men. With these troops Mamari overcame all his rivals and neighbours – Soninke, Fulani, Malinke, Mossi and others.

Yet in building this military power, Mamari again created rivals for power. After his death in about 1755, events took a new turn. His son Dekoro became king of Segu, but had ruled for less than two years when the commanders of the soldiers took over. According to the traditions, King Dekoro was killed by the professional soldiers, bound together as they were in their condition of being a caste or group of 'slaves'. Then the king's power was taken by the *Ton-Mansa*, or 'commander of the slaves', who was the senior army general.

But this *Ton-Mansa*, like other ambitious generals then and since, fell victim to his own methods. He set an example which others could repeat. Three years later the soldiers killed him too, and elected in his place another general called Kaniuba Niuma, Kaniuba the Handsome, who was commander of the cavalry at Segu.

Kaniuba's reign was likewise no more than three years. Then the soldiers overthrew him in his turn and elected yet another king, Kafa Diugu, from among their number. Only in about 1766 did this disorderly soldier's rule come to an end. Then an outstanding leader called Ngolo Diara seized the throne. Ngolo Diara reigned for more than 30 years, put an end to the soldiers' political plots and plans, and restored the state of Segu to its former position of power.

Segu under King Ngolo became a large and busy city. In 1796, two years after Ngolo's death, the Scottish traveller, Mungo Park, the first European to come this way, estimated that Segu contained as many as 30,000 people. He found them living in four closely adjoining towns which consisted of clay-built houses with flat roofs, sometimes of two storeys. Segu's prosperity and size greatly impressed Park. 'The view of this extensive city,' he wrote, 'the numerous canoes upon the river, the crowded population, and the cultivated state of the surrounding countryside, formed altogether a prospect of civilization and magnificence, which I little expected to find in the centre of Africa.'[4]

The Fulani reforming movement

The Bambara states of Segu and Kaarta were a part of the political recovery in the Western Sudan after the collapse of Songhay and the final decline

---

[4] From Mungo Park, *Travels in the Interior of Africa in the Years 1795, 1796 and 1797*. Drawn from Park's published journals, these composed his first great journey in West Africa. He embarked on a second journey in 1805, and perished during the course of it.

of Mali. But they were not the only part. Another of great importance was the rise of a new set of states under Fulani leaders, and, combined with this, a renewed effort to strengthen the powers and the ideas of Islam.

Most of the Fulani were cattle-breeders who followed a wandering way of life. Now and then, linked with other peoples, some of them had settled down and grown used to living in towns. Mixed with Mandinka allies, the Fulani of Takrur had done this in the middle of the sixteenth century.

Other groups of Fulani had also done the same, and, in doing so, had likewise changed their methods of government. Living in one place for long periods, they had accepted the authority of some of their ruling families; and these families regularly elected men to rule them as chiefs. In this, of course, they behaved like many other wandering peoples who had settled down and found that they needed chosen men to rule over them. Many Fulani ruling families now took part in a movement for Muslim revival. Unlike the Bambara leaders and their people, these Fulani became devoted Muslims.

Historians differ on the exact reasons for this. Broadly, however, we can see in this Fulani acceptance of Islam the same kind of motives that had inspired earlier kings and peoples in the Western Sudan. Islam's unified system of ideas about religion, law and order, and trading customs could be valuable to men who suffered from the confusion of the times, for it promised a way of overcoming conflicts and rivalries. And many men undoubtedly remembered how the empires of Mali and Songhay had become strong under Muslim rule, or at least under Muslim influence.

Among the Fulani, their new faith had what we can now see was a revolutionary effect. First, it gave them a new unity among themselves. Secondly, it brought them into touch with the wider current of Muslim thought, whether from West Africa, from Egypt, or within the Western Sudan itself, and made them think about international as well as local questions. In this way they acquired new ambitions. There emerged what we may call the Fulani reforming movement. At its best, this held out a common vision and idea of how people in community should behave and live together, and of what they should strive to do for the betterment of life.

This new vision inspired in turn a revival of the power and law of Islam throughout the Western Sudan. Little by little, Fulani leaders gathered warrior bands. They began to set up new states in the countries where they lived, in those same countries which had suffered so many troubles since the decline of Mali and the ruin of Songhay.

We should note two important points. The first is that although this Muslim revival was often the work of Fulani people (or their close relations, the Tucolor), these were by no means alone. Others also took part. Among these the most important were the Mandinka, whose ancestors had built the empire of Mali and whose traders, the Dyula, had done so much for the trade of West Africa. The Mandinka will generally have understood, far better than the Fulani, how to revive trade and why it was necessary to build up the strength of the market-cities once again. They had more relevant experience.

Another point to remember is that this reforming movement was a complicated process. Much good came out of it; but also much misery. In the minds of the best of the reformers there was manifest an intention to open a new period of social justice, security for all Muslims, and prosperity by trade. The whole of the Western Sudan should come within the *Dar al-Islam*, the 'home' of Islam, the place where people should obey the rules of Allah and live at peace together. But it did not work out like this.

A great deal of progress was made in several ways: in trade and education, and in the spread of law and order. The Western Sudan regained its international connections. Muslim scholars once more travelled from capital to capital, including some who came from distant lands outside West Africa. Yet this progress was purchased at a bitter cost to many non-Muslim peoples who were raided, plundered, or turned into slaves. Later, in the nineteenth century, there were more wars; and not a few of these wars were the work of kings and warriors who used their devotion to Islam simply as a cover for seeking loot and privilege.

In the eighteenth century, however, the changes were impressive in a number of new states.

The western imamates

The first of these reforming states, of these Fulani-led states of Muslim revival, was the imamate of Futa Jallon. We call it an imamate because it was ruled by an *almamy* or *imam* of Islam. It lay in the hillside country that is now in the central part of the modern republic of Guinea. Muslim reformers of the Fulani – *Mujaddadin*, 'revivers of Islam'[5] – together with allied groups of Mandinka and other local peoples founded this state in about 1725. They subdued the non-Muslim farmers who were living in the neighbourhood, members of a branch of the Mandinka language-family called Dialonke.

This was a state of a new kind. It was organized in nine provinces (*diwal*) and many sub-districts (*miside*), and its political power was wielded by a religious leader, the *almamy*, while its military power, also commanded by the *almamy*, was based on a strict system of compulsory service. But the imamate of Futa Jallon was not simply a dictatorship of religious leaders.

---

[5] *Mujaddadin*, revivers of Islam, must be distinguished from *Mujahiddin*, warriors of Islam.

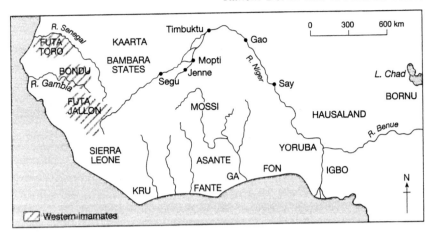

Map 6.4 The western imamates.

It retained many traditional features of West African political life. These included a measure of democracy. The *almamy* was very powerful, and claimed to rule in the name of God. But he still had to listen to the opinions of his counsellors; and these counsellors, at least when they were effective, spoke up for the complaints and needs of ordinary people.

Yet the part democracy played grew less with time. A new *almamy* was chosen every two years, at least after 1800; but the election was always from one of two ruling families, the Alfa or the Sori. With this narrow method of choosing their ruler, the leading families won more and more privilege and wealth. In the nineteenth century this was to lead to many revolts and changes. Here we need only note that the imamate of Futa Jallon, strong in its defensive hills, survived more or less intact until French colonial invasion later in the nineteenth century.

A second imamate was formed in Futa Toro, in the land of old Takrur far to the west, among the northern neighbours of the Wolof. Here along the south bank of the Senegal river the Denianke kings had ruled since the Fulani–Mandinka invasion of 1559. Yet here too the influence of Islam had remained alive, though the Denianke kings were not Muslims; and Islam now acquired new power. In the 1770s there arrived in Futa Toro a group of Muslim reformers. They belonged to the clan of the Torodbe, and were led by a famous marabout, or religious leader, called Suleiman Ba. This *almamy* or *imam* defeated the ruling *silatigui* (a Mande word which means 'commander', and was the title of the Denianke rulers) at a decisive battle in 1776. The Torodbe then formed the imamate of Futa Toro. They ruled it severely and owned or controlled all the fertile land. But they also gave peace to the people of Futa Toro, and introduced Muslim schools for children. Later, when these Torodbe grew more numerous and so became

87

short of land, they began to take themselves and their ideas about government and religion to other parts of the Sudan.

The Torodbe belonged to the Tucolor, a West African people closely related to the Fulani. Once established in Futa Toro, they began to expand the trade with French merchants who came up the Senegal river, as well as with other Muslim centres of trade in the western region of the Western Sudan. They gave attention to Muslim learning and founded many schools for teaching the laws of Islam although, like their Fulani neighbours, their belief in Islam was combined with many ideas drawn from traditional customs. This included a great reverence for 'holy men' or marabouts who were supposed to possess magical powers, an aspect of life in that part of West Africa (as in some other parts) which may still be observed today.

A third new Muslim state, or *imamate*, was founded by another Fulani group soon after 1770 in the region of Bondu, lying between Futa Toro and Futa Jallon. The Scottish traveller Mungo Park, who passed through Bondu in 1795, has left us a good description of the country. He found it prosperous and at peace, though threatened by many dangers. The king, who lived in a set of clay-built houses surrounded by a high wall, received him hospitably and introduced him to his wives, who found their first sight of a European very surprising.[6] Park also found Bondu well provided with village schools, and visited many of them. He thought the children very well behaved and attentive. The cattle-breeders of the countryside, he observed, were quite wealthy, 'and enjoy the necessaries of life in a high degree'.

A traveller's story

What was it like to travel in those days? Mungo Park met with difficulties through the actions of some of the kings across whose lands he travelled – not surprisingly, for he reached them through the territories of rival kings, and was easily suspected of being a spy. But he met with much kindness from ordinary people, and one of his stories about this deserves telling here.

Arriving at Segu for the first time, he had to wait on the bank of the Niger opposite that large and prosperous city while the king of Segu decided whether or not to let him go across. He was hungry and alone. At sunset, while he was sitting under a tree and wondering whether he would

---

[6] They teased him good-humouredly about the whiteness of his skin and the size of his nose, saying that both were artificial. 'The first, they jokingly said, was produced when I was an infant, by dipping me in milk; and they insisted that my nose had been pinched every day till it had acquired its present unsightly and unnatural conformation.' Park, *Travels in the Interior of Africa*.

ever see his own homeland again, a woman who had been working in the fields came up and spoke to him. She asked him why he looked so sad and tired. When he explained, 'she took up my saddle and bridle, and with looks of great pity, asked me to follow her'. Leading him to her hut, she lit a lamp and spread a mat upon the floor, and told him that he should rest there until the next day. Meanwhile she would find him some food.

In a little while, Park wrote afterwards, this kindly and hospitable woman returned with well-prepared fish, which she baked on the embers of her fire and gave him to eat. After this she told the other women members of her family to go on with their spinning, and they worked through most of the night. While they were spinning, they made a song about their hungry visitor. This song 'was sung by one of the young women, the rest joining in a sort of chorus'. The words, Park tells us, went something like this: 'The winds roared and the rains fell, the poor white man, faint and weary, came and sat under our tree. He has no mother to bring him milk, no wife to grind his corn. Let us pity the poor white man: no mother has he . . .'[7]

This little story shows once again how false an impression may be given by the bare record of events. Wars and quarrels between leaders, the rise and fall of states and kings and generals: all this can suggest that life was one long tale of violence. But in times of peace it was not like that; and times of peace were more frequent than times of war.

The eastward spread of Muslim reform

While these three new Muslim states were taking shape in the west, others of a similar kind began to appear further eastward. Here, too, formerly subject peoples made new states of their own; and here, too, the Fulani and their allies played a leading part.

Some of these Fulani lived in the Masina plains which lie in the neighbourhood of the Niger market-town of Mopti. Like their Bambara neighbours, with whom they were sometimes on good terms and sometimes bad, they made a bid for independence. In about 1629 their chiefs, the Ardo, who were not yet converted to Islam, broke away from the overlordship of the Moroccan *pasha* or governor of Timbuktu, allied themselves with the Songhay of Dendi, southernmost province of the old Songhay empire, and waged war on every Moroccan or part-Moroccan garrison they could reach. Afterwards, they became subject to the overlordship of the rising power of Segu. Much later, in the nineteenth century, Muslim Fulani in these Masina plains built an empire of their own.

---

[7] Park, *Travels in the Interior of Africa*.

Further eastward again, beyond the Masina plains, other Fulani groups established themselves on the plains to the south-west of Gao. There, too, they were able to set up a little state of their own.

Other groups went on down the banks of the Niger. Not long before 1800 the religious leader of some of these, a marabout called Alfa Muhammad Diobo, founded the town of Say, not far from modern Niamey, which is the capital of the Niger republic today. Alfa Muhammad's idea was to make Say into a centre for Muslim revival.

With the foundation of Say, by 1800 the Muslim revival movement had moved right across the Western Sudan as far as the borders of Hausaland.

Early Senegambia

Early Senegambia

A long way to the west of the old grassland empires lay the country and coastland between the Senegal and the Gambia rivers, long since named Senegambia by European travellers and writers, but first reached by Europeans only in the fifteenth century. They found a complex of African peoples and states, and opened a sea-trade with some of these. But it was a long time before Europeans understood anything real and reliable about these states of Senegambia. When they did, they placed the Senegambian states high on their list of useful partners.

The Wolof empire

Soon after AD 1300 the Wolof people come into history as the makers of a small state, called Jolof, in the central part of inland Senegal. Though little is known about their relations with Ancient Ghana or other states of the Western Sudan, it seems that their political methods were influenced by their neighbours. Jolof was ruled by a king, whose title was *burba*, through ruling families in much the same way as had been adopted by the Soninke of Ghana and the Mandinka of Mali. Here again was a case where an important descent-line chief who had religious duties, as the leader of ceremonies by which one people linked themselves with their 'founding ancestors' in the world of the spirits, was given political duties as well. Fulfilling these political and religious duties, the king became powerful.

Like early Ghana long before, Jolof began to form a number of little 'daughter states' during the fourteenth century. This was a type of political development which happened in many lands. It occurred at much the same time, for example, among the Yoruba of Western Nigeria: the Yoruba 'mother state' of Ife set the pattern for the formation of other Yoruba

Map 7.1 The Wolof empire and some neighbouring states.

states which were governed in the same way. So the *Burba* Jolof, like the *oni* of Ife, came to have religious and political power over lesser Wolof states, of which the principal ones were Cayor, Walo and Baol. These the *burba* and his government of Jolof joined into a powerful Wolof empire during the fifteenth century. At the same time a related people, the Serer, formed a state called Sine-Salum; this became an outlying part of the Wolof empire.

Wolof government and trade

Up to the middle of the sixteenth century this empire was held firmly together by the government of the *burbas*. This government may be described, again like that of the Yoruba, as an aristocratic one. It was ruled by privileged men or nobles who drew their power from being born into ruling families. Their political strength came from their leadership in warfare, their control of trade, and their close alliance with one another under the rule of the *burba*. They also had religious power that came from Wolof beliefs about the spiritual character of their rulers.

This aristocratic system was well described in 1455 by the earliest European to visit the Wolof, a Venetian called Cadamosto. He explained that the *Burba* Jolof was not chosen simply by birth. Usually, he said, 'three or four lords (of whom there are many in this country) choose a king whom they like . . . and who reigns as long as he pleases them. [But] they often dethrone their kings by force, and [on their side] the kings often try to make themselves so powerful that they cannot be dethroned . . .' Like other kings in other kingdoms then or since, the Wolof kings did this by appointing their own officials and servants to positions of power.

Most people had no political rights of much value. They were obliged to serve the lineage chiefs, pay tribute in cattle and other goods, and work for the lineage chiefs when required. Within these limits, however, the Wolof system was prosperous and stable. It endured for many years. How strong it was is shown by a Portuguese report of 1506.[1] This says that the *Burba* Jolof had an army of 10,000 horsemen and 100,000 foot soldiers, no doubt another exaggeration but pointing nevertheless to the existence of a big military power.

After the development of European sea-trade along the coast of Senegal, there came a gradual dissolution of Wolof power. European contacts had begun in the 1440s, at first as little more than piracy. Portuguese sailors and soldiers fortified the little island of Arguin, on the northerly coast of Mauretania, and raided the mainland for captives whom they took back to Portugal and sold into slavery. By the 1450s, however, this piracy had begun to give way to a regular partnership in trade between the Portuguese captains and the agents of the *Burba* Jolof and his subject-kings. Like other rulers, they proved willing to sell captives to the Europeans in exchange for the advantage of being able to buy European goods such as metalware, cotton cloth and weapons.

Partnership in trade led to a political alliance with the Portuguese. One interesting example of how this worked occurred when Biram became *Burba* Jolof in 1481. Biram favoured as his heir a man who was his own mother's brother. This was resented by Biram's brothers who were the sons of other wives of his father. After Biram's death they revolted and deposed the prince whom Biram had chosen. This prince is known in the European records as Bemoy, from the Wolof word *bumi*, 'the chosen one'. Bemoy fled for help to Portugal. There in Lisbon he was splendidly welcomed and promised aid if he would become a Christian. The Portuguese records describe Bemoy as 'forty years old, a man of great stature, very dark, with a long beard, finely built and of a very noble appearance'.

---

[1] That of Duarte Pacheco Pereira, *Esmeralda de Situ Orbis*.

Intending to make Bemoy their puppet ruler, and so gain indirect power in the Wolof empire, the Portuguese sent him back to Wolof with a fleet of twenty ships and many soldiers. But this attempt at warlike infiltration, a method which the Portuguese were afterwards to try in other African lands and sometimes with success, failed disastrously in Wolof. Bemoy was killed, and the expedition went home defeated.

Rivals to Jolof: the rise of Cayor

Although the Wolof proved strong enough to keep the Portuguese out of their country, they were unable to hold their empire together. The main reason for this lay in the advantages which the leading men of Cayor, the biggest of the 'daughter states' of Jolof, could now win from coastal trade with Europeans. As this trade expanded, the nobles of Cayor grew more powerful; and, growing more powerful, they became more independent. Finally, in about 1556, they rebelled against the *Burba* Jolof of that time and set up an independent kingdom under one of their number, whom they chose to be king, and whose royal title was *damel*. Encouraged by this success, Cayor then invaded Baol, and the *damel* of Cayor then became ruler of Baol as well. Their success in this was crowned a little later when Cayor defeated a Jolof army and killed the *burba* who was leading it.

From this time onwards the prosperity and therefore the power of Jolof declined because it was cut off by Cayor from contact with European trade.[2] Yet the *damel*s of Cayor proved incapable of building a strong empire. This was partly because Walo and Baol also shared in the advantages of European trade, and partly because they failed to form a firm alliance against Mauretanian Berbers, who repeatedly attacked these trading states from across the Senegal river.

In 1686, Baol threw off its subjection to Cayor. Not long afterwards Jolof again invaded Cayor, seeking to re-establish its former power, and this time with partial success because they were able to kill the *damel*. Many Cayor Wolof then fled to Baol. In subsequent fighting the *Burba* Jolof was himself killed in battle and his army thrown back. After this the king or *teny* of Baol took control of Cayor and became its *damel*. This ruler, Latir Fal Sukabe, continued to rule over Baol and Cayor until 1702 when he was succeeded by two sons, the older of whom became *damel* of Cayor while the younger became *teny* of Baol.

Though with many wars such as these, and therefore with a great deal of misery for the mass of ordinary people, all these states maintained

---

[2] Here again there is an interesting parallel with Yoruba history. There, too, during the sixteenth century the Yoruba of Oyo, thanks to their command of long-distance trade with the Western Sudan, were able to outshine the power of Ife and its traditional ruler, the *oni*.

their independence of the Europeans until the late nineteenth century, when they were invaded and subjected by the French. They had formed a notable part of West African civilization. But they had failed to overcome the quarrels between their aristocratic rulers, or to resolve the great conflict between the interests of the nobles and the interests of the majority of ordinary folk within their kingdoms.

Futa Toro and the Fulani

One other development in Senegal should be noticed. This was the rise of a new state in old Takrur, north-east of the Wolof states. With this the Fulani and their near-relations, the Tucolor,[3] now made a decisive entry on the scene of history.

As we have seen the Fulani had made their mark in earlier times. They were concerned in the fall of Ancient Ghana and the rise of its successor states. But by this time they had spread far across the grasslands of West Africa from their original home near the Upper Senegal river and the Upper Niger.

They had sent out nomad groups of cattle-breeders both eastward and westward. These groups were certainly small in the beginning, but they built up their numbers. Some of them settled down and formed states of their own, so that, in the course of time, there came to be two kinds of Fulani: 'cattle Fulani' who lived the old nomad life of the countryside, and

Map 7.2 The Fulani and Mandinka movements in the sixteenth century.

---

[3] 'Tucolor' means 'people from Takrur'.

'town Fulani' who preferred to live in towns. Because of this, and because of their wandering habits, the Fulani have played a special and at times a leading part in West African history.

What some of these Fulani did, soon after 1500, is told by traditions which may be accepted as truthful in outline, though not in detail. A group of Fulani cattle-breeders, ruled by a prince called Tenguella, was living at this time in the broad plains between Termes and Nioro, lands that were once the homeland of Ancient Ghana in the country between the Upper Niger and the Sahara. This area had passed from the control of Ghana to the control of Mali, and was now under the authority of the emperor of Songhay whose capital lay at Gao. This emperor, as we have seen in Chapter 5, was the vigorous and efficient *Askia* Muhammad, afterwards called *Askia* the Great.

Tenguella Koli and the Denianke

Tenguella, the Fulani leader, revolted against the overlordship of *Askia* Muhammad. No doubt he and his people wanted freedom of movement for their cattle. Perhaps they also objected to the taxes which they were supposed to pay their Songhay overlord or his officials. Tenguella led his warriors across the plains against Diara, one of the old successor-states of Ghana whose king was now a vassal (that is, a tax-paying under-king) of the Songhay emperor. There is reason to think that Tenguella was encouraged by the reigning emperor of Mali, who was now a declining rival of *Askia* Muhammad of Songhay.

Askia Muhammad's brother, Amar, led an army against this Fulani raider. The two armies met near Diara in 1512. Amar won, and Tenguella was killed. But this proved to be only the beginning of the Fulani adventure.

Tenguella had a son named Koli by a wife who belonged to the ruling family of Mali. Tenguella Koli led his father's warriors south-westward, crossed the Upper Senegal river and arrived in Badiar, a region which lies to the north-west of the Futa Jallon Mountains.[4] Here he was joined by many Mandinka soldiers, who saw in him a bold leader as well as a relation of their own overlord, the emperor of Mali.

Seeking a new home, these Fulani and Mandinka allies marched north-westward into Senegal, passed round the fringe of the Wolof states, and fell upon the ancient state of Takrur in Futa Toro. This state was then ruled by a family of Soninke chiefs who owed loyalty to the king of Diara. Tenguella Koli and his Fulani–Mandinka army overthrew these Soninke chiefs in 1559 and set up a new line of kings.

---

[4] In the modern republic of Guinea, and not to be confused with Futa Toro.

These new rulers in Futa Toro were called the Denianke. They proved strong and capable, and remained in control of this country until 1776, more than two centuries.

Notice, here, three developments.

Firstly, these Fulani had changed their way of life. Those who had set out to invade Diara at the beginning of the century were little more than a raiding band of cattle nomads. They were after revenge for real or fancied hurts; even more, they were after loot in the settled lands of Diara. They behaved no differently from the nomad Tuareg of the southern Sahara, who often attacked the settled lands and cities of the Western Sudan. But the Fulani who conquered and settled in Futa Toro some 50 years later were a people ready to abandon their wandering ways and build a state of their own. It seems that this change was largely due to their long contact with Mandinka people who were not nomads.

The second development, flowing from the first, was that these Fulani had adopted new ways of living together. They had accepted the political authority of chiefs and ruling families settled in one place. They had adopted city manners, and acquired an interest in trade.

Thirdly, these Fulani–Mandinka state-builders in Futa Toro held fast to their own religions. They resisted Islam. And because they resisted Islam, the Muslim traders of Futa Toro (of old Takrur) began to quit the trading towns which had long existed there. This kind of thing, we may recall, had occurred before, when the non-Muslim rulers of old Takrur had attacked and taken Kumbi, Ghana's ancient capital. Then the Muslim traders of Kumbi had retreated northward and founded a new trading centre in the southern Sahara at Walata, a market that was still important in the sixteenth century.

There followed from this clash of religions a real decline in the commercial importance of Futa Toro, and one that was to last for some time. It was at this period, it seems, that ancient and famous markets like Takrur itself, Sila and Berissa began to disappear from the map. The writers of North Africa had often mentioned these markets in the past. Today we do not even know exactly where they lay.

Thus the sixteenth century in Futa Toro may be seen as a period of both advance and retreat. The new rulers brought strong methods of government, but they also provoked a serious decline of trade.

The Gambia, Futa Jallon, Sierra Leone

Southward from the Wolof states and Sine-Salum,[5] along the Gambia river and the coast towards Sierra Leone, there lived small populations in the

---

[5] See map 7.1 on p. 94.

scrublands and forests. Like their neighbours, by AD 1000 these peoples had long since entered their Iron Age. They had developed their own methods of farming, fishing, metal-working and other skills, and their arts of dancing, music and sculpture.

Little is known of their early development. Deep in their forests, safe in their valleys or along their remote river banks, they remained for a long time on the margin of the busy world of the inland country. Most of them lived at what was then the back door of West Africa, facing an empty ocean that was not yet crossed by ships from other continents. We may imagine that they lived quiet lives, keeping to their ancient ways, warring with one another from time to time for land to cultivate, but generally content with their ancient methods of social and political organization in small family groups.

After 1300 there came a change. Many of these peoples began to feel the influence of the growing empire of Mali, and of the expanding power of the southerly Wolof states. Some of them had valuable products to sell, among these being the wax, for example, of the Diola people as well as a great deal of dried sea-fish. The Dyula trading companies of the Mandinka of Mali began to link them with the Western Sudan. They found new and bigger markets. Their country also began to be penetrated by wanderers from the inland country.

New states emerged. Around 1400 the Susu people, for example, formed a state in the Futa Jallon, the hill region that lies in the centre of the modern republic of Guinea. Other Susu afterwards moved down to the coast where most of their descendants live now, while a branch of the Fulani won control of Futa Jallon, remaining there to the present.

Others took the same route. In Sierra Leone, partly by migration from outside the area, new states began to be formed by the Bulom, Temne and Mende peoples on either side of the Scarcies river. Most of these incoming groups mingled with the populations they found in the country, adding to their numbers, sometimes keeping their own language and sometimes adopting the language of the local people among whom they settled. So while it is true that some of their distant ancestors undoubtedly came from the grassland country of the north, most were the descendants of peoples who had lived in Sierra Leone since distant Stone Age times.

New sea-trade

Revolutionary changes began when European ships sailed in from Portugal and Spain, England and France. They brought the coastal peoples a new and previously undreamt-of chance of sharing in long-distance trade. But they also brought firearms and new forms of warfare; and, not much later, they brought the beginnings of the Atlantic slave trade.

These visitors from Europe did a good service to history: they wrote many reports of what they found, saw and heard along the coast. Thus the same Cadamosto who had visited the Wolof empire in 1455 came up the Gambia river a year later and described what he found there. He made his base on an island in the estuary of the Gambia[6] and got in touch with local rulers, who included the *mansa*s or kings of Baddibu and Niumi (Barra).

After disputes and difficulties, European trade with these small river-side states of the Gambia became regular and peaceful. Portuguese ships now began coming here several times a year. In 1506 Duarte Pacheco Pereira wrote about the Gambian markets of his time. Far up the river, he wrote,

> there is a country called Cantor [probably between Basse and Yarbutenda]. It has four villages of which the biggest is called Sutucoo and has 4,000 inhabitants. The others are Jalancoo, Dobancoo and Jamnan Sura. They are surrounded by palisades of timber ... At Sutucoo there is held a big market. Mandinka traders come there with many donkeys. And when times are peaceful, these traders visit our ships [in the river], and we sell them red, blue and green cloth of cheap manufacture, linen and coloured silks, brass rings, hats and beads and other goods. Here in peaceful times we can buy five to six thousand *dobras'* worth of good quality gold. These lands of Sutucoo and their neighbours are part of the Wolof kingdom, but the people speak the Mandinka language ...

Such reports were made on most parts of the Guinea seaboard. They show how these coastal peoples, having long had trade with the inland country, now found new and useful partners from the sea. They also indicate that these peoples were well able to defend themselves. Pereira says that the Bulom of Sierra Leone, for example, were 'a warlike people' who dealt in gold, which they bought from the traders of the empire of Mali in exchange for salt, and which they now sold to the Portuguese for brass rings, large metal basins, and cotton goods. 'And in this country you can buy ivory necklaces that are carved better than anywhere else.' So greatly did the Portuguese admire the skills of West African ivory-carvers that rich traders and noblemen commissioned many beautiful objects, such as salt-cellars, for their own use at home.

Pereira explains how Sierra Leone, the Mountain of the Lion, got its name: 'Many people think that the name was given to this country because there are lions here, but this is not true. It was Pero de Sintra, a knight of Prince Henry of Portugal, who first came to this mountain. And when he saw a country so steep and wild he named it the land of the Lion, and not

---

[6] At first called St Andrew's Island, then James Island when the British made a base there in 1661.

for any other reason. There is no reason to doubt this, for he told me so himself.'

Behind the Bulom (or Sherbro, as they are sometimes called) was the kingdom of Loko, speaking a related language. To the north of them were the Temne; and behind these again, over the modern frontier of Sierra Leone with the republic of Guinea, were the Susu and the Fulani of the Futa Jallon, as well as other Mande-speaking peoples.

Methods of government

Another early Portuguese report, that of Valentim Fernandes written between 1506 and 1510, throws light on the political methods of these states. He mentions villages which had kings of their own, and explains that these kings also had councils of elders. 'If the king wants to go to war, he gathers the elders and holds his council. And if it appears to them that the war is unjust, or that the enemy is very strong, they tell the king that they cannot help him, and give orders for peace in spite of the king's disagreement.'

Not only were some people in these states more powerful than others, whether by their birth or their position in such associations as the Poro; they were also more prosperous. 'The houses of the poor are made of stakes stuck in the ground, hardened with mud and covered with thatch. [But] the houses of the rich are made of hardened clay and brick, well white-washed in the interior and outside covered with chalk or white clay, and the interior is very well adorned, and these are the best houses in all Guinea.'

Reasons for the rise and fall of states and empires

Underlying all these changes in West Africa were social and historical reasons, for the rise and fall of states, that can be analysed as clearly as in the case of changes in other parts of the world. These reasons were:

1 *Economic* A people who happened to control an important source of wealth found that they needed to defend it against rivals. Then they found that this wealth could give them the power to expand their control over the wealth of their neighbours. This led in turn to the development of wider trading systems, and these, in turn, to wider political systems. Small states grew into big states. Big states grew into empires (into states, that is, which control the life of other peoples as well as their own peoples).

Example The Asante empire. In the beginning, around AD
1400, Asante was a group of very small states where there was
gold in the ground and rivers. They began to export this gold to
the north. For a long time they were weak, and had to pay tribute
(taxes) to their neighbours. Then they found they could use the
wealth they got from gold to build a strong army. They used this
army against their neighbours. From about AD 1700 they went on
to build a very big trading system. They built the Asante empire.

2 *Military* A people who happened to occupy a good trading position
found that they could become stronger, and make their trading
system bigger, by getting control over their neighbours. They could
do this by buying military supplies or equipment which they did not
have or could not produce at home. Their good trading position
enabled them to pay for these supplies.

Example The Oyo empire. In the beginning, when the northern
Yoruba state of Oyo was founded, perhaps around AD 1300, the
Yoruba of Oyo were farmers and craftsmen. Then their chiefs found
that they occupied a key position on the long-distance trade routes
between the southern Yoruba states and the states of the Hausa
and others to the north of Oyo. This 'middleman' position gave
them a good basis for expansion. They had wealth enough to buy
horses from Hausaland and form an army of cavalry (horseriding
soldiers), although, because of tse-tse fly, they could not breed horses
themselves. This cavalry army made it possible for Oyo to expand
into an empire.

3 *Political* A people who happened to occupy a bad position for
defending themselves, or for developing their own political system,
found that they could gain from going to war with their neighbours.
If they won that war, then they also found that it would be wise to
remain strong. But to remain strong they had to dominate their
neighbours. This led them into building a bigger state than before.

Example The rise of the Fon state in Dahomey. After about AD
1600 the people who lived inland from the coast of Dahomey were
the Fon. They had to pay tribute (taxes) to the Yoruba of Oyo. They
were also raided for slaves by their small neighbours on the coast
of Dahomey. These small coastal states could do this because they
bought guns from the European sea-traders. So the Fon decided to
invade these small states in order to win control of the trade with
the Europeans. They did this in 1727 and after. This led to the rise
of the military state of the Fon. In the end, after AD 1800, this Fon
state helped towards the destruction of the empire of Oyo.

Of course, there were plenty of other reasons why small states
grew into big states or empires. But the chief causes of this development were economic, military and political.

The Forest Kingdoms: in the Delta of the Niger and its Peripheries

The Forest Kingdoms: in the Delta of the Niger and its Peripheries

With improved navigational skills and better sailing ships, European mariners now embarked on a remarkable period of discovery about the then unknown globe and its distant peoples; and this was to be the great triumph of the late fifteenth century. In what then seemed a climax to that period of discovery, Christopher Columbus reached the Caribbean in 1492 and brought in the New World, as it would be said, so as to 'right the balance of the Old'.

But another famous discovery had been made in 1472, twenty years earlier. A Portuguese captain, Ruy de Siqueira, reached the Bight of Benin on the far remote coastland of West Africa. This at once opened the way to the discovery of an unknown Africa beyond the southern skylines. These Portuguese ships were small, and their captains seldom sailed out of sight of land from fear of losing their route of return. But courage and determination were not lacking; and where the Portuguese led, other European sailors quickly followed. Up to now, the African peoples who lived along this West African seaboard had faced an ocean empty of visitors. Now they began to have visitors in plenty.

It would still be a long time before the full import of this news from Africa could be understood in Europe. But what the Portuguese found in the Bight (or wide bay) of Benin proved of sensational interest. For the little 'port' of Ugwato on the Benin river, where the Portuguese first landed, was found to be only a day or so's easy ride from a wealthy and imposing city. This turned out to be the capital city of a powerful kingdom called Benin.

That was good news; still better news followed. In 1486 another Portuguese mariner was able to buy a quantity of malagueta pepper; and this was at a time when pepper was valuable in Europe as a much sought after means of keeping meat edible, for artificial refrigeration was still far ahead. The Portuguese hastened to open a regular trade in malagueta pepper.

Curious to learn more about this unknown land called Portugal, the King of Benin sent one of his chiefs as an ambassador to Lisbon; and the visit was a notable success. The Portuguese official archives of that time say that this ambassador 'was a man of good speech and natural wisdom'. Great feasts were held in his honour (at the Portuguese royal court), and he was shown many of the good things of Portugal and Spain. 'He returned to his own land in a ship of the Portuguese king's, and at his departure they made him a gift of rich clothes.'

These and other such records have given us an outline of Benin history in those times. More knowledge soon made it clear that other such kingdoms, fully developed, were to be found along or near this West African coastland – kingdoms which had been formed and had flourished before any European influence arrived, and which displayed a native African civilization of great capacity and skill.

Reporting home, whether to court historians or to other European traders, these rare travellers returned to Europe with information that was often puzzling, strange or hard to understand. Europeans knew nothing about West African languages; in any case, they were often confused and misled by their own ignorance or superstition. They often reported gossip which proved to be baseless. Any truly reliable information that came to hand had to make headway against more or less wild or foolish reports, as when the Italian traveller Antonio Malfante came back in 1447 from the big oasis of Tuat, far away in the central Sahara, with news that further south again, beyond the great desert, there were peoples 'who have innumerable great cities and territories'. This was fairly close to the truth, but Malfante, repeating the tall tales carried by the long-distance caravan trade, added that those peoples 'breed greatly, for a woman bears up to five at a birth', along with other fantasies such as that 'they are eaters of human flesh'.

Yet sound information gradually spread as the long-distance trade widened in scope. It became known that Benin had other kingdoms in its neighbourhood, and other countries which had states of their own but which preferred to get along without kings. They had 'governments without rulers', as it became slowly understood. The complexities of African self-government could now begin to be examined.

Broadly stated, these kingdoms belonged to what may be termed 'the Yoruba group', and the 'government without rulers' states to 'the Igbo group'. Roughly dividing their territories in these densely forested lands, the wide River Niger came down from the far interior to its outflow in the Niger Delta, a land of many creeks and estuary rivers. Magnificent forests clothe these lands, even today, with hardwoods such as iroko and mahogany often rising to gigantic heights above the forest floor.

Early Yoruba history

Not far west of Benin, in ancient times just as today, lay the home of the Yoruba, another West African people who took shape several thousand years ago and whose political development followed distinctive patterns of its own.

This important people have several traditions about how their life began. One of them says that it was at Ile-Ife, an ancient town in Yorubaland, that mankind was first created. Another tradition tells the story of a great ancestor and hero called Oduduwa. He is said to have settled at Ile-Ife and sent out his descendants to rule the various branches of the Yoruba. One of his sons, for example, is said to have become the first *alafin* of Oyo, as well as being the father of the first *oba* of Benin, while another was the first *onisabe* of Sabe; his eldest daughter is remembered as the mother of the first *alaketu* of Ketu (in modern Dahomey), while another daughter gave birth to the first *olowu* of Owu.

What historical truth lies behind such beliefs? They point to the early arrival of newcomers who settled in Yorubaland and merged with the more numerous people whom they found there. The people who were already living in Yorubaland had certainly been there since distant Stone Age times. Archaeological evidence suggests that they were pioneering metal-workers and fine artists in baked clay and that they were possibly related to the people of the Nok Culture[1]. Experts in language explain that the Yoruba language (like other languages nearby) probably came into existence several thousand years ago.

Then who were the ancestors, personified by Oduduwa in the traditions, who joined these people and built the Yoruba civilization of historical times? Here again, modern experts in the study of language have something useful to say. They think that there were two main movements of incoming ancestors, one towards Ekiti, Ife and Ijebu in the zone of dense tropical forest, and the other towards Oyo in the much more open country to the north of the forest. The earliest of these migrations probably started soon after about AD 700.

Where did these incoming ancestors come from? Some Yoruba legends say that they came from Arabia, and quite a few Yoruba customs may perhaps reflect the ideas of ancient peoples who lived along the Middle Nile, notably the people of the ancient kingdom of Kush. No doubt the truth, however, is that these incoming ancestors came from the Western Sudan, more probably from a little way to the north of Yorubaland, where they had been influenced to some extent by the Nile civilizations which had sent out traders and travellers in ancient times. Entering Yorubaland, they brought new political ideas and methods with them. They introduced or

---

[1] See map on p. 12.

developed new types of government. We perhaps see the reflection of this process of early political development in the story of how Oduduwa sent out his children to rule the various branches of the Yoruba in new ways.

In any case, Yorubaland entered on a new stage of development before about AD 1000; and, partly because of these influences, this development launched the people of Yorubaland into forms of political life that were different from those of their neighbours.

Like the Igbo, the Yoruba relied on forest farming for their livelihood. Unlike the Igbo, their political life was dominated by town government and not by village government. Many Yoruba towns were founded in the forest lands to the west of the Niger and, somewhat later, in the more open country north of the great tropical forest. These towns varied in size, power and wealth.

Yoruba achievement: the growth of towns

Yoruba towns evolved from the rich complexity of Yoruba ways of life. In many fields the Yoruba shared the skills of their neighbours in forest farming, iron-smelting, brass-work, cotton-weaving and other valuable handicrafts. Yet their special contribution to West African civilization, as a modern Yoruba writer has rightly claimed, consisted in 'their remarkable urban centres, unparalleled anywhere else in tropical Africa'.[2] They had, of course, many villages and small settlements: *abúlé* (hamlet), *ìletò* (village), *ìlú ọlójà* (small market town); but it was in their big towns, their *ìlú aládé*, that their urban achievements were greatest.

The *ìlú aládé*, of which Ife was the most important in ancient times, were the seat of powerful rulers: of *oba*s whose ancestors were believed to be descended from Oduduwa, and who had the right to wear crowns with bearded fringes as a symbol of authority. Little is known of the size of these 'crowned' or capital towns in the distant past, but they certainly had large populations. They were usually surrounded by a defensive wall. The wall round Old Oyo, once the capital of a Yoruba empire, was as much as 40 kilometres round and 7 metres high at the beginning of the nineteenth century.

Yoruba methods of government

Externally, the capital towns of Yoruba states were linked together during ancient times in a confederation under the spiritual and political leadership

---

[2] G.J. Afolabi Ojo, *Yoruba Culture* (London, 1966), p. 104.

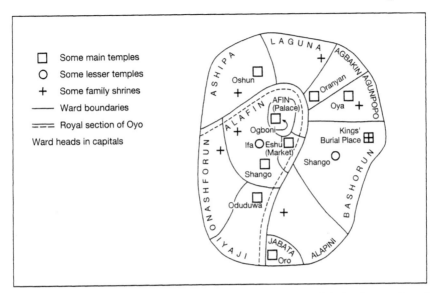

Map 8.1 Plan of the city of Old Oyo, capital of the powerful Yoruba empire of that name, in around 1650.

of the senior Yoruba ruler, the *oni* of Ife, and by arrangements between ruling families.

This confederal system left each state to run its own affairs, while providing means for keeping the peace between them. Only with the rise of Oyo in northern Yorubaland, during the sixteenth century, did the central influence of Ife begin to decline. Even then, the arrangements between ruling families continued.

'All these kingdoms', writes a Yoruba historian, 'believed in and practised the *Ebi* system of government. Under this system, a kingdom was regarded as a larger version of a family, and a country as a collection of kingdoms whose rulers looked on one another as relations'. Seniority was based on the believed ages of the various kingdoms. To some extent, the Oyo empire cut across these arrangements by asserting the leadership of Oyo, historically a 'junior' kingdom.[3] The Oyo empire and the *Ebi* system were thus in conflict.

Internally, these populous and busy capitals were organized in a way which combined segmentary patterns of authority, such as those of the Igbo, with government by ruling families and *obas* (kings). This combination of different types of self-rule was reflected in the architecture of the

---

[3] I.A. Akinjogbin, 'The Oyo empire in the 18th century', *Journal of the Historical Society of Nigeria* (December 1966), p. 451.

towns, whether they were capitals or not. At first sight these might appear as a mere confusion of dwellings, densely packed together and divided only by narrow roads. But the apparent confusion had an order of its own. Each family – each 'extended family', that is, of grandparents to grandchildren – lived in its own cluster of homes, its compound or *agbo'le*. Each *agbo'le* was gathered round the house of the head of its *agba ile* or descent-line (in this case a descent-line through fathers and not, as in Asante, through mothers). At the centre of the town, if it was a capital, stood the *afin* or *oba*'s palace, often a big building.

Government and religion

Political organization developed in the same way. Each head of a descent-line or 'big family' was in charge of his own quarter of the town. All the descent-lines sent representatives to sit on a council of chiefs who owed their positions to their birth. These chiefs, usually known as the *iwarefa*, had important political powers of decision. Often these included the right to choose the man who should be *oba*.

But it was seldom the work of the *iwarefa* to take action on decisions. Political action, as distinct from political decision, was the duty of the *oba* and his officials (civil servants). This formed another aspect of the Yoruba system. So the *oba*'s government consisted mostly of the servants and messengers of the *oba*. These might be very numerous in wealthy states. They took their orders only from the king. It could also consist of men who belonged to one or other of the special societies who were in charge of the various age-sets of the Yoruba. One or other of these age-sets carried out public works and performed services of value to the whole community. Inside the towns the various heads of descent-lines looked after purely local affairs.

In practice, the system was more complicated than any brief description could show. Though democratic in small matters, Yoruba government differed from Igbo government in being aristocratic wherever important decisions were concerned: power in big matters, that is, always rested in the hands of a minority of nobles.

Government by kings and nobles made it possible to unite the people of each main town firmly together, but difficult or impossible to unite the different towns. Each town's nobles tended to feel themselves in rivalry with those of neighbouring towns, even though the *Ebi* 'family system', as mentioned above, made all the towns part of the same big Yoruba 'family'.

Politics was mixed up with religion, even more than among other West African peoples. The Yoruba system of government in this respect, like other systems, rested on the political power of appointed rulers among leading families, but also on their religious power. In the distant past all the Yoruba states felt strong loyalty to the ancestors of Oduduwa, and so to the *oni* of Ife who was the senior living representative of those ancestors. But as civilization grew, and Yoruba populations became more numerous, this common loyalty to Ife proved difficult to maintain. Each state tended to develop its own separate loyalties, and to worship the spirits and gods in its own separate ways. This is one reason why some of the leading Yoruba spirits and gods have taken different forms. In some places, for example, Oduduwa is thought of as a man and in other places as a woman. According to a modern writer,

> The real keynote of the life of the Yoruba is neither in their noble ancestry nor in the past deeds of their heroes. The keynote of their life is their religion. In all things, they are religious ... As far as they are concerned, the full responsibility of all the affairs of life belongs to the Deity; their own part in the matter is to do as they are ordered through the priests or diviners whom they believe to be the interpreters of the will of the Deity ...[4]

This emphasis on the religious powers of their rulers has been reflected in Yoruba life by the beauty and excellence of Yoruba sculpture in wood and brass, clay and ivory. The 'home-city' of the Yoruba people, Ife, has yielded many splendid things that were made long ago in honour of Yoruba beliefs and rulers. At Ife, for instance, Yoruba artists were called on to celebrate the *oni* of Ife and his kinsmen, and evolved one of the greatest schools of sculpture the world has known. They modelled works in clay and brass that are of great power and beauty.

A study of these sculptures shows that some of their features relate back to those of the baked clay sculptures of the Nok Culture people in earlier times. On the other hand, the Ife brass sculptures were made by a special method, using wax, which was certainly used by the sculptors of the ancient civilizations of the Nile. Yoruba civilization was thus a creative combination of many ideas, customs and beliefs that were born in different parts of Africa.

Later Yoruba history: the growth of Oyo

It seems likely that Ife reached the height of its artistic and political achievement soon after AD 1300. By this period there were many Yoruba towns and a much larger Yoruba-speaking population than in earlier times, while the language they spoke varied from place to place. States created by the

---

[4] E. Bolaji Idowu, *Olúdùmarè: God in Yoruba Belief* (London, 1962), p. 5.

Yoruba existed far westward in Dahomey and northward through the rolling country beyond the edge of the forest, as far as the Niger above its confluence with the Benue. Here in the north there was Oyo, founded after most of the forest towns to the south but now destined, because of its favourable trading position and its local wealth, to become the strongest of them all, and the capital of a powerful empire.

Early in the sixteenth century, Oyo was still a small state scarcely able to hold its own against two strong neighbours, Borgu to the north and Nupe to the north-east. Nupe even conquered Oyo in about 1550. The king (*alafin*) of Oyo and his senior chiefs retired into Borgu, but soon returned south again and built a new capital at Igbohu. But now they began to consider ways of making themselves strong enough to prevent further defeats. One solution, it was clear, would be to build a strong cavalry army such as was repeatedly used by Borgu and Nupe.

Yet here there was a difficulty. Northern Yorubaland, like some other parts of West Africa, harboured two types of tse-tse fly that were very harmful to horses. The northern Yoruba could keep horses, but they could not breed them. The answer, then, was to buy steady supplies of horses from north of the Niger, and to train soldiers in the tactics of cavalry warfare. This was the policy adopted by *Alafin* Orompoto who laid the foundations of Oyo power towards AD 1600.

Fortunately for Oyo, it was able to pay for the needs of this policy. Its wealth came from two economic facts. In the first place, the Oyo Yoruba were particularly well placed to win success in the long-distance trade. Living not far south of the Middle Niger, they were linked to the whole trade of the Western Sudan by grassland routes running northward to the markets of Hausaland in one direction and to those of Gao, Timbuktu and Jenne farther west. They could feed these markets with the export goods of all Yorubaland, for, as Professor Ajayi tells us, 'Oyo traded with all parts of the Yoruba country' and became 'an important centre for gathering the produce of the rain forests to sell to people of the drier savannahs'.[5]

But the Oyo were not only fortunate traders: they were also valuable producers on their own account. They were skilled in the spinning, dyeing and weaving of cotton, and their cloths were prized in many lands. Their iron smelters and blacksmiths were famous, as were their makers of calabash bowls and jugs. They traded in these goods with the peoples of the north and were able to import 'such articles as salt, leather goods, antimony and glass ware. But the most significant imports were horses, which formed the basis of the political power of Oyo'.[6] By the seventeenth century Oyo had used this power to build a large empire.

---

[5] J.F. Ade Ajayi (with Robert Smith), *Yoruba Warfare in the Nineteenth Century* (Ibadan/ Cambridge, 1964), p. 3.
[6] Ibid.

The empire of Oyo: a great power

Under its supreme leader, the *Alafin*, the empire of Oyo grew in strength and influence during the seventeenth century. It reached the peak of its strength soon after 1650, and continued as a great power in this region for more than 100 years, dominating most countries between the Volta river in the west to Benin and the Niger in the east. It maintained during this time, through Egbado, a firm hold on the coastal trade with Europeans at Ajase (Porto Novo); and it increased its authority over its subject peoples by a big and efficient army, consisting of a full-time cavalry force together with part-time levies of troops from all its tributary states. The Oyo cavalry became famous and much feared.

High among Oyo's successes in this main period of expansion was the domination of Dahomey. This was completed in two phases: first, in four successful expeditions between 1724 and 1730 and secondly, to reassert these successes, between 1739 and 1748.

After these years of military expansion, Oyo's leaders had to decide whether to go on with expansion or concentrate on building up the trading wealth of the empire. This problem was not resolved until the reign of *Alafin* Abiodun (1770–89). He won a bitter struggle against the militarist views of *Bashorun* Gaha. Then he turned vigorously to policies of economic development, especially of the trade in slaves with Europeans along the coast. There were now said to be 6,600 towns and villages under the *alafin's* direct or indirect rule.

But *Alafin* Abiodun, concentrating on trade, neglected his army. This weakened the real power of the central government. Under the next ruler, *Alafin* Awole, there came a period of decline. Local revolts broke out and proved difficult to put down. By this time the *alafin's* authority was supported in Oyo itself by a complicated public service under leading officials such as the *Ona Efa*, in charge of justice, and the *Osi Efa*, who controlled the financial affairs of the empire. Elsewhere the *alafin* ruled through representatives, the *ilari* and *ajele* chiefs, who lived at the court of each of the subject-states, enjoyed religious power as priests of the shrines of Shango, and acted as the *alafin's* political spokesmen.

So long as the army was strong, the *ilari* had much power. Now, they began to lose it. Besides this, the empire had grown so large that it was very difficult to govern through officials who made no use of writing. Orders and reports had to be sent back and forth by word of mouth, because Oyo had no-one who could read and write.

The *alafin* was still by no means a dictator. His personal power was limited even in the eighteenth century, when the empire stood at the height of its power. As a constant check on his actions and decisions, there was his council of senior 'big family' nobles, the Oyo Mesi, under their leader the *bashorun*. As with other Yoruba states, the whole system was based on a balance between the *alafin* and his 'king's men' or appointed officials, on one side, and the Oyo Mesi and other nobles on the other side. And the power of the latter could be decisive because they kept the right to say that an *alafin* had lost the confidence of the ancestors, and must therefore commit suicide,[7] whereupon they could choose another *alafin*. Yet here again the system developed another 'built-in' balance. This took the form of chiefs who controlled the Ogboni association. If necessary these chiefs were able to countermand the Oyo Mesi's decision that an *alafin* should be deposed. Rivalries between these various holders of political and religious power now added to Oyo's difficulties.

In the last years of the eighteenth century, many disputes broke out between the ruling *alafin* and the powerful Oyo Mesi nobles. The chiefs of other Yoruba states now took a hand in these disputes, siding with either the *alafin* or the nobles according to local interest or calculation. So the careful balance of political power within the empire became increasingly upset. Here we see another aspect of the long conflict between the traditional *Ebi* system – of family relations between the Yoruba rulers – and the Oyo drive for a single great Yoruba state.

The troubles of the *alafin*, like those of the *oba* of Benin, were also increased by the growth of the coastal trade in slaves and firearms. This helped to spread warfare and raiding. These in turn tended to promote revolt among the less loyal subject-states of Oyo. There were increasing calls on the military and financial power of the *alafin*. These led to greater demands on the subject states for soldiers and taxes. Such demands were not popular.

The challenge to Oyo came in fact from three directions:

1 There was first of all a growing difficulty in keeping control of the trade routes to the coast. These ran through forest lands where Oyo had never enjoyed much power, mainly because its cavalry could not operate in the forest. Growing strong in their middleman position between the sea-merchants and Oyo, and taking advantage of the troubles between the *alafin* and his nobles, the little states along and near the coast grew increasingly rebellious. They took advantage of the disputes at court between the Oyo Mesi and the *alafin*.

2 At about the same time the power of Oyo began to be challenged from a new direction. For a long time the Fon people of Dahomey (now called the republic of Benin because it lies in the wide Gulf of Benin) had paid tribute to Oyo. Now they too entered the coastal trade in firearms, and, gathering their strength, made a bid for their independence. Oyo's armies were

---

[7] The method of announcing this decision to an *alafin* was to send him parrot's eggs.

able to master the situation for many years but in the end, largely because of the disputes in Oyo, they failed. During the nineteenth century, when the power of Oyo had very greatly declined, the Fon were to turn the tables and themselves invade Yorubaland.

3 Thirdly, soon after 1800, there came a threat from the north. The rising strength of the Fulani rulers of Hausaland began to press down on the northern states which were subject to Oyo. The *alafin* of that time lost Ilorin in this way. Nupe threw off its loyalty. By the early years of the nineteenth century the empire of Oyo, for all these reasons, had really ceased to exist outside the northern region of Yorubaland; even there its power was declining.

As elsewhere in West Africa, the old systems were now in crisis or collapse; and new forms of government, shaped more closely to the needs of the new times, would begin to rise and take their place.

The Edo and Benin

The beginnings of the state of Benin, like those of the Yoruba states, lie deep in the forgotten past. It seems that the first rulers of Benin, a trading settlement and afterwards a city of the Niger Delta, acquired their power soon after the forming of the first Yoruba states, or soon after about AD 1000. Tradition knows them as the Ogiso dynasty or line of kings.

There is no doubt that the Edo people of Benin took some of their political ideas from their Yoruba neighbours. Tradition says that hundreds of years ago the Edo of Benin became dissatisfied with their own kings. They accordingly sent to Ife and asked Oduduwa for one of his sons to rule over them. He sent them Prince Oranmiyan; and Oranmiyan started a new period in the political life of the Benin state.

This does not mean, of course, that the Edo took over Yoruba ideas completely. In fact, this change probably happened long after the time when Oduduwa is supposed to have lived; perhaps as late as AD 1400. Even if there was a close connection between some of the rulers of Benin and those of the Yoruba states, the Edo have been very much a people with ideas of their own. Their artists, whether at Benin itself or in other Edo towns, were especially brilliant in the skills of working metal, and developed many styles of much distinction.

Edo expansion at Benin dates back to a period long before the first European written reports were made, and was no doubt linked to Benin's strong trading position on the Niger Delta. Tradition suggests that the political system and customs of Benin were already well established by the fourteenth century. By the fifteenth century Benin had become an important power in the land. It was at this time that the artists of Benin, like those of Ife before them, were called on to celebrate the power and authority of their rulers. In doing so, they developed a special style of royal sculpture that was different from the more popular (and often more beautiful) styles which were liked by ordinary folk. As well as producing many fine heads and figures, the royal artists also designed and made many splendid brass plaques, or large rectangular pictures in metal, which were used to decorate the *oba*'s palace. Many of these fine old sculptures, whether in the royal style or in other styles, have survived and become famous throughout the world.

Here again we find an interesting point. The sculpture of Benin was mainly in brass. Yet brass cannot be made without copper, and there is no copper in southern Nigeria. So the copper must have come from somewhere else, and it must have come in exchange for goods produced or sold by the Edo of Benin. Benin, in other words, was deeply concerned with foreign trade. This trade seems to have consisted of buying copper and other goods from the Western Sudan in exchange for Edo cotton stuffs and other goods. Once again we see how the rise of states and empires was linked to the *production* of goods and the *exchange* of goods. The power of the empire of Benin, like that of other big states and empires, was built on economic foundations of this kind.

By the middle of the sixteenth century, perhaps earlier, the *oba* of Benin ruled over an area which spread from the region of modern Lagos to the Niger Delta. Even when the Portuguese first came in touch with Benin in 1486, they were impressed by the large size of the empire and the strong power of its ruler. Benin soon became the largest of the political systems of the lands near the West African coast. It traded far and wide. It received ambassadors from Portugal and sent its own ambassadors to Europe.

The Benin empire

Written down early in the twentieth century by Chief Jacob Egharevba, the royal traditions of Benin speak vividly of this period. One of the most famous *oba*s of this time of expansion was Ewuare, who came to the throne in about 1440. He is said to have travelled widely in Guinea and to have visited the Congo.

Ewuare was 'powerful, courageous and wise', say the traditions.

He fought against and captured 201 towns and villages in Ekiti, Ikare, Kukuruku, Eka and Igbo country. He took their rulers captive, and he caused the people to pay tribute to him.

He made good roads in Benin City . . . In fact the town rose
to importance and gained the name of city during his reign . . .
It was he who had the innermost and greatest of the walls and
ditches made round the city, and he also made powerful charms
and had them buried at each of the nine gateways of the city so as
to ward against any evil charms which might be brought by people
of other countries in order to injure his subjects.[8]

But Ewuare is remembered as an outstanding ruler not only for his
conquests and breadth of contact with the world. He also presided over
important political changes. For it was under Ewuare, according to tradition, that the State Council of Benin was formed, together with other new
political bodies. And it was from this time that the empire of Benin acquired not only a central ruler but also a central government, with officials
and departments and regular means of ruling the empire.

New links with Europe: *Oba* Esigie

These changes were carried further under Esigie, who came to power in
about 1504 and added to the empire the state of Idah, lying between Benin
and the Benue. Esigie is especially remembered for having taken several
important steps in changing political power in Benin from the basis of
ascription to that of achievement: from men who wielded power, that is,
simply because they were members of noble families, to 'commoners' who
were appointed to positions of power as servants of the king.

Esigie is also remembered as the *oba* who entered upon good relations
with Portuguese envoys who were now arriving more frequently on his
coasts. Missionaries also came from Portugal and were well received. One
of them, Duarte Pires, wrote to the Portuguese king in 1516, telling how
generously the *oba* had shown them hospitality, and how he had 'sat them
at table to dine with his son'. This *oba* is remembered as a man of learning,
and as having practised astrology (*Iwe-Uki*), forerunner of the science of
astronomy, the study of the stars. He could speak and read Portuguese.
He is said to have reigned for nearly half a century. Benin was now a city
of great size and wealth.

Orhogbua followed Esigie in about 1550, Ehengbuda in about 1578,
and Ahuan in about 1606. All three are praised in the royal traditions as
sensible and forward-looking rulers, the memory of *Oba* Ahuan being
especially honoured as a herbalist and skilful maker of charms.

---

[8] J. Egharevba, *A Short History of Benin* (Ibadan, 3rd edn 1960), p. 14.

The first Englishmen to reach this powerful Edo empire arrived at Ugwato, the port of Benin, in 1553 during *Oba* Orhogbua's reign. A Portuguese who was with them wrote afterwards that the *oba* (like Esigie before him) could speak, read and write Portuguese. These Englishmen bought a cargo of Benin peppercorns in exchange for English metal pots and other goods.

Westward of Nigeria, in what is modern Dahomey,[9] the states of the Yoruba, notably Ketu, and the empire of Benin shared control over much of the inland country and over the little states along the coast. The Fon people had yet to make their successful bid for independence. The Ewe were already well established in the southern country of what is modern Togo.

Nupe and Jukun

North of Oyo and Benin, other states developed along the Middle Niger and Benue rivers, Nupe and Jukun were two of these.

The Nupe today number about a million people. Their early state began a very long time ago, perhaps as early as the eleventh century. But it took historical shape only around 1400. One story, which we cannot be certain is true, is that a great Nupe leader called Tsoede or Edigi united several small Nupe states into a single and much stronger state at about this time.

The Nupe gained from their position along the River Niger because they became middlemen in trade between the south and the north: between southern Nigeria, that is, and the Hausa states. But they also lost from this position, because they were often brought under the control of Oyo or of the Hausa states, and had to pay tribute to these stronger states.

The history of the Jukun kingdom, lying east of Nupe, is much the same. The Jukun became middlemen in the south–north trade. But this attracted the interest of their rivals. The Jukun were often at war with Zaria, to the north of them.

Between 1500 and 1600, Zaria had the upper hand and made Jukun pay tribute to its strong rulers. After about 1600 the Jukun rulers reversed this position. They invaded to the north, and are even said to have brought Bauchi and Gombe under their control for a while, and to have raided as far as Kano. After 1800, the Fulani also brought Jukun under their control.

---

[9] Now renamed Benin.

The prosperity of Benin, and beginnings of decline

The power of the *oba*s of Benin, at least outside their city and its neighbourhood, diminished slowly after about 1650. The reasons for this are to be found in the changing nature of politics and trade along the coastland of the eastern region of West Africa (often called Guinea).

The sea-merchants from Europe were now bringing many more openings for profitable trade. These, in turn, led to more attempts by local people to win their independence from the *oba*'s rule. There were new wars. As the wars multiplied, so also did the number of firearms that were bought from the sea-merchants. Gone were the days when the *oba* could hope to keep the control of expensive weapons in his own hands. Now these weapons were also getting into the hands of rivals and rebels.

With the rising quantity of firearms in many different hands it became less and less easy for the king of Benin, or any other powerful ruler in this region, to make sure that his peoples remained obediently loyal. The traditions of Benin speak of bad or harsh *oba*s in this period; behind such traditions we can glimpse the mounting problems of government, as warfare and rebellion spread across the land.

But these disturbing events did not necessarily mean a decline in general prosperity. At least until the middle of the eighteenth century, and perhaps later, Benin remained a city of wealth and comfort. Benin chiefs and their families continued to live very well. A Dutch visitor, David van Nyendael, wrote about them in the year 1700:

> The rich among them wear a white calico [cotton] cloth about one yard [1 metre] long and half as broad . . . Over that they wear a finer white cotton dress that is often as much as sixteen or twenty yards [15–19 metres] in length. This they pleat neatly in the middle, casting over it a scarf about a yard [1 metre] long . . .
> Wives of great chiefs wear calico cloths woven in this country. These cloths are very fine, and very beautifully patterned in several colours. The women wear necklaces of coral that are very nice to look at. Their arms are decorated with bright copper or iron bangles. Some of them wear bangles on their legs, while their fingers are thickly crowded with copper rings . . .

This Dutchman's report shows that local industries still prospered in Benin, especially the crafts of weaving and metal-working, just as they had in the past. It also underlines the self-respect and dignity of the people of this famous city. Van Nyendael wrote that the inhabitants of Benin were generally 'good-natured and very civil', as well as generous in their treatment of strangers.

But they certainly expect that their good manners shall be repaid in the same way, and not with arrogance or rudeness. And to think of forcing anything out of them is to think of arguing with the moon.

They are very prompt in business, and they will not allow any of their ancient customs to be set aside. But once we [foreign merchants] comply with these customs, then the people of Benin are very easy to deal with, and will leave out nothing needed for a good agreement . . .

History has many examples of great cities which continue to be comfortable while the states and empires around them totter and fall. So it was with the great and ancient city of Benin.

Its dignified way of life, the result of centuries of social and political growth, continued to surprise and please the strangers who came here from beyond the seas. They admired its government, its courtesy, its laws, its tolerance. They praised its hospitality and care of visitors. They respected its sense of independence.

Yet the seeds of political decay were sprouting many weeds by the end of the eighteenth century. Gradually, this old empire fell apart. And as it fell apart, the security and comfort of Benin itself began to fail. The rulers and their priests, threatened by many perils, became more dictatorial. Their wisdom shrank. Their civilization narrowed. One may see this even in the changing styles of Benin's wonderful art of sculpture in brass. These styles became less sensitive and delicate, more warlike and crude, closer to the spreading insecurity and confusion of the times.

The Niger Delta and its peoples

The history of the Delta peoples – that is, of all these most southerly lands that are watered and divided by the many outflow channels of the great River Niger – may be said to have begun in the sixteenth century. Groups of Ijọ fisherfolk and saltmakers had lived here since early times. Their ancestors had probably come from the region of Benin and Igboland. Pressures of population in Igboland, always fertile in people, now combined with the new attraction of coastal trade with European sea-merchants to carry more people into the delta lands. These newcomers were of many origins, Ijọ, Igbo, Edo, Jekri, Ibibio, Efik, and even some Tiv and Fulani from the distant north.

These delta peoples lived on islands in the swamps and along the banks of their creeks and rivers, and relied greatly on canoe transport. Facing special problems of their own, they became a population with notably different ideas and ways of life from their neighbours of the inland country. They were called *Ndu Mili Nnu*, the People of the Salt Water, by the inland Igbo; and it was they who dominated the trade of the whole Niger Delta from the Cross River to the River of Benin, along a coastline of more than 500 kilometres from east to west. They it was, too, who opened the channels of sea trade to the Igbo of the inland country.

The People of the Salt Water were all organized on segmentary lines, even though some of them, in later times, had kings of their own. As time went by, they found special and often very interesting solutions to the problems of living together in the Delta, a land of creeks and islands, dense vegetation, and many other natural difficulties. These Delta institutions took their rise in the seventeenth century, though they flowered fully only in the nineteenth, and will be discussed in a later section.

These many small states of the Niger Delta and Cross River, formed from many different peoples, took full advantage of the quickly growing trade with European sea-merchants. As the ships from Europe and the Americas entered creek after creek along this maze of ocean-fronting waterways, market after market sprang into being.

The late Professor Onwuka Dike[10] has described this energetic process. He explains that the places where these markets grew were widely separated from each other. After all, there was plenty of room in the Delta: going along the coast, it is more than 450 kilometres from the Cross River in the east to the River of Benin in the west, and there are many useful creeks and river outlets in between. Usually, the points of settlement were 'islands like Bonny dominating the mouth of a river which linked the hinterland to the sea. In time, each community developed the independence and individualism so typical of island dwellers. Every river mouth, every centre of trade, and, in some areas, every town had its overlord'.

Government in the Delta

As these Delta states continued to develop, new methods of government took shape. A local people would combine together to form what is called a 'city-state'. This meant just what it says: a state composed of a city or big central settlement, founded for reasons of trade or other interests, but governing only itself, its surrounding villages, and nearby land or waterways. History has many examples of city-states, the most famous in Europe being those of the ancient Greeks: Athens and Sparta and their like.

There were many such states in the Delta after about the middle of the seventeenth century. As Dike explains, 'each city-state had all the apparatus of rule which enabled it to maintain law and order, administer justice, make war and peace, organise and prosecute peaceful commerce'.

---

[10] In his pioneering book, *Trade and Politics in the Niger Delta, 1830–85* (Oxford, 1956).

Map 8.2   The city-states of the Niger Delta.

But the city-states of West Africa, like those of ancient Greece, also had various different forms of government. Some, like Athens, were republics. Others, like Sparta, had kings or their equivalents. Among the second were Bonny (a word corrupted by sea-merchants from Ibani), New Calabar (Kalabari) and Warri: these were ruled by kings elected from members of their wealthiest and most prominent families. Among the republics were Brass and the market towns of Old Calabar in the Cross River (Creek Town, Henshaw Town, Duke Town and Obutong); these were ruled as republics by members of special political associations.

The Old Calabar towns, for example, were governed by Ekpe, an Efik word for leopard. The Ekpe or Leopard association was a shrewd means of government by a minority of powerful men, but all local men could find a place on one or other level of seniority. Its main job was to protect the interests of the merchants of these towns. Everyone who could afford to pay its entrance fees could join Ekpe. But the merchants made sure that fees for entry to the top or ruling grades were high enough to keep power in the hands of the wealthiest among them. This 'merchants' government' supervised all dealings with the European traders, punished the latter when they misbehaved, and at the same time made and enforced the laws for lesser men. This was a mixture between a limited democracy and rule by wealth.

Whether their government was monarchic or republican, the day-to-day life of the people was organized through the *House System*. This was another new development. It took the place of traditional ways of rule through clans of big families. The House was a kind of co-operative trading company based not so much on kinship as on commercial association between the head of the House, his family, his trading assistants and his servants.

There were many such Houses in the Delta, although their full development came only after 1800. Some of them, like those of the Pepples of Bonny, became known throughout the western world. Often they were very large. They included not only the members of the House family itself, but also a large number of workers and servants or slaves. All these were employed not only in trading with the sea-merchants and with other Africans, but also in clearing and planting land, in founding new settlements, and in manning the trade-canoes and war-canoes of each House. The House system was a good example of the way in which new solutions were invented for the new problems of the times.

The Igbo and their neighbours

There is a rich belt of forest country between the ocean and the grassland plains that was the scene of many important developments in the distant past. Today the region has some of the densest countryside populations in any part of Africa, and this appears to have been the case in much earlier periods as well. Archaeology and the study of languages support the opinion that it was from this region that pioneering groups of early Iron Age people carried the knowledge of iron-working into the distant lands of the Congo basin. Even local tradition has a little to say on this. The Yoruba, for example, have an interesting legend about the creation of man. According to tradition, it was at their holy place of Ile-Ife that the gods first created men and women, and it was from here that men and women spread out to populate the earth.

Many political systems of Africa did not develop into states or empires, and the Igbo were among them. They continued to live peacefully together, to defend themselves and enlarge their wealth, with the help of very little central government.

Does this mean that peoples without chiefs or kings were any less successful than the peoples who formed themselves into states with central governments? Far from it. Some of these peoples without kings were to be among the most go-ahead of all the peoples of Africa: very active in trade, very skilful in politics, very clever in dealing with their neighbours.

Prominent among them were the Igbo who have lived, since times beyond the reach of history, in these fertile lands to the east of the lower part of the Niger. In historical times the Igbo were always divided into five large groups who differed somewhat from one another in language, customs, ways of work, and religion.[11] These differences are certainly very old. So are the various types of Igbo government. Most Igbo have governed themselves without giving power to chiefs. Some, however, like those of Nri Awka towards the Niger, have had kings of their own; while their Cross River neighbours of the eastern Delta have made much use of political associations such as Ekpe. Nearly all Igbo have divided themselves into regular 'age-sets', with each set having its own special rights, duties and responsibilities.

Some of these differences have been in response to varying natural conditions and problems of everyday life. The Nri-Awka Igbo were influenced by what happened along the Niger, and perhaps by the centralized methods of rule adopted by the Edo of Benin even before 1400. Other Igbo, notably those of the Cross River, were far more concerned with local activities in the eastern Delta, and afterwards with the specialized challenge of the ocean trade. All had skilled craftsmen in weaving, metal-working and other activities, and were interested in local trade. But the great formative influence on Igbo politics has undoubtedly been their forest life. They have lived in forest villages and practised forest agriculture with outstanding

---

[11] Northern or Onitsha (and Nri Awka) Igbo; southern or Owerri Igbo; western Igbo, eastern or Cross River Igbo; north-eastern or Ogoja Igbo.

success. As long ago as 1789 an Igbo writer published an excellent description of his country that was also true for still earlier times:

> Our land is uncommonly rich and fruitful, and produces all kinds of vegetables in great abundance. We have plenty of Indian corn [maize], and vast quantities of cotton and tobacco . . . We have spices of different kinds, particularly pepper; and a variety of delicious fruits that I have never seen in Europe, together with gums of various kinds and honey in great abundance.
>
> All our work is exerted to improve these blessings of nature. Agriculture is our chief employment; and everyone, even the children and women, are engaged in it . . . The benefits of such a way of living are obvious . . . Those benefits are felt by us in the general healthiness of the people, and in their vigour and activity.[12]

Government without kings: the Igbo achievement

This emphasis on farming helps to explain why nearly all Igbo, though divided into several cultural groups, were united in more basic ways. They ran their affairs reinforced through the formation of 'age sets' to which all men and women belonged, or by special political associations whose leaders had power throughout the area of the government in question. Many village governments might also join together, through religious ties and ceremonies, in respect for the ancestors of still bigger units, usually called 'clans'. Igboland had many hundreds of clans, the product of a few village governments which had grown in size and split up, during the distant past, into many governments.

For the affairs of everyday life, however, fairly small numbers of people worked together in separate village governments. This could be a disadvantage to them in times of danger from invaders: unlike peoples organized in big units under kings, they could not rely on big armies. But it also had an important advantage. It was stubbornly democratic. The village governments of the Igbo, and others like them, were popular governments. Every grown-up man (and women in some but not all cases, feminism in Africa being for a distant future) could and did have a say at village assemblies where matters of common interest were decided. Governments like these were good for individual development. People accustomed to a

---

[12] Olaudah Equiano, *The Interesting Narrative of . . .* (London, 1789), p. 20. This remarkable Igbo was born in about 1745, sold into slavery, but was able to win his freedom and escape to England. There he took a leading part in the great campaign against the slave trade. In 1792 he married the daughter of James and Ann Cullen of Cambridge.

great deal of everyday democracy are people with a great deal of individual self-confidence: they tend to be enterprising, always ready to deal with new problems, easily adaptable to new conditions.

Of course the amount of democracy varied. Some of the Igbo, like the Tiv, Konkomba, Tallensi and other West Africans with village governments, had much democracy. There was less among the Igbo who developed 'title societies', such as those of Ama at Nsukka and Ozo at Awka. These were run by a minority of men who were rich enough to pay high fees for the privilege. The same was true among the Cross River Igbo, whose Ekpe association worked on the same principle. Yet a man's own skills and ambitions were still the important things. Systems with 'title societies' might be dominated by a handful of rich men. But it was always possible for other men to enter the ruling group by hard work, and not, as in most governments with kings, simply because they had been born into one or other ruling family. Promotion, in other words, was by *achievement* and not by *ascription*. In this way, if not in others, village governments of this type were very much in line with the democratic habits of the modern world. All this helps to explain why the peoples of the Igbo country, most of whom had segmentary governments of one kind or another, acquired a well-founded reputation for enterprise in trade.

On the Threshold of Modern Times: the Economy of West Africa in 1600

Overleaf

One of a pair of ivory leopards decorated with bronze studs from Benin, placed on either side of the Oba's throne on state occasions. (Werner Forman Archive and British Museum)

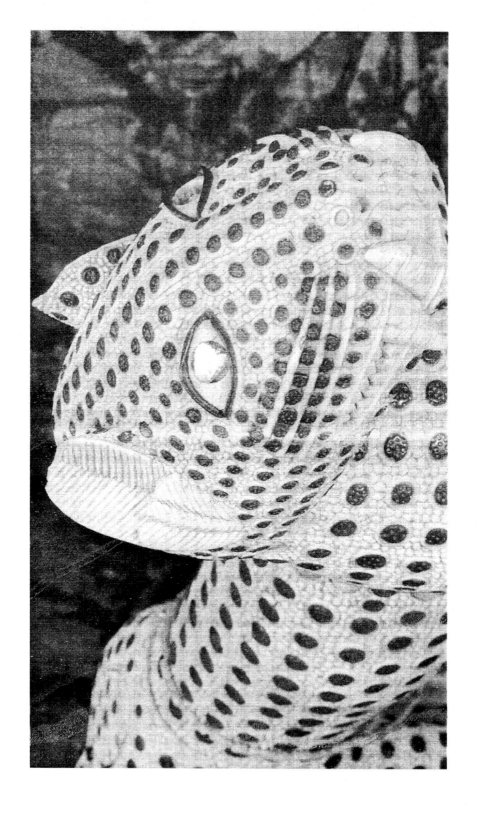

On the Threshold of Modern Times: the Economy of West Africa in 1600

The first eight chapters of this book have covered the period of early times, until AD 1600 or thereabouts, and have followed the main political and social events of the West Africa story in those centuries. Here we turn aside to look at the nature of the African cultures that took shape in these countries and among these peoples. In broad outline we shall look at how people lived and worked, at their arts and sciences, at the ways in which they organized their communities and government, and at their forms of religion and spiritual belief. In short, we shall look at the nature of their civilization.

Until about AD 1600 all this proceeded with little impact from the world outside West Africa. South of the great desert of the Sahara, West Africa was by no means cut off from developments elsewhere, because the long-distance caravan trails to and from North Africa continued to operate. Yet they could operate only with immense effort and difficulty, so that the peoples of West Africa were largely left to their own devices.

Of all this the world outside Africa as yet knew little or nothing, while most of what it thought it knew was to be proved wrong or even absurd. But with the advance of European sea-going navigation, rulers and businessmen in Europe now began to hear about West Africa, and see that West Africa could become a valuable region with which to trade and exchange ideas.

Progress was difficult because communications were slow, and the European sea-going nations, at that time principally Portugal and the Netherlands, Britain and France, were in more or less permanent and often violent competition with each other. Each kept their commercial intelligence to themselves, and fought each other on the seas whenever they met and clashed.

Any thought of a European invasion of the African mainland was still far ahead; and if the Europeans were masters of the seas, the Africans

131

remained masters of the land, and were well able to defend the independence of their countries. News and knowledge about Africa spread in Europe, gradually, by the publication of books. These were the work of European or Arab writers such as Leo Africanus (Hasan al-Wazzan) of Muslim Spain, and then especially of Dutch travellers and chroniclers. The people of the Netherlands were generally more advanced than other Europeans of the time in the skills of writing and publishing. They also possessed a better commercial economy than other Europeans, and needed widespread information about lands beyond the seas.

Gradually, after about AD 1600, there developed between the sea-going Europeans and the Africans at home a period of peaceful exchange and partnership. This proved of great advantage to both sides. It was only with the rise of the Atlantic slave trade, and its massive expansion as African workers were more and more needed in the Americas, that peaceful partnership collapsed into loss and sorrow, above all for Africa.

Unity and variety

Big events and useful dates are the skeleton of history: the rise and fall of states and empires, the reigns of kings and queens, conquests and invasions, victories and defeats. But the skeleton by itself is not much use. To enjoy the living reality of the past, we must put the flesh of life on these bare bones. We must turn to vital questions about how people lived and worked, believed and thought, built and evolved the historical civilization of West Africa in times past.

The peoples of West Africa lived and worked in many different ways, spoke many different languages, created many different gods, served many different rulers. All this, and much else besides, was part of their civilization. It was therefore a civilization of great *variety*. Some peoples lived well; others lived badly. Some made much progress in finding better ways of working and of governing themselves; others did not.

But it was also a civilization, however varied in appearance and in detail, of great underlying *unity*. This underlying unity came from the common origins and formation of nearly all West African peoples. They were all, or nearly all, shaped and influenced by the same general conditions and opportunities, by the same kind of handicaps and advantages, by the same West African land and life.

In many ways it is impossible to distinguish the civilization of West Africa during the sixteenth century, as at other periods, from that of a much larger part of Africa. The peoples of central and southern Africa, of eastern and even to a large extent of northern Africa, all built their ways of life on the same deep foundations.

132

West Africa can therefore be regarded as a separate historical unit only for purposes of study. Yet the achievements and experience of West African peoples have been so rich and interesting, so fertile and full of meaning for the future, that it is reasonable to speak of a West African civilization, so long as one remembers that this was always a part of the wider unity of African civilization as a whole.

Continued growth

There is a third important point. West African civilization enjoyed great *continuity*: it was a process, in other words, of continual change, development and growth. It is easy to see why. For many centuries, because of the wasteland of the Sahara on one side and Central Africa's vast forests on the other, West Africans were left to work out their own problems in their own way.

They suffered very few invasions from outside. Of major importance we can count only three: the Berber invasion of the eleventh century, aimed at the wealth of Ancient Ghana; the Moroccan invasion of the late sixteenth century, aimed at the wealth of Songhay; and the nineteenth-century conquest by the Europeans, aimed at the wealth of the whole continent. Yet the first two of these invasions were soon over. They were painful, even disastrous, to the West African countries which they touched; but these countries were few. Safe behind their seas of sand and water, most West Africans were unaware of or barely disturbed by these invasions.

But safety from outside interference had one disadvantage: while the seas of sand and water certainly protected West Africa from many dangers, they also cut off West Africans from close contact with the outside world. This meant that these peoples had no share in the great advances of scientific thought, and in the new uses of machinery, which began to appear in Europe long before the sixteenth century. While Europe discovered ever more profitable and skilful ways of producing goods and of mastering nature, West Africa remained largely in the age before mechanical science. This scientific backwardness was to prove a very great handicap.

West Africa's isolation was not complete. Many links with North and Central Africa were never broken. On the contrary, as we have seen at many points in this book, trade between North and West Africa was often of great value to both. New kinds of useful plants came into West Africa in this way, notably cotton. So did new ideas about religion and government, those of Islam being the most obvious example, and the arts of writing and scholarship. By 1500, West African civilization had absorbed many ideas from North Africa. It had taken over these ideas, and put them to West African use. In all this we can see the mixture of unity with continuity.

133

How the people lived

There were fewer people in those days, and fewer kinds of food. But more were now added. Valuable plants and fruits like maize and pineapples were brought from Central and South America in Portuguese ships after about 1500, and cultivated in West Africa for the first time. These new crops were eagerly accepted, and they spread rapidly.

Though they had no knowledge of modern science, West Africans had already solved many hard problems connected with living in their vast and often difficult region. They had learnt the secret of many medicinal herbs and how to use them to cure sickness. They had discovered how to look after cattle in very dry weather. They had become experts at growing food in the forest. They had found out how to recognize minerals in rocks, how to sink mines, how to get the ore and smelt and work it. They had developed a wide range of hand-manufacture in many materials. They had formed religions of their own. They had evolved effective methods of government, though mostly without the use of writing.

These skills impressed foreign visitors. A Portuguese report of 1506, that of Duarte Pacheco Pereira, tells how high-quality cotton goods could be purchased at many points along the Guinea coast. An English captain called William Towerson wrote in 1556 of the 'fine iron goods' that were hand-made in West Africa: 'spears, fish-hooks, farming tools, and swords that are very sharp on both edges'.

Of all their material skills, *tropical farming* and *mining* were the most important. In both these fields, West Africans were far advanced among all the peoples of the sixteenth century. They were so far advanced, indeed, that it was to be Africans who later pioneered the development of tropical farming and mining in South America after the Colombian discoveries.

There was one great difference between then and now in the way people obtained the goods they needed. Today most people work partly or entirely for money, for wages or salaries or business profits. With this money they buy the goods they need or can afford. This is what we call a *money economy*. In the distant past, however, very few West Africans worked for money. They did not have a money economy. They had what we call a *subsistence economy*. This means that most West Africans worked in order to grow or make the goods they *personally* needed, and not in order to earn money with which to buy such goods.

A farmer then would grow enough food for his family's needs, but little or no more. A blacksmith would make enough hoes or spears to be sure that he could get what he and his family needed in exchange; but he seldom exchanged these for any kind of money. He took them to market and exchanged them *directly* for the goods he wanted. This kind of economy was a stage of development which occurred nearly everywhere in the world.

Of course the detailed picture is far from simple. There was a growing quantity of home and foreign trade in the sixteenth century; and this trade was carried on in foods that were grown, and goods that were manufactured, with the idea of exchanging them for other goods or for various kinds of money. The beginnings of a money economy did indeed develop wherever traders gathered in markets and began to deal in goods for sale.

The fact remains that nearly all West Africans still lived outside the centres of this small though steadily expanding money economy of the towns and big markets. Even inside these centres the idea of employing men and women in exchange for wages or salaries was still in the future. The only form of city employment that was known then was a kind of servitude, which historians call domestic or household slavery, in which wages played no part. Employment outside the towns and market-centres was also in the same forms of servitude, or else, as in the forest areas, in work provided by customary duties and age-grade organizations. Money and wages still played no part.

This is not the place to discuss the full effects of this absence of wages and of the habit of working for money. One main effect, though, was to keep the production of goods at the same general level as before. Most people were content to live as they had always lived. They felt no need for the invention or use of machinery which would enable them to produce more goods, or at a much cheaper price. All the goods that were required for a normal everyday life could be grown well enough or made with the equipment that was already known.

Making goods and trading in goods

Other West Africans, mostly those who lived in or near towns and big market-centres, were busy making goods for local and long-distance trade, as well as trading in these goods with their neighbours or with North African traders.

Even before 1600, many were producing goods for trade, and not because they needed these goods for their own use. By 1600 this local and long-distance trade was very large and had become an important part of daily life.

People on the coast caught and dried fish for sale to inland peoples. Forest peoples traded in kola nuts and other items. Grassland peoples traded in cattle and skins.

They also traded in manufactured goods: goods produced by turning raw materials into useful things. Two such raw materials became very important. One was cotton. The other was gold.

Cotton was widely grown in West Africa before AD 1000. Many West African peoples – for example, the Yoruba of southern Nigeria, the Akan and their neighbours in the country now called Ghana – became expert in the spinning and dyeing of cotton for clothing. When European sea-merchants came to West Africa after about 1450, they found that some of this West African dyed cloth was better than any that was made in Europe.

More and more cotton cloth was made. We can get some idea of the amount from the writings of a German traveller called Henry Barth. He wrote about the cotton-cloth production of the busy Hausa city of Kano in northern Nigeria during the 1850s. But what he said about Kano then was also true of cotton-producing towns in earlier times.

> The great advantage of Kano is that trade and manufacture go
> hand in hand. Almost every family has a share in them. There
> is something grand about this kind of industry. It spreads to the
> north as far as Murzuk, Ghat and even Tripoli [on the coast of the
> Mediterranean Sea]. It spreads to the west not only to Timbuktu,
> but in some degree even as far as the shores of the Atlantic, the
> very inhabitants of Arguin [on the coast of Mauretania] dressing in
> the cloth that is woven and dyed in Kano. It spreads to the east all
> over Bornu . . .[1]

And it also spread to the south.

So cotton cloth was a big part of the long-distance trade, as well as of local trade. What about *gold*?

The prosperity of several of the states and empires of this wide African region depended largely on the mining of gold ore and the sale of gold. How much gold did West Africa produce?

West Africa today can still show many thousands of old gold-workings, especially in Asante and the northern part of the modern republic of Guinea. Gold was also 'panned' from rivers in those two regions. Men stood in the water and sieved the gravel of the river-bed for the little bits of gold that it contained. French archaeologist Professor Raymond Mauny, who has studied this question, believes that West African miners and 'panners' got about nine tonnes of gold every year during the sixteenth century, and by then they had been doing this for a long time.

Of these nine tonnes of gold produced every year, about four tonnes came from the goldfields of Asante, and about four tonnes from the (modern republic of) Guinea. 'The total amount of gold produced in West Africa from ancient times till 1500', the pioneering Mauny has estimated, 'may be placed at several thousand tons [tonnes]; with an amount of about the same size, perhaps 3,500 tons [tonnes], for the period between 1500 and 1900'.[2]

---

[1] Henry Barth, *Travels and Discoveries in North and Central Africa*, 1849–55 (London, 1858). In five volumes; quote here from volume IV.
[2] R. Mauny, *Tableau Géographique l'Ouest Africain* (Dakar, 1961), pp. 300–1.

Map 9.1 The gold-producing areas of West Africa.

It was hard to produce this gold. West Africa's miners had to be able to find the places where gold-bearing ore existed under the ground. They had to dig shafts into this ore, and get it out, using hand tools. They did not have any machines to do this for them. They had to crush the ore by hand. Yet throughout the sixteenth century, year after year, they produced nearly half as much gold as was produced by modern machinery in the colonial period. As late as 1938, for example, the production of West African gold by modern methods and machinery was only 21½ tonnes.

The *export* of goods pays for the *import* of other goods. In exchange for their cotton-cloth and gold and other goods, West Africans were able to buy many foreign products that they wanted or needed.

They bought a lot of Saharan salt, something that everybody needed. They bought luxury goods, such as silks that came from Asia. They bought thoroughbred horses from Egypt and Tripoli. They bought swords and knives and kitchen things from the little workshops of early industrial Europe, or from the craftsmen of the Arab countries of the Middle East. They bought hand-written books of learning for their Muslim schools and libraries. And as trade grew with European sea-merchants, especially after 1600, they bought guns and gunpowder, bars of iron, rings of copper, jewellery, hats, and a host of other items.

Trade routes and traders

We have seen how trade routes across the Sahara were opened in the distant past. Inside West Africa, other trade routes were opened. They were used especially by the Dyula traders of the Mali empire, the Hausa traders of northern Nigeria, and other trading peoples. By 1600 you could say that every region of West Africa was part of this internal trading network.

Transport in the Sahara was by camel, while camels and donkeys were used in the Sudan. South of the Sudan, in forest country where tse-tse fly prevented the breeding of horses, transport was by men and women carrying things on their heads along the forest trails.

Where cities grew, the biggest merchants often became the rulers of the countries in which the cities stood: kings and their counsellors, chiefs and elders. These were men (and sometimes women) who needed wealth in order to pay for governments and soldiers, maintain their courts, make gifts to visitors, and live well themselves.

As we have seen, King Tunka Manin of Ancient Ghana monopolized the gold and salt trade. Other kings did this, too. This was why, when European ships sailed up the Benin river, for example, and dropped their anchors at Ugwato, the river-port of Benin, they entered into trade not just with anyone they met but only with agents and merchants selected by the king of Benin. 'Nobody is allowed to buy anything from Europeans on this coast,' observed a Dutch report of the seventeenth century, 'except the agents and merchants whom the king has named for this purpose. As soon as one of our ships drops anchor, the people inform the king, and the king appoints two or three agents and twenty or thirty merchants whom he empowers to deal with the Europeans.'

It was much the same in the grassland plains of the Western Sudan. Passing through Bornu at the beginning of the sixteenth century, an Arab visitor reported that the king of that empire was especially interested in buying horses from North Africa and Egypt. He paid for these horses in various ways, but notably in war-captives who were used as servants in North Africa and the Mediterranean countries. Yet the merchants who brought the horses and took away the captives were allowed to deal only with the agents of the king himself. If the king happened to be away when they arrived at his capital, they simply had to sit down and wait until he came back again.[3]

What did the kings and merchants do with their wealth? Nobody thought of rich men *investing* their wealth; of handling it, that is, in such a way as to produce more wealth. They mostly used it for their expenses, for gifts with which to ensure the loyalty of allies and servants, and for displaying their power. The emperor of Kanem-Bornu, according to Leo Africanus, had the equipment of his cavalry made in gold, 'stirrups, spurs, bits and buckles'. Even his dogs had 'chains of the finest gold'. But the giving of gifts was perhaps the most important way of using wealth. Taking their wealth with one hand, and giving it away with the other, the kings and chiefs helped to keep it circulating among people.

How they traded

Whether they worked for local trading companies, or for kings or chiefs, or on their own account, West Africans were keen traders. The European sea-merchants soon found this out. They had thought it was going to be easy to get the better of African traders; they soon discovered they were wrong.

'These people', an English sea-merchant called John Lok reported to his friends in England, after getting back from a voyage to the Guinea coast in 1553, 'are very clever in their bargaining. They will not overlook

---

[3] This visitor, Hasan al-Wazzan, afterwards wrote a valuable travel book, eventually published in Italy in 1550, entitled *The Description of Africa*. This writer was called Leo Africanus by the Italians, who had captured him in the sea-piracy of those days, and installed him in a monastery in Rome. He was born in Granada, a splendid city of Muslim Spain.

a single bit of the gold they offer for sale. They use their own weights and measures, and they are very careful how they use them. Anyone who wants to trade with them must do so honestly, for they will not trade if they are badly treated.'

As we have seen, this trade was mostly done by *barter*: that is, the exchange of one lot of goods for another lot of goods, without using money. Barter trade called for great care. Prices often changed. Traders had to be on the lookout not to 'lose their bargains'.

In certain trades, as John Lok observed, Africans used their own weights and measures. The gold-traders of Asante, for example, had long developed a very complicated set of weights for the sale of gold-dust. For a long while these were made in the measures of weight used by the traders from the Western Sudan. After about 1600, they began to be made for measures of weight used by the European sea-merchants as well.

West African traders also used various measures of value: or of what we call money. These measures were seldom or never coins or paper-notes, such as those of today. They were cowrie shells, or pieces of brass, or lengths of iron bar, or cloths of cotton.

This West African 'money' of those days was useful, but it was clumsy. Here is a table that shows the value of cowries in the 1850s:

40 cowries	= 1 string	= $\frac{1}{4}$d to 1d
5 strings	= 1 bunch	= 3d to 6d
10 bunches	= 1 head	= 1s $9\frac{1}{2}$d to 2s
10 heads	= 1 bag	= 18s to £1

So you had to have 20,000 cowries in order to buy something worth 18 shillings in the English money of that time.

Cities

In the year 1602, a Dutch visitor described the city of Benin (now in southern Nigeria). It seemed very big to him.

> When you go into it you enter a great broad street, which is not paved, and seems to be seven or eight times broader than the Warmoes street in Amsterdam [the chief city of Holland]. This street is straight, and does not bend at any point. It is thought to be four miles [6$\frac{1}{2}$ kilometres] long.
> At the gate where I went in on horseback, I saw a very big wall, very thick and made of earth, with a very deep and broad ditch outside it ... And outside this gate there is also a big suburb.

140

Inside the gate, and along the great street just mentioned, you see many other great streets on either side, and these also are straight and do not bend...

The houses in this town stand in good order, one close and evenly placed with its neighbour, just as the houses in Holland stand... They have square rooms, sheltered by a roof that is open in the middle, where the rain, wind and light come in. The people sleep and eat in these rooms, but they have other rooms for cooking and different purposes...

The king's courtyard is very large. It is built around many square-shaped yards. These yards have surrounding galleries where sentries are always placed. I myself went into the court far enough to pass through four great yards like this, and yet wherever I looked I could still see gate after gate which opened into other yards...[4]

Little or no stone was used in building the cities of West Africa, for it was easier and cheaper to build in wood and clay. This is why West Africa has so few ancient ruins, even though, as in Yorubaland, it had many cities that were large and prosperous. The wealthy city of Jenne, for example, was built entirely of short-lived materials. Leo Africanus tells us that 'the king, the men of religion, the doctors of learning, the merchants and those of wealth and authority' lived in 'houses made like huts, of clay and thatched straw'.

Yet absence of stone was not a sign of absence of civilization. This same traveller found that the people of Jenne were 'very well dressed'. That is not surprising. They enjoyed a big trade with the Akan peoples in the south and with those of the Western Sudan in the north. 'It is because of this blessed city of Jenne', wrote the author of the *Tarikh as-Sudan*, Abd al-Rahman as-Sadi, in 1665, 'that caravans come to Timbuktu from every side', for Jenne, standing where it did, had long been 'one of the great markets of the Muslim world'.

The architecture of the important desert city of Timbuktu, on the caravan trail to North Africa, was much the same, though it had some buildings in brick as well. Soon after 1500, Leo Africanus found 'many handicraft workers, merchants and cotton-weavers' there. European goods were much in use. There was also an abundance of grain and other foods. Milk and butter were in good supply. The king possessed a big treasure in gold. 'The royal court', Leo wrote, 'is very well organised and splendid. When the king goes from one town to another with his train of courtiers, he rides a camel; but horses are walked behind by his servants. Should

---

[4] Recorded in O. Dapper's *Description of Africa*, first published in Amsterdam in 1668. Dapper was a geographer who collected reports from travellers.

there be any need for fighting, the servants take charge of the camels and all the soldiers mount horses.' The king had about 3,000 horsemen and a much larger number of infantry. The best of these horses were brought across the Sahara from North Africa.

Gao, capital of the Songhay empire, was described by the same traveller as 'a very large town without any defensive wall'. He thought that most of its houses were poor and ugly, but reported that there were 'several fine ones where the king and his courtiers live'. Gao's inhabitants included many rich traders who spent their time in travelling on business. 'Bread and meat are very abundant, but they have no wine or fruit. Yet their melons and cucumbers are excellent, and they have enormous quantities of rice. Fresh-water wells are numerous there.'

Leo considered that the revenues of Songhay in the sixteenth century were large, but so were its expenses. Luxury goods brought across the Sahara for the kings, nobles and rich merchants were very dear. Imported horses, woollens, swords, cavalry harness, medicines and jewellery all cost far more than they did in the countries where they were made.

Yet the cities grew, in the northern grasslands as well as in the forests of the south. They became a fruitful part of West African civilization.

Religion, the Arts, and Learning

Religion, the Arts, and Learning

Even today, when times have greatly changed, the beliefs and customs of West Africa (like other parts of Africa) continue to reflect the social and spiritual development of the past. Out-of-date though many of these customs and beliefs may seem, they were a vital and necessary part of everyday life in historical times. They explain much of the success and power of West Africa's wealth and importance.

The values of religion

The origins of religion in Africa, as in other continents, lie far back at the beginning of human society. They took shape in remote times when mankind first multiplied and spread across the world.

This means that some of the origins of West African religion were formed in that very early but remarkable 'nursery' of early cultures which grew up in the green and fertile Sahara during Stone Age times. That is one reason why African religions often resemble each other, at least in some of their ideas of worship. The sacred ram, for example, was a symbol of the supreme god of the pharaohs of ancient Egypt; but so it was for the Berbers of the Sahara and old North Africa also; and so it still remains for some West African peoples today. The python was honoured in ancient Meroe, capital of the African empire of Kush on the Middle Nile more than 2,000 years ago; and the great snake has been similarly honoured in other African lands.

By the sixteenth century, however, West African religions had long since grown into forms of their own. These were extremely varied, for they reflected the great variety of ways in which men and women lived and worked. We can think of them, briefly, as having served a double purpose.

In the first place, they provided an *explanation* for how people came to be what they were and the world what it was. Secondly, going on from this religious explanation, they provided the *social power* by which people could make laws and customs and ensure that these were respected.

How did they do this? The answer is complicated. It rests in the fact, already noted at various points in this book, that religion and politics went hand-in-hand in traditional civilization. Like the Europeans of the Middle Ages (AD 600–1350), Africans lived in an 'age of faith'. They believed, in short, that political authority came not from men or women but from God and the spirits. Those who exercised power on earth could do so, in other words, only if they were accepted as speaking and acting with the good will of their departed ancestors, who, in turn, were their protectors and helpers in the world of the spirits. Rulers could rule only if they were spiritually appointed to do so; and their subjects obeyed them not simply from respect for the king's power and law, but also for reasons of religion.

There are many examples of this. Among the Asante, the office or position of chiefship was referred to as *akonnua*. This may be interpreted as the 'stool', though it also had a spiritual meaning. Asante who were appointed to be chiefs went through various ceremonies, but the final ceremony or ritual was the 'enstooling' of the chief with the supreme ancestral stool of his particular chiefdom. From that moment the appointed chief, duly enstooled, could speak with religious as well as with political power. The power inherent in the ancestral stool was regarded as belonging to the whole people and no longer only to his own descent-line or 'big family'. Such attitudes were common to many peoples.

Governments without kings, such as those we have discussed for the Igbo, also relied on religion as the basis for political power, though they did so in ways different from the Edo, Yoruba, Asante or other centrally organized peoples. The Tallensi of northern Ghana ruled themselves in a number of village governments without kings. Power was shared out among different descent-lines, but these were held together by religious rituals. Underpinning all these rituals were those that affected the men who held senior offices in village government. These were the chiefs and the Earth-priests. Only if proper ceremonies were carried out, and religious duties observed between chiefs and Earth-priests as between 'men and their wives', could the Tallensi prosper. Otherwise, it was believed, disasters such as sickness or famine would strike at all the Tallensi.

An old idea about Africa in the West is that Africa's peoples possessed no religions deserving of respect. Nothing could be more mistaken. On the contrary, their religions expressed the values by which history had steered them through their long years of development. Consider the case of the Yoruba of south-western Nigeria, a people with a history reaching back through several thousand years. 'The real keynote of the life of the Yoruba', says a distinguished expert in Yoruba beliefs, Bolaji Idowu, who writes from a Christian Yoruba standpoint, 'is neither in their noble ances-try nor in the past deeds of their heroes. The keynote of their life is their religion. In all things, they are religious.' They pay especial respect to wor-ship at shrines to Oludumare, their word for the Creator. As far as Yoruba are concerned, 'the full responsibility of all the affairs of life belongs to the Deity; their own part in the matter is to do as they are ordered through the priests and diviners whom they believe to be the interpreters of the will of the Deity'.[1]

This being so, people in Yoruba society (as in many African cultures) do not live their daily lives happily unless they pay attention to the rules of good behaviour in Yoruba life. These teach that sensible persons will try to behave according to these rules, because behaving otherwise is to invite trouble and failure. 'Let us not run the world hastily', goes one of their ritual songs: 'let us not grasp at the rope of wealth impatiently. What should be treated with mature judgment, let us not treat in a fit of temper . . .'. This is not to say, of course, that Africans in traditional society, in the society 'before modern times', always behaved according to accepted rules, any more than anyone else ever has or does. But it is to say that the religions of Africa had at their heart the firm idea of a moral order. They taught that people could prosper only if this moral order were preserved in every-day behaviour.

They taught, for example, that greed was the source of great evil, because greed unbalanced relationships between people, upset society, and threatened trouble. Popular sayings argued against greed. Among the Bemba of Central Africa, the sociologist Max Gluckman reported half a century ago, 'to find one [wild] beehive is good luck, to find two is very good luck', but 'to find three is witchcraft'. Beehives full of honey are rare, so to find three wild beehives in the bush you will have to have searched deliberately so as to advantage yourself and disadvantage your neighbours; this would be an anti-social action. The greed will invite divine punishment.

Such attitudes and beliefs were designed as practical guides to the sensible behaviour that enables people to live together in community. Many grassland peoples, unlike the forest-living Yoruba and their neighbours, had in their history a record of movement or migration from one place to another in search of fresh pastures for their cattle. Their religious beliefs therefore sought to provide a sense of reassurance, psychological reassur-ance, such as 'changes of base' do usually require. So it was that their beliefs, applied in Africa's limitless bush, were expected to supply 'answers to the questions: "Where did I come from? Who cares if I live or die? Upon whom can I depend for food, land, and shelter? Who will remember me?"' This example comes from the Tiriki of East Africa; but it might

---

[1] E. Bolaji Idowu, *Oludumare: God in Yoruba Belief* (London, 1962), p. 5.

have come from any region, for such beliefs give people a 'sense of social affiliation and continuity, and are thus a source of economic and super-natural support'.[2]

And so these ways of belief could be a practical guide to successful living in community, and be altogether different from empty or foolish superstition even if it has taken a long time for non-African peoples to understand this. Many such beliefs have remained important, though they have also gone along with outmoded belief in magic and witchcraft, the latter being nonetheless always concerned with the age-old struggle between good and evil.

These explanations may seem strange in our modern world. Yet they could and did reflect the deeper moral truths of life, the difference between right and wrong, between good and evil, between the rights of the individual and the duties of society. Often they were expressed in proverbs and stories. Much moral and practical wisdom may be found in the traditional sayings or proverbs of West Africa, linked as these often are to religious beliefs. The traditional wisdom of the Akan, for example, is expressed in more proverbs than will be found in the Bible or the Koran.

Many such sayings took the form of sharp comments on people's behaviour. 'A lot of mice may dig a hole,' ran the Akan proverb, 'but it does not become deep'. Or, 'when your guns are few, so are your words'. There were innumerable stories, too, which told 'home truths' about good or bad behaviour, folly or wisdom, arrogant pride or decent humility. Of Ananse Kokrofu, the Great Spider in ancient legend, the Akan used to tell this tale:

> Ananse collected all the wisdom in the world and shut it up in a gourd. Then he began climbing the trunk of a tree so as to keep this precious gourd safe at the top. But he got into difficulties only half-way up, because he had tied the gourd to his front, and it hampered him in climbing. His son Ntikuma, who was watching at the bottom, called up: 'Father, if you really had all the wisdom in the world up there with you, you would have had the sense to tie that gourd on your back'. His father saw the truth of this and threw down the gourd in a temper. It broke on the ground, and the wisdom in it was scattered about.
>
> Men and women came and picked up what each of them could get and carry away. Which explains why there is much wisdom in the world, but few persons have more than a little of it, and some persons have none at all.

---

[2] W.H. Sangree, *Age, Prayer and Politics in Tiriki, Kenya* (Oxford, 1966), p. 44.

Creative arts

The many arts of West Africa, dancing, singing, the playing of musical instruments, sculpture and the like, were also an important part of everyday life. Sometimes they were only for amusement or for adding to the fun of things. But often they were inspired by moral and religious beliefs, and were placed at the service of social and spiritual customs. In being thus linked to religion, West African arts were no different in *content* – in what they meant and did for people – from the arts of all other peoples who lived in an age of faith. But they were very different in their *form* – in their shapes, fashions and styles.

By the sixteenth century, West Africans had long developed many art forms of their own, often of very great skill and beauty. Today these masks and dances and sculptured figures have an honoured place in all the great museums of our Western world. Yet they are worthy of much respect, quite apart from their artistic beauty, because they, like the religions and proverbial wisdom of West Africa, helped to express the beliefs and hopes by which men and women lived.

In any good museum you can find splendid carvings in wood and ivory that illustrate the skill of those old artists who worked in clay and wood and metal. Think of the energy and life that speak in traditional music and dancing. Consider the discipline that is needed for all that, the restraint and modesty, but also the power and daring. Or listen to the drums that men had learned to make and play so well. With their drum language, skilled artists could speak of many things. Here, for example, is the fragment of a drummer's song of praise to Tano, the river god of the Asante, as recorded many years ago:

> The stream crosses the path
> And the path crosses the stream:
> Which of them is the elder?
> Did we not cut a path to go and meet the stream?
> The stream had its beginning long long ago,
> The stream had its beginning in the Creator:
> He created things,
> Pure, pure Tano . . .

Many of these old arts and songs have passed away, together with the beliefs, ideas and customs which gave them birth. A new life has opened. But the depth and value of the old life, so much a parent of the new, can be seen only when we give these arts of the past the honour they deserve.

Education and schooling

Outside the cities, teaching was restricted to popular instruction in the skills and customs that were used in everyday life; to training in traditional law; and to the preparation, also by example and by word of mouth, of priests, practitioners in herbal medicine, and other specialists.

All West African religions possessed a body of complex beliefs which trainee priests had to learn and know how to use. They learned this either from the priests of shrines in their home and nearby villages, or sometimes in regular 'academies' established at a regional centre. In the same way, all who wished to practise as doctors, whether in the use of herbs or at shrines, had to be taught their art by men and women who possessed the necessary qualifications and reputation. Metal-workers, weavers, boat-makers, drummers, warriors and others had to be schooled not only in the material techniques of their respective crafts, but also in the spells and special rituals which were believed to be essential to success in their work.

Apart from these requirements about rules of behaviour, of religion, and of craftsman skills, there were also the needs of government. Many peoples had organized themselves in communities which gave much power, for the taking of community decisions and the keeping of law and order, to special associations or groups of men and women. Entry into these groups or societies was generally by rites that were secret. These rites had to be taught to would-be members.

All the members of such associations also had to know about the history of their own people or branch of a people. They were expected to know about their law, their methods of enforcing the law, and their punishments for those who broke the law. Where peoples had organized themselves in states with central governments and kings, there had to be schooling in the skills and methods of administration by civil service. Many states had groups of elders whose duty it was to learn the traditions of their country, to recite these on proper occasions, and to teach them to younger persons.

Altogether there was a great deal of schooling in sixteenth-century West African civilization. But with some exceptions, important though few, it was a matter of the teaching of skills, customs, laws, traditions and the like by word of mouth. It was done for the most part without the aid of writing and reading.

This was also a stage of society in which education was generally thought of as being a part of religion. It was not based on modern science, and so could do little to promote technical progress. Skilled craftsmen were trained in the methods of the past, and were content to follow the old methods. They felt no need to experiment with new methods. Having a religious attitude to their methods of production, they could also be against experiment.

So we have to think of this civilization as both moving forward and standing still. It was moving forward all the time because of its energy and growth and wealth; yet it was also standing still because of its conservative attitude to methods and techniques.

This aspect of standing still should not tempt us to underestimate the achievements of West Africa. The farmers who grew food, the miners who found metals, the smiths who worked so skilfully in these metals, the weavers and woodcarvers, the artists and musicians, the chiefs and counsellors, the traders and tellers of tales: all these, and their fellow-specialists, were successful because they had discovered and learned to understand their work and its problems.

Important centres of Muslim learning

Two universal religions were also at work in West Africa: Islam and Christianity. We call them universal religions, open to all, because they differed in this important respect from the religions created in West Africa. Muslims and Christians believed (as, of course, they still do) that it was their duty to send out missionaries to convert everyone else to their faith. People who believed in West African religions generally did not think like this. They thought of their religion as belonging only to themselves and their own people.

Christianity had little influence. Apart from a handful of missionaries along the coast, it was absent from West Africa. Islam, on the other hand, was by now important in the Western Sudan and was already pushing its believers into the forest lands and down to the coast. Yet in this period Islam still remained chiefly a religion of the cities, towns and big market-centres. Outside these there were very few Muslims.

In the towns and cities where Islam was widely accepted, literacy and book-learning appeared in West Africa. There is no knowing when Islamic schools, founded for the teaching of the Koran and the *sharia*, the laws of Islam, first appeared. Muslim teaching of some kind certainly existed in the city of Gao as early as the beginning of the tenth century, and many Muslim missionaries were at work in the Western Sudan during the eleventh century. We hear of the growth of Islamic schools in the empire of Mali during the fourteenth century, as well as in the Songhay cities of the fifteenth century. By the sixteenth century, West African Muslim scholars were writing on many historical, legal, moral and religious subjects.

The book by Leo Africanus, referring to the years around AD 1500, has much to say on this. Of the old capital of Mali, Niani on the Upper Niger, Leo wrote that 'they have many mosques, priests and professors who teach in the mosques'. As we know from other sources, they taught to a high level of Muslim erudition.

151

'In Timbuktu', Leo tells us, 'there are many judges, professors and holy men, all being generously helped by the king, who holds scholars in much honour. Here, too, they sell many handwritten books from North Africa. More profit is made from selling books in Timbuktu than from any other branch of trade.' Gao, on the other hand, could boast of no such brilliance. 'The people here', Leo considered, 'are absolutely ignorant. There is probably not one in a thousand who knows how to write. But the king of Gao', he adds with a touch of humour, 'treats them as they deserve. For he taxes them so heavily that they are scarcely left with enough to live on.'

In these and other cities of the Western Sudan, learning drew not only on the talent and work of local people, but also on those of Muslim scholars from other lands. 'God has drawn to this fortunate city', wrote a Timbuktu author about Jenne, 'a certain number of learned and of pious men, strangers to the land, who have come to live here.' This was another reason why the Islamic schools of Timbuktu and Jenne became famous in the whole Muslim world.

Three famous writers

Timbuktu and Jenne had many well-known writers. The most renowned of the sixteenth century was probably Ahmad Baba.

Born in Timbuktu in 1556, Ahmad Baba composed many works on Islamic law as well as a biographical dicitionary of Muslim scholars. At least thirteen of his works are still in use by the *ulama*[3] of West Africa. His library was so good that it was held in high esteem for many years after his death. His bravery and independence of mind were also much respected. It is easy to see why.

When invaders from Morocco seized Timbuktu in 1591, Ahmad Baba refused to serve them. Fearing his influence and accusing him of organizing a rebellion, the Moroccan invaders took him in chains across the Sahara to their capital of Marrakesh. There they held him for many years before allowing him to come home again. So it may be said that Ahmad Baba, who never ceased to protest against the invasion of his native land, was not only an outstanding scholar but was also in his daily life one of the forerunners of West African nationalism.

Two important histories of the Western Sudan were also written by scholars of Timbuktu. They are the *Tarikh al-Fattash*, the History of the

---

[3] This is an Arabic word meaning 'men of learning'. Its singular is *mu'allim*. In West Africa this word often appears in its Hausa form, *mallam*.

Seeker for Knowledge, completed in about 1665 and the *Tarikh as-Sudan*, the History of the (Western) Sudan, also completed in about 1665. Both were written in Arabic, for this was the literary language of the scholars of Islam. Both were the work of West Africans born in Timbuktu. The chief author of the first was Mahmud Kati, who was born in about 1648 and is said to have lived to a very old age; the second was Abd al-Rahman as-Sadi, who was born in 1596 and lived until about 1655.

Both scholars had good careers. Kati was only 25 when the Songhay ruler, *Askia* Muhammed the Great, took over power from *Sunni* Baru; Kati became a member of the *Askia*'s personal staff. He went to Mecca with the emperor and was thus well placed to see and understand the events of his time. He began his great book in about 1519, but his sons and grandsons, who were also scholars, continued to work on it and brought the story of Songhay and Timbuktu down to about 1665.

Abd al-Rahman as-Sadi was born only five years after the Moroccan invasion, the results of which he saw when still a child. He tells us in the *Tarikh as-Sudan* that it was because of all the sad events he had witnessed in his youth that he decided to write his book. In a moving preface he recalls how he saw 'the ruin of learning and its utter collapse' under the hammerblows of Moroccan onslaught. He explains:

> And because learning is rich in beauty and fertile in its teaching, since it instructs men about their fatherland, their ancestors, their history, the names of their heroes and what lives they lived, I asked God's help and decided to set down all that I myself could learn on the subject of the Songhay princes of West Africa, their adventures, their story, their achievements and their wars. Then I added the history of Timbuktu from the time of its foundation, of the princes who ruled there and the scholars and saints who lived there, and of other things as well.

For some of these 'other things' we can be very thankful; they include, for example, many of the early stories of Ancient Ghana and Mali.

This long history of Muslim learning and writing has never ceased in West Africa. On the contrary, it has grown and spread with the passing of the years. Today the *ulama* of West Africa, whether in the northern country of the plains or the southern country of the forests, have many libraries and pupils. Their libraries contain works by West African and other Muslim authors, and range from books written centuries ago to books of the present time.

In later years, Christian scholarship began to make its powerful and lasting contribution to West African education and schooling; but in the sixteenth century, this was still to come.

153

Islam and politics

The introduction of the ideas and beliefs of Islam have proved valuable to West Africans in the fields of literacy and of politics.

So far as literacy is concerned, Islam is based on a book, the Koran, which Muslims are enjoined to know and study. So Islam called on West Africans to learn how to read and write. Muslim teachers set up schools where students read the Koran and learned to recite passages from it by heart. They also founded centres of learning where books written by Muslim scholars were studied and discussed, and new books were written.

So it came about that important centres of book-learning arose in West Africa, the first of their kind: after 1300 at Niani, the capital of the Mali empire; after 1400 at Timbuktu, which became a city of the Songhay empire; and elsewhere. The Muslim schools of Timbuktu became especially famous; they formed an early kind of university.

Different branches of learning were taught and studied. One was *tawhid*, the study of the unity of God. Another was *tafsir*, the study of the Koran. A third was *fiqh*, the study of law and administration. History and geography were also taught.

All Muslims have a code of basic rules for behaviour. This is the *sharia*. In West Africa, after about AD 1000 (or 391 in the Muslim calendar, which begins in AD 622 and has a slightly shorter year), the *sharia* was taught according to the ideas of the Maliki school of religious teachers.

The ideas and beliefs of Islam helped to build larger states than before. One reason for this was that when people became Muslims they could join together more easily across 'ethnic' boundaries or separatist loyalties. Islam was a means of creating unity between them. Another reason was that Islam provided the kind of laws that were useful to bigger states and larger market-towns. Such laws were about the administration of justice, the inheritance of property, the improvement of market organization, and other matters that became important as civilization developed.

Famous scholars taught these things. One of them was al-Maghili, a North African who wrote a book of advice about new methods of government for the benefit of King Muhammad Rumfa of the Hausa state of Kano in about 1490. He called his book *The Duties of Kings*.

When long-distance trade with North Africa, across the Sahara, became important for West Africans, new methods of conducting this trade were required. North African Muslims had already developed useful techniques for credit and exchange, for reckoning in values based on coins, when they were trading with other peoples who lived far away. These techniques began to be adopted by West African traders as well; and many of these West African traders became Muslims.

After about AD 900 the standard measure of value in North Africa became the Almoravid *dinar*, sometimes in West Africa called the *mitcal*.

Although West Africans continued to use their own standards for measuring value – the cowrie shell became the most important of these – they also began measuring in dinars or mitcals when they were trading with North Africans. Such developments encouraged long-distance trade and also helped to spread Islam.

But if Islam has often been of positive value to the enlargement of the political culture of West Africa, it has also had its negative side. In certain ways the teachings of the *sharia* have proved both violent and destructive. Forced conversion to Islam was widely resisted by Africans who possessed viable religions of their own. Bitter conflicts have emerged from the clash between non-Muslim beliefs and those of the Muslim *sharia* code of behaviour. These conflicts have often become, as in our own times, very destructive of peace and goodwill. Muslim dogmatism has made this hard to avoid, for the Muslim rules of law and social behaviour were composed 1,000 years ago, and they have not been revised for modern conditions. These rules demand that Muslims must make war on non-Muslims, a demand that no modern society can sensibly accept.

Some useful dates concerning Islam in the history of West Africa

AD

622	Foundation of Islam in Arabia. Year One of Muslim Calendar.
641	Muslim Arabs capture Babylon, at that time (Christian) capital of Egypt.
670	Muslim Arabs, under Uqba ibn Nafi, occupy Ifriqiya (Tunisia). In 711 a Muslim Arab army under Tariq crosses into Spain at Gibraltar (Jebel al-Tariq: the Hill of Tariq). They conquer most of Spain and Portugal, and go raiding into France. This leads to the rise of a brilliant Muslim state in Spain, with its capital at Cordoba (756–1031).
c.750	Small Muslim trading states in North Africa (especially Tahert in Algeria) are active in the trade with West Africa across the Sahara.
773	Muslim Arab geographer al-Fazari writes of Ancient Ghana as 'the land of gold'. Muslim traders from North Africa become active in cities of the Western Sudan: Takrur, Audaghost, Gao.
c.1010	King of Gao becomes a Muslim. So do some other kings of the Western Sudan, including the king of Mali (Barmandana) and of Kanem-Bornu (Hume).
1076	Almoravids (Mauretanian Berbers) capture capital of Ancient Ghana.

1324	Famous pilgrimage of *Mansa* Kankan Musa of Mali.
1335	*Sunni* line of Songhay kings begins at Gao. They are Muslims.
1400	Rise of Timbuktu and Jenne as centres of Muslim learning and of trade in gold with the Akan people of central (modern) Ghana.
1490	Al-Maghili writes *The Duties of Kings*.
c.1550	Kings of Kanem-Bornu enter into good relations with the great Muslim empire of the Ottoman Turks. (In 1517 the Ottoman Turks completed their conquest of Egypt. In 1529 they dominated Algeria. In 1534 they set up a new (Ottoman) state in Tunisia.)
1665	The writers of Timbuktu complete two important histories of the Western Sudan, the *Tarikh al-Sudan* (History of the Sudan) and the *Tariqh al-Fattash* (History of the Seeker for Knowledge).
1725	Fulani Muslims of Futa Jallon (modern republic of Guinea) form new religious state. Beginning of the revival of Islam in the grassland plains of West Africa. This continues after 1800.
c.1775	Foundations of Muslim state of Futa Toro (in the north of modern Senegal).
1804–11	Muslim Fulani conquer Hausaland. Origins of the caliphate of Sokoto.

The Organization of Society

The Organization of Society

Ways of life had changed greatly even before the onset of modern times. Bigger food supplies had become available because of better tools, improved farming methods and wider markets. Already West Africa contained far more people than at the beginning of the Iron Age, and most of them were better fed.

These social changes had led to political changes. Many different ways of self-rule were now on the scene. Often these were strengthened by dividing people into age-sets which gathered together persons belonging to different descent-lines, or 'big families'. Always they were strengthened by the worship of gods through revered ancestors. There were many systems of rule by chiefs through 'title societies', such as those of Awka and Nsukka, or special associations such as Ekpe among the Cross River peoples, Ogboni among the Yoruba, and Poro among the peoples of Sierra Leone.

Big states and empires had been built by powerful kings. For a long time these rulers had continued to be appointed by councils of chiefs who were the heads of senior 'big families'. This produced what may be called an early form of 'constitutional monarchy'. The emperors of Ancient Ghana and Mali, for example, were obliged to rule according to the 'constitutional' laws and limits laid down by tradition and safeguarded by councils, consisting of the heads of 'big families'.

As time went by, the kings and chiefs got more power over the mass of ordinary people. There arose new forms of government by groups or classes of nobles who tended to alter the traditional rules to their own advantage. Throughout the Western Sudan the rise of Islam after the fourteenth century did much to change the customs of former times, in government as in trade and religion. We have noted important examples of the way in which Muslim kings strengthened their positions against the descent-line chiefs: in Songhay under *Askia* the Great, or in the Hausa states under rulers such as Muhammad Rumfa of Kano. This trend continued,

159

and there came the rise of 'king's men'. These were appointed officials who were not members of the 'big families', and who were loyal only to the king their master.

This strengthening of the authority of kings at the expense of senior chiefs did not happen only in areas influenced by Islam. We shall see that the *alafins* (kings) of Oyo also strengthened their personal authority with the growth of their empire in the seventeenth century, and the same thing happened elsewhere. The old ways, in fact, were continually being modified into new ways. Nothing in any of these systems of government was ever 'standing still'. On the contrary, all these varied methods of self-rule, ranging from popular rule in village governments to rule by chiefs or kings, were constantly going through a *process of change*.

The dividing-up of society

As this *process of change* went on, and more peoples formed themselves into states under elders, chiefs or kings, something very important happened to society. Its old natural equality began to disappear. It became *stratified*. It became divided, that is, into different social *strata*: different 'layers' of power and wealth. Some persons, usually because of their birth, had the right to become chiefs. Others could not become chiefs, but had the right to elect them. Others again could not elect chiefs, but only had the right to say how chiefs ought to behave. Still others were pushed down into a lowly position where they had to obey their masters without question.

These 'layers' may be thought of as *horizontal* divisions, with all the senior chiefs, for example, on one level of power, all the free farmers on a second, all the unfree servants or slaves on a third. Together with these different 'layers' there remained, however, older divisions of another kind. These were *vertical* divisions which separated all the people of one clan from the people of other clans, all the inhabitants of one village from their neighbours, all the descendants of one set of ancestors from the descendants of other ancestors. These vertical, or 'up-and-down', divisions were in some ways even more important to West African social development than the horizontal divisions or 'layers', and they were already very ancient by the sixteenth century.

There also took place a third kind of dividing-up of society, caused by the changing and better ways in which people worked together. Craftsmen formed themselves into different groups, according to their skills: metalworkers, boat-builders, fishermen, farmers, diviners, priests, singers of songs, and many others. Some of these groups of craftsmen and specialists possessed much social power; others possessed little. How much social power each group possessed varied from place to place. Among some peoples, for example, metal-workers were greatly honoured; among others, they were not.

This dividing-up of society had already gone very far in West Africa by the early years of the sixteenth century. There had appeared in West Africa, as elsewhere in the world, a form of social organization in which some people were masters and other people were servants. People had built, in other words, a ladder of social power. Kings stood on the top rung, slaves on the bottom. In between there was everyone else, standing on rungs that were higher than the rungs below them, but lower than the ones above.

This dividing-up of society into different 'levels' or 'layers' was not, of course, a chance invention by clever kings and chiefs. It reflected the new ways in which people worked together, produced wealth, exchanged goods, and lived in society. It marked an important if often painful stage in history; and it happened in nearly every part of Africa as in nearly every part of the world. And, of course, we are still in this stage.

But men were seldom able or content to go on standing for long on the same rung of the ladder of social power. Slaves pushed upward into freedom. Kings were sometimes pulled downward. Poor men climbed to wealth. Rich men became poor. This movement up and down the social ladder greatly influenced the events of political history. It could not, for example, always be a peaceful one. Quite often it set one people or state against another, and promoted wars and conquests. The progress of one people had to be at the expense of some other people.

One further point. We have said that the dividing-up of society occurred nearly everywhere in the world. But it needs to be remembered that it went much further, and became much more painful, in many of the countries of Europe and Asia. There, because of much greater development in production and exchange of goods and wealth, society became rigidly divided into separate *classes* of masters and servants, with a few people having great wealth and power, and most people having little or none. There, too, movement up and down the ladder of social power became difficult or rare.

This stiff and harsh dividing into classes had not yet happened in West Africa. The horizontal divisions into 'layers' of power remained less influential than the vertical divisions into different clans, descent-lines, and communities. This is why most West African governments during the sixteenth century and onwards were much more democratic, much more respectful of the rights of individual persons, than were the governments of Europe.

By the sixteenth century, for example, most of the land of Europe was becoming the private possession of a landowning class. In West Africa there was no such class. Yet the horizontal 'layers' in West African society were of growing importance; and we shall now discuss them a little further.

Masters and servants

Old records and traditions tell us little of the way that ordinary folk lived, but much of the magnificence of kings. Travellers from North Africa were greatly impressed by the power and wealth of West African rulers. Here, for example, is a North African description of the court of the emperor of Mali. It is that of Ibn Batuta, who travelled through Mali in 1352 during the reign of *Mansa* Suleyman, but it remained true of later times as well:

> The lord of this kingdom has a great balcony in his palace. It is called the Bembe. There he has a great seat of ebony that is like a throne fit for a large and tall person. It is flanked by elephants' tusks. The king's arms stand near him. They are all of gold; sword and lance, quiver of bow and arrows. He wears wide trousers made of twenty pieces of stuff, and they are of a kind which only he may wear.
>
> Before him stand about twenty Turkish or other pages, who are brought from Cairo. One of these, standing on his left, holds a silk umbrella that is topped by a dome and bird of gold. The bird is like a hawk. The king's officers are seated in a circle near him, in two rows, one to the right and the other to the left. Beyond them sit the commanders of the cavalry.
>
> In front of him there is a person who never leaves him and who is his executioner; and another who is his official spokesman, and who is named the herald. In front of him there are also drummers. Others dance before their king and make him merry . . .

There we have a glimpse of some of those groups of men who had the right to serve the king and the state in special jobs or offices according to their training and position in society: counsellors, military officers, spokesmen, drummers and others. But what about the mass of ordinary people?

They were generally divided into the 'free' and the 'unfree'. We have to treat these words with care, because the actual amount of freedom and unfreedom greatly varied with time and place; and it was always possible for free men to become unfree, mainly by being captured in war, or for unfree men to become free by hard work, loyal service, or good luck. All the same, these big divisions into 'free' and 'unfree' became more widespread and important during the sixteenth century.

In Nigerian Hausaland, for example, men understood very well the difference between the mass of ordinary folk who were free, the *talakawa*, and all those who were not free, the *cucenawa*. In Bornu, the nobles ruled over three big social groups known as the *kamba, kalia* and *zusanna*, whose amount of freedom got less from the first to the second, and less again from the second to the third. Writing of the people of the seaboard of modern Ghana in 1700, a Dutchman called William Bosman observed five main 'layers' among the peoples he knew there. The first were kings and rulers. The second were chiefs whom 'we should call civic fathers, their duty being to take care of their city or village, and to maintain law and order'. The third 'layer' were those who had 'acquired a great reputation by their riches, either got by inheritance or obtained by trade'. The fourth were farmers and fishermen. The fifth were slaves.

Free men seldom lived or worked just as they liked. Their freedom usually needed the protection of chiefs and lords. This protection was given in exchange for taxes or regular payments of one kind or another. In this way, free men often became vassals or subjects of sub-chiefs, or of big chiefs, or of kings and emperors. These vassals owed service to their lords; but their lords owed them protection in return. It was on this two-way system of service that many big political systems were founded.

Unfree men were in much the same general position as the majority of free men, except that they had fewer rights and were often pushed down into very humble positions in society. They seldom or never had any political say in deciding how chiefs should behave. They were usually 'tied' to a certain place and occupation, and were forbidden to move away or change their work. In the empire of Songhay, for example, unfree women were even forbidden to marry free men, a ban that was applied so as to ensure that the children of slaves should remain slaves, and not be free because the father was free. *Askia* Muhammad slightly changed this law about the marriage of the unfree (or slaves), but the result was much the same. He laid it down that a slave women might marry a free man, but that her children would still be slaves. The point about laws of this kind was to ensure that the king and his chiefs should continue to have a large source of free or cheap labour.

Kinds of service

It is often difficult to draw a clear line between men who were counted as being free, and men who were considered as slaves. Since nobody worked for money, free men as well as slaves had duties they could not escape, and often these duties made them do very much the same kind of work. One helpful way of seeing how things were is to consult the *Tarikh al-Fattash*, which gives a detailed picture of everyday life in the Songhay empire around AD 1600.

The *Tarikh al-Fattash* tells us at one point that *Askia* Muhammad, who became emperor in 1493, acquired 24 special peoples as part of his estate. It describes who these peoples were, and what they did in return for the emperor's protection. We can regard them either as vassals or slaves.

They served in different ways. Some of them had to cut fodder for the Songhay ruler's cavalry. Others were riverfolk and fishermen. These owed the ruler of Songhay a certain amount of dried fish every year. 'It consisted', says the *Tarikh al-Fattash*, 'of ten packets of dried fish to be paid by those who could afford as much . . . And every time the king was asked for river transport, he got it from the canoes of this people, and they also supplied the crews.'

Another of these vassal or slave peoples of the *Askia* were called Arbi. Their job was to be bodyguards and house-servants of the king. As many as five subject peoples (groups of people whose exact numbers we do not know) were metal-workers. 'They owed a duty to the king of one hundred spears and one hundred arrows every year for each family of them.'

And so it went on, each vassal or subject group having to provide this or that service to their chief or king, and each chief or king, in his turn, having to protect them from enemies and to help them in times of trouble. Good rulers were men who fully accepted this two-way system of service. Bad rulers were those who took what was due to them, but gave no help and protection in return.

There was, we should remember, a lot of movement up and down the ladder of power. Free men were taken prisoner in wartime, and were thrust down to the bottom rung; they could be used or sold as slaves. The Muslim rulers of West Africa often raided their non-Muslim neighbours so as to secure supplies of free labour; and their non-Muslim neighbours now began to do the same in reverse. Lawbreakers were also reduced to slavery for serious offences. Regular slave markets were held. In the city of Gao, for example, Leo Africanus observed 'a market where many slaves, men and women, are sold every day. A girl of fifteen is worth about six ducats.[1] Little children are sold for about half the price of grown-ups.' Many such slaves were sent northward across the Sahara.

We should note, however, that slavery in West Africa was seldom the harsh and pitiless fate that was reserved for those who were later taken across the Atlantic to the mines and plantations of the Americas. There, across the Atlantic, slaves were treated worse than cattle. Their fate was a hopeless one. Few could become free men and women.

Traditional slavery in West Africa was a much milder affair.[2] Seldom if ever was it *chattel* slavery, suffered by the Africans taken to the Americas by the Atlantic slave trade. We will come back to this subject. Often it scarcely deserved the name of slavery at all, being only a form of service which carried special duties and obligations. Slaves could easily work

---

[1] A ducat was a coin in use among North African traders.
[2] This was untrue of some countries, such as Mauretania, where Berber peoples continued to treat their slaves with cruelty and contempt.

themselves into freedom. They could marry into their owners' families. They could become rich. Sometimes they even became chiefs and kings, like *Mansa* Sakuru of Mali.

Civil service developments

Government through a highly trained and educated civil service is a modern development. But states and empires of this period had civil services of a less complicated sort. Their rulers governed through a system of governors and sub-governors; and each of these had his own *bureaucracy* (a word that comes from the French for office). These office-holders or officials operated an early form of civil service.

This started a long time ago, certainly in the days of Ancient Ghana. There are no detailed accounts of how the lords of Ghana organized their government. But they must certainly have had some kind of civil service, for they were able to secure law and order over a very wide region of the Western Sudan, and to draw tribute from many peoples.

With the passing of the years, we learn more about the old methods of government. A writer of the early fourteenth century, al-Omari of Cairo, has described how *Mansa* Kankan Musa of Mali (1312–37) carried on his rule. It was one of this emperor's customs, we are told by al-Omari, 'that whenever someone who has been charged with a certain task or important affair reports to the king, the latter questions him on everything that has happened from the time of his departure to the time of his return, and in great detail. Legal cases and appeals also go up to the king who examines them himself. Generally, he writes nothing himself, but gives his orders by word of mouth. For this, he has secretaries and offices.'[3] Already, in fourteenth-century Mali, there were the beginnings of a regular civil service.

Yet early forms of civil service such as these tended to be easy-going and unreliable. The officials might be prompt and obedient when the king or governor was present. When the king or governor was absent, they might stop bothering about his orders. Or they might simply go on doing things as they had always done them, no matter what the king or governor had ordered. The governments of these early states, in short, were very loosely organized.

After about AD 1500, there came new developments in government. Kings and governors began to need more reliable methods of giving their orders, and of having these orders carried out. Life got more complicated

---

[3] Al-Omari's encyclopaedic writings date to the 1340s and are a major source for the history of the empire of Mali. The most useful, *Masalik al-absar*, is available in partial English and French translation; it was written in Arabic around AD 1337, or 737 in the Muslim calendar.

as wealth and power grew. The rulers of Benin, for example, introduced important reforms in methods of government. These were, it seems, especially the work of *Oba* Esigie, who came to power at the beginning of the century and ruled for nearly 50 years. Esigie emerged as victor in an old power-struggle, which had been fought by many Benin kings before him, against Benin's strongest group of nobles, the Uzama. These Uzama nobles had previously enjoyed the right to choose, by election among themselves, who was going to be the king of Benin. Now they lost this right, and from this time onwards the eldest son of a dead king took the throne.

Kings, nobles, governors

In this particular change we can see not only how the power of the king of Benin had grown, but also how the traditions of the Edo people influenced political ideas that had come from Yorubaland in earlier times. The Uzama nobles of Benin had been in many ways like the Oyo Mesi nobles of Oyo, whose power continued to include the right to elect the *alafin* of Oyo. But while the Oyo Mesi among the Yoruba continued to enjoy this right, the Uzama among the Edo did not.

At the same time as taking away some political power from the Uzama, the king of Benin created two new kinds of noblemen: palace chiefs and town chiefs. In this he was no doubt seeking to balance two important influences in the state. While the palace chiefs were usually connected with the court, the town chiefs were often self-made men who had done well in trade or warfare, or in some other specialized way of life which did not depend on having court connections.

With all this, the sixteenth-century kings of Benin became more powerful in their city. Yet they do not seem to have strengthened their hold over the Benin empire. Benin princes became rulers of different parts of the empire, even outside Edo-speaking areas, but they ran their own affairs very much as they pleased.

All this emphasized a basic principle of West African government: wherever possible, power should be decentralized into the hands of local people. If rulers were not obliged to decentralize, they would be tempted to act as dictators, and social disaster would follow.

Somewhat similar changes were taking place in Yorubaland. In Oyo itself the hereditary council of nobles, the Oyo Mesi, retained their former powers as the chiefs of senior descent-lines, but these powers were not increased when the empire grew larger in the seventeenth century. While the subject-kings of outlying parts of the Oyo empire continued to enjoy a fair measure of self-rule in local affairs, they were bound to the *alafin*, but not to the Oyo Mesi nobles, in a number of new ways:

1 The *alafin* appointed resident officials in the different provinces. Their duties were to look after the collection of taxes, settle political quarrels, and stop the development of plots against the *alafin's* rule. These officials were usually men who had the status of slaves or permanent servants; they were called the *Ilari*.
2 The *alafin's* authority was strengthened by the spread of worship of Shango, the god who was regarded as the special protector of the *alafin* and his power.
3 All chiefs had to supply troops for the *alafin's* wars, attend the *alafin's* yearly festival at Oyo, and serve him in other regular ways.

In the grassland countries of the Western Sudan, too, there was a steady improvement in methods of government. Here the customs of Islam helped towards the formation of regular civil services staffed by 'king's men': by officials, that is, who owed their appointments not to their birth but to individual skill and service to the king. *Sunni* Ali of Songhay (1464–92) had divided Songhay into provinces and had appointed governors and commanders with staffs of their own. *Askia* Muhammad (1493–1528) developed this system further still, improved it and increased the number of officials. Songhay was thus divided into the provinces of Kurmina, Dendi, Baro, Dirma and Bangu. Each had its own governor, called *fari* or *farma* or *koy*; the senior among them was the *kurminafari*.

At the seat of central government, the *askia* governed through a 'civil service' of officials. There was a large number of military chiefs, as we shall see in a moment; but a still larger number of civil chiefs. The latter, for instance, included the *barey-koy*, who was in charge of all court arrangements, and was assisted by the *kukura-koy*, whose job it was to provide food and other necessary supplies, and by the *garei-farma*, master of the camp. There was also the *katisi-farma*, head of the 'finance department', assisted by the *waney-farma*, responsible for questions of property, by the *bara-farma*, who was concerned with wages, and by the *dey-farma*, who looked after such buying and selling as had to be done on behalf of the government. Farming problems were likewise the business of the *fari-mundia*; forestry matters that of the *sao-farma*; while the *asari-mundia* was head of the 'department of justice'. Besides these, there were many other officials. Similar civil service systems were built in the Kanem-Bornu empire under *Mai* Idris Alooma (about 1580–1617), in the Hausa states, and elsewhere.

Professional armies

Another way in which the means of government developed was in the methods of making war. These became more destructive, more highly organized.

167

Chiefs, kings and emperors of earlier times had relied on simply 'calling up' their subjects, their vassals, or their allies. Some of them, like King Tunka Manin of Ghana in the eleventh century, could put very large armies into the field by this means of 'call-up'. But these were temporary armies. They were *amateur* armies. They served for a campaign or a war, and then everyone went home again until the next time.

The rulers of the sixteenth century found that this method of amateur war-making placed a narrow limit on their powers. They began to create full-time armies, *professional* armies.

They did this for several reasons. With the growing development of central government, kings needed troops who were always available, who could move at once, and who could be relied on to obey orders. This last point, incidentally, explains why kings often employed their unfree men as professional soldiers. Another reason was that the weapons of war were becoming more expensive and more difficult to handle. Firearms, for example, cost a lot to buy, while cavalry horses were expensive both to buy and to feed. They also called for special skills in using them; and only regular training could provide these skills. Kings saw that if they were going to lay out wealth on cavalry horses and firearms, they had better give these to men who were going to spend their life as soldiers, who would be properly trained, and who would stay closely under the king's own command.

Askia Muhammad of Songhay seems to have led the way in forming professional armies. His famous predecessor, *Sunni* Ali, had relied on the old-fashioned 'call-up' of earlier times. Muhammad, taking over a large empire and determined to make it larger, was not content with an amateur army: he wanted a full-time army, and he built one up.

How he did this may be seen from the *Tarikh al-Fattash*. Briefly, a full-time army was raised and placed under the command of a full-time general, the *dyini-koy* or *balama*. The *Askia* also formed a full-time navy on the Niger. *Sunni* Ali had included Niger boatmen in his amateur military system. The *Askia* turned these into professional sailors. This Songhay navy on the Niger he placed under the *hi-koy*, or admiral of the canoe-fleet. Another officer, the *tara-farma*, had command of a full-time force of cavalry.

Mai Idris Alooma of Kanem-Bornu was another sixteenth-century ruler who took advantage of all this development in the means of making war. He imported muskets and instructors from Tripoli, and built up a small group of musketeers. He found these useful for three reasons. First, they were professional soldiers, and so were always available for duty. Second, they trained regularly with their weapons, and so were good at using them. Third, they were war-prisoners who had become the king's slaves, and so were bound to obey him.

Some of the governments of the forest states along the coastland also raised full-time military forces. Special groups of professional warriors emerged in Igboland. These were men who sold their war-making or defensive services to other countries or rulers who might need them. Such warrior-mercenaries, or professional soldiers, were also busy along the great trade routes, providing escorts for the caravans, defending markets, chasing off raiders.

It should be remembered that these long-service troops were only the core or nucleus of the army. Every state still depended on calling up amateur soldiers during time of war, for none of them had enough professionals. What sometimes happened now, in contrast with the past, was that the skill of the professionals was learned to some extent by the amateurs, especially in conquering states like Songhay where large armies fought many wars.

All this had mixed results. War became more frequent and more destructive. Ordinary folk suffered accordingly. Professional armies strengthened the power of kings and governments, and, in doing so, made it easier to impose law and order over wide regions. Ordinary people could sometimes gain from this. The same contradictory process of loss and gain was part of the building of the modern world.

Law and order

Some people had many laws, many social rules and regulations, and went to great trouble to enforce them. Other peoples got along with far fewer laws, and bothered far less about applying them. It depended on where people lived, and how they lived. The sixteenth century saw changes in this field, too.

There was a growth in the means of *enforcing* law, whether by specially appointed officials, by special associations elected or recognized for the purpose, or by the formation of soldier groups who took their orders from judges or kings (though judges and kings were often the same men). But there was also a growth in the means of *making* law. This development of African law, or what is sometimes called customary law because it was not written down, was an important aspect of the sixteenth century.

It has been little studied; and it is not a subject we can follow here. But one unusual problem in this development of law does call for special comment. There came a clash between Muslim law and traditional African law. (Later on, a similar though more limited clash would occur between African law and European or Christian law.)

Clash of beliefs

These differences in custom and belief had important political results. There was often an outright clash between those who continued to believe in their traditional religions, and those who accepted Islam.

169

The force of this clash varied with the times. Often there came a compromise, or settlement, between the two kinds of religion. Some peoples accepted Islam, but none the less kept many of their old beliefs and customs. As well as the *sharia*, in other words, they also had the *'ada* (traditional or customary law, as distinct from *sharia*, or Muslim religious law). In the sixteenth century, however, the clash was often acute in the Western and Central Sudan, because the late fifteenth century had seen a big expansion of Islam in the towns and cities.

Before leaving this subject, we can usefully return for a moment to the case of Songhay, which we discussed in Chapter 5. By the time *Sunni* Ali came to the throne in 1464, Islam was becoming strong among the merchants and leaders of the Songhay cities and market-centres. *Sunni* Ali accordingly made concessions to their beliefs and customs, and he went out of his way to declare his respect for Muslim scholarship. 'Without learned men', he is said to have remarked, 'there would be no pleasure in life.' But *Sunni* Ali based his political and military power on the support of the non-Muslim farmers and fishermen of the countryside; and his tremendous record of success shows that in this he calculated wisely.

Yet Islam went on gaining converts and influence in the cities and market-centres, so that *Askia* Muhammad, coming to power at the end of the century, found himself in the opposite position to that of *Sunni* Ali. Although the *Askia* was careful not to offend non-Muslim feelings, at least on questions of court ceremonial, he ruled as a strict Muslim and introduced many legal reforms.

This pro-Muslim policy served *Askia* Muhammad well. He built a still larger empire than *Sunni* Ali had done. But the conflicts between Muslims and non-Muslims, in Songhay as elsewhere, continued. They had their full effect after the Moroccan invasion of 1591. For the *ulama* of the Songhay towns then tended to accept the Moroccans as their natural Muslim allies against the non-Muslim people of the Songhay countryside. When *Askia* Ishaq II faced the Moroccan army at the disastrous battle of Tondibi in 1591, his chief secretary and adviser, Alfa Askia Lanbar, actually persuaded him to abandon the field. Later on, this Muslim official even betrayed some of the Songhay chiefs to the leader of the Moroccan invaders. In behaving like this, of course, the *ulama* of cities like Timbuktu were really trying to recover their old independence. They backed the Moroccans against the Songhay rulers, although, once the Songhay were defeated, they turned round and became hostile to the Moroccans. But their attitude during the invasion tells us a lot about the political importance of the conflict between Islam and West African religion at that time, and in later times.

New Pressures from Outside

Head in brass of Queen Idia of Benin, in ancient times renowned for her mystical powers. (National Museums and Galleries on Merseyside (Liverpool Museum))

New Pressures from Outside

By AD 1600, at the end of the sixteenth century, West Africans had solved the great problems of everyday life. They had developed efficient ways of growing food under tropical conditions, and were able to provide for the basic needs of a steadily expanding population. Even to this day their evolved farming methods and farming management have shown little need for essential improvement. The coming of cocoa and other new crops has greatly widened their overall means of production. These peoples had meanwhile discovered how to locate and mine the underground ores of valuable minerals and of gold, and their gold production had already become famous for its value in many distant countries and cities. They had built original and efficient systems of community life and government, and had long been skilled in ways of keeping the peace among themselves.

Whether in the grassland plains or the forest states of the coastland, new states took shape under the pressures of social and political development. We can usefully look at several of the more important of these new states, for each of them, in different ways of detail, revealed the creative capacity of these West African peoples as they left their early origins far behind them. Where they chiefly differed from the European states of the same period was in the fact that they had not as yet developed any mechanical industries, nor, save marginally, the use of writing and therefore of reading, which were arts still narrowly known even in the advanced European states of the same period.

Bono and the trade in gold

Among these early states we can usefully give attention to the state of Bono in the Takyiman region (of modern Ghana), for it was through the little state of Bono that the West African trade in gold production and gold export built a vital centre in early times. The long-distance traders of the empire of Mali had their base in the forest regions of Bono. Bono therefore stands for us in a kind of ancestral relationship with the great African empires of the distant past.

There are Bono historical traditions which indicate that their state was founded by a famous leader, King Asaman, and by his queen-mother Amayaa whose reigning dates are remembered as lying between AD 1297 and 1329. They are said to have made their first royal capital at Tutena, a word in the Twi language which means 'new settlement', but soon moved it to a site judged more suitable, called Nkoranza. Meanwhile other peoples of the West African grouping called Akan developed in the same region.

These early Akan states were small, and it is important to see why. They were formed in dense forest country. There was no chance of building big states and empires which could be controlled by fast-moving cavalry, for the tse-tse fly hampered the breeding and keeping of horses. Movement was difficult. Political authority could not stretch very far, at least in those early days. Later on, with the expansion of political ideas and trade, this would change. In the eighteenth century, when long-distance trails were established, the Asante empire would include nearly all of modern Ghana, together with some of the Ivory Coast and Togo as well.

The traditions of early Bono say that gold was discovered in the Twi river and around Perembomase during Asaman's reign, and this discovery led to a new prosperity and progress. The truth behind this particular tradition is no doubt rather different. Gold was almost certainly *discovered* in this area long before Asaman's reign, but it was probably not much *worked*. Now, however, soon after 1400, there came a greater demand for gold from the grassland country, itself responding to a bigger demand from North Africa and Europe. This led the Dyula traders from Mali to travel south in search of gold, and it was offered to them in Bono. So the founding of Bono was partly the result of a growth in the gold trade. Once again, new ways of earning a livelihood went hand in hand with new ways of political organization.

Along the coast of modern Ghana: early states

The earliest peoples whom we hear of along the coast of central West Africa are those who formed their states in the fifteenth and sixteenth centuries. Although probably few in number, they were not without resources. They lived at what was then the backdoor of West Africa, faced with the empty ocean, but they evolved a stable way of life. When Portuguese sailors first arrived on this coast in the 1470s, they found people who were eager to trade with them. We have records of how the Portuguese were first received at Elmina. There, in 1482, the Portuguese asked for permission to build a castle, and this permission was given them by the chief of the Elmina district, whom the Portuguese records call Caramansa. Some scholars have seen in this word Caramansa a sign of Mandinka–Dyula presence on the coast of modern Ghana in the fifteenth century. They point out that the second part of the word is the same as the Mandinka word *mansa*, meaning king or chief. Others say that Caramansa was only a mistaken way of writing Kwamina Ansah, a name borne by several later rulers of Elmina.

Here is how the Portuguese of 1482 described their meeting with Kwamina Ansah at Elmina:

> He was seated on a high chair dressed in a jacket of brocade, with a golden collar of precious stone, and his chiefs were all dressed in silk ... These noblemen wore rings and golden jewels on their head and beards. Their king, Caramansa, came [towards the Portuguese] in their midst, his legs and arms covered with golden bracelets and rings, a collar round his neck, from which hung some small bells, and in his plaited beard golden bars, which weighed down its untrimmed hair, so that instead of being twisted it was smooth. To show his dignity, he walked with very slow and light steps, never turning his face to either side.

The Portuguese went on to describe Kwamina Ansah as a man

> of good understanding, both by nature and by his dealing with the crew of the trading ships, and he possessed a clear judgment. And as one who not only desired to understand what was proposed to him, who not only listened to the translation of the interpreter, but watched each gesture made by Diogo de Azambuja; and while this continued, both he and his men were completely silent, so perfectly disciplined were they ...

For a long while the trade with the north remained more valuable than the newly growing trade with the European sea-merchants. Now, as from Bono, the Dyula traders from Mali conducted their commerce from a base at Begho on the north-western outskirts of the forests where the gold was mined. From Begho the main trading route went north-westward through Dyula towns and little states, such as Kong and Bobo-Dioulasso ('the house of the Dyula traders of Bobo'), that lay in the northern part of the modern Ivory Coast, and then on to Jenne. Another main route went north-eastward from the Akan forests to Hausaland. Both were used for the export of gold, kola and other items, and for the import of salt, copper, and manufactured products from the north.

Coastal trade grew ever more important during the sixteenth century. The gold trade began to move southward as well as northward; not much at first, yet in steadily growing volume. In 1554, for example, three English ships bought no less than 400 lb of gold of fine quality on the coast of modern Ghana (known then to Europeans as the Gold Coast), as well as 36 barrels of peppercorns and about 250 elephants' tusks.

This shift in the movement of gold exports began to have political consequences. As coastal trade expanded, previously weak peoples along and near the seaboard began to evolve a new power of their own, helped by their control of the trade with Europeans.

The founding of Gonja: warriors and settlers

One of these consequences was the founding of Gonja. At some time between 1550 and 1575, *Askia* (Emperor) Dawud of Songhay found that his supplies of gold from the southern country were getting smaller. The main reason, as we have just seen, was that Akan gold-producers had begun selling some of their production to Portuguese and other European traders along the seaboard. *Askia* Dawud accordingly despatched a force of Mandinka cavalry to see what could be done about stopping up this 'leak' in his supplies.

It soon turned out that nothing could be done. Dawud's armoured horsemen rode south from the neighbourhood of Jenne until they reached the scrub and grassland country of the Black Volta region of modern Ghana. But they got no farther. They discovered that cavalry could not operate in the dense forest country where the Akan lived and smelted gold.

Unable to affect the movement of the gold trade, Dawud's warriors settled in the Black Volta lands and founded there, in the course of time, no fewer than seven little states of their own. Dyula traders joined them and helped to turn these states into new trading centres. Of these the most important was Gonja. Two others which took shape around 1600 and were ruled by Dagomba chiefs were Wa and Buna; and these, too, became centres of trade and Muslim learning.

Changes in North Africa

West Africa's many-sided political development throughout the sixteenth century, with colonial invasions still far in the future, was entirely the work of West Africans, but it was influenced, sometimes with deep effect, by new pressures from outside. Important among these, as before, were the demands and opportunities that arose from the long-distance trade.

Map 12.1 Caravan routes across the Sahara in the fifteenth and sixteenth centuries.

For century after century, the gold and other export products of West Africa were carried across the Sahara by 'ships of the desert', the slow but persevering camel caravans which brought back, in exchange, salt and other things of value in West African markets. This interaction between producers and buyers in West and North Africa had first become important during the early times of Ancient Ghana and Kanem.

In the sixteenth century, more or less after AD 1500, these old and valued links of trade were much disturbed by new political troubles. These troubles especially affected the trans-Saharan trade-trails. The older routes across the Sahara had been in three main geographical groups: those in the west, the centre and the east. The first of these, the westerly groups, linked far western Africa, by way of Mauretania, with powerful Muslim states in Morocco and southern Spain (al-Andalus) and, beyond these, with the cities of western Europe across the Mediterranean Sea. The second group of trails, again going from oasis to oasis wherever this was possible, or otherwise across the waterless wilderness, linked the valuable markets of the Middle Niger by way of Tuat with Algeria and the markets of the central Maghreb (Tunisia, Algeria and Morocco). The third group, the easterly routes, linked the Hausa states and Kanem by way of Ghat with the Fezzan (in southern Tunisia today), Tripoli and Egypt. Another important route went eastward from Kanem-Bornu by way of Darfur to the Middle Nile, and so to Egypt.

177

There were cross-routes as well. Caravans from the Middle Niger, for instance, could and often did go westward so as to take the westerly routes to the north; or they went north-eastward to Aïr and then to Tripoli by way of the great oasis of Tuat.

Events now worked together to disturb the trade along nearly all these routes. So far as the westerly routes were concerned, this was largely the result of wars between Muslims and Christians in Spain and Morocco. Pushing the Muslims out of Spain, the Portuguese and Spanish came south across the Mediterranean. In 1471 the Portuguese, lured on by tales of easy wealth in Africa, captured some of Morocco's Atlantic ports, including Tangier; in 1505 they captured still more of these ports. The Spanish, meanwhile, seized some of Morocco's Mediterranean ports. At the same time new conflicts broke out inside Morocco itself.

Later, in the second half of the sixteenth century, the Moroccans recovered most of their ports and began a slow recovery. But much had been destroyed. Sijilmasa, the ancient market city which lay at the northern end of the westerly caravan routes, had been reduced to ruins and never recovered. Even more serious for West African trade, there was now a frontier of warfare between Muslim Morocco and Christian Spain. Trade continued between the two; but it lost much of its former freedom of movement. In losing this, it became smaller in value.

Made poor by these costly wars, the Moroccan kings looked about for means of filling their empty treasuries, and picked on Songhay. They strove to capture the wealth of the Western Sudan. Their venture had little success; but it meant another big interruption in the peaceful flow of trade between West and North Africa.

At the same time a new power was rising in the eastern Mediterranean. This affected the central and easterly caravan routes, though with varying impact, as the Ottoman rulers of Turkey began to expand westwards into Africa. Egypt became their target. Ruled since 1250 by a line of powerful soldier-kings, the Mamluks, Egypt had known prosperity and freedom from invasion, especially under Sultan Baybars (1260–77) and Sultan Kala'un (1279–90). But since then, military rule had weakened Egypt. It was now attacked from two directions.

In 1509 a Portuguese fleet under Francisco de Almeida fought and defeated an Egyptian fleet in the Indian Ocean. This gave Portugal control of the narrow straits which lead from the Indian Ocean into the Red Sea.

In 1517 the armies of an expanding Turkish (Ottoman) empire conquered Egypt. In 1551 they occupied Tripoli. Irregular raiding companies[1] carried the power of their country still further westward through North

---

[1] The Europeans of the Mediterranean, who often fought these companies, called them corsairs or pirates.

Africa. They made themselves the masters of the coast of Tunisia and Algeria, founding new Turkish-dominated states along this seaboard.

A bitter Mediterranean rivalry now developed between the Christians of southern Europe and the Muslim Turks. Much of the sixteenth century passed here in small, harsh battles between the two sides, each seeking to win control of sections of the North African coastline and so acquire mastery of the trade with West Africa.

All these wars and upheavals damaged the trans-Saharan trade, especially on the western routes. After the ruin of Songhay and the establishment of Turkish power along much of the North African coast, the long-distance trade was slow to recover. The movement of goods between West Africa and southern Europe by way of Tunis and Algiers, and between West Africa and western Asia by way of Egypt, was repeatedly barred by new frontiers of war or hindered by new imperial rivalries.

And when, finally, trade could again flow easily between West Africa and North Africa, the world had greatly changed. The 'ships of the desert' were fast giving way to the ships of the ocean. Because of their progress in long-range sailing and ocean navigation, the sailors and merchants of Europe were firmly on the scene.

Europe comes to West Africa

Not many Europeans had sailed to West Africa before 1500. After that, their numbers rapidly and regularly increased. They also sailed increasingly to India and other Far Eastern lands, as well as to the Americas, having first reached those countries at the end of the fifteenth century.

This overseas enterprise was by no means an accident. It was the product of important developments in Europe. One of these was the *national growth* of western and southern Europeans, notably the Spanish, Portuguese, Dutch, English and French, together with their expanding financial and military power. Another was the *commercial interest* with led these peoples, firstly the Portuguese and Spanish, into trying to break the Muslim hold on international trade with Asia and West Africa. Faced with Muslim control of North Africa and Egypt, the Europeans now tried to 'get round the back of the Muslims' by sailing far to the south and east. A third and decisive development was Europe's new *technical ability* to build ocean-going ships and sail them out of sight of land.

Until the 1430s the seaboard nations of Europe possessed no ships that were good enough for long-range voyages.[2] Before that time, only the

---

[2] Vikings of Scandinavia had sailed and rowed to North America several hundred years earlier. But these Viking voyages were not followed up.

Map 12.2 The Turkish (Ottoman) advance in North Africa.

peoples of the East knew how to make long voyages by sail. Of these peoples, the Chinese were the most advanced. It was the Chinese who made the great naval and navigational inventions which led to the building of large ships that could survive the storms of the ocean. It was they who designed sails which could enable these ships to sail against the wind, 'into the wind' as sailors say; and it was they who first used instruments, like the compass, which could tell seamen in what direction to steer, even when their ships were far from any coast.

These Chinese inventions were taken over by other peoples who sailed the empty waters of the Indian Ocean and the eastern seas. Foremost among these other maritime peoples were the Arabs. Through the Arabs, inventions of this kind became known to the Europeans of the Mediterranean. Now moving into the age of modern science, Europeans borrowed the new methods of sailing and navigating, improved on them, and began to build long-range ships of their own. In this the Italians, Spanish and Portuguese took a leading part.

Until the 1430s the sailors of Portugal had never managed to come beyond the coasts of southern Morocco. They had feared to come any further, because, apart from superstitious beliefs about the climate and conditions at sea and on land beyond Cape Bojador, the winds along this coast blow nearly always from the north to the south. The Portuguese could sail southward with the wind behind their ships and sails, but these ships and sails were not yet good enough for them to turn round and go back northward against the wind. They had a saying which sums up the situation:

Who sails beyond the Cape Nun shore,
Turns back then, or returns no more.

Now they built ships and sails which could master the winds, and in 1434 they came far south beyond Cape Nun. Year by year, they sailed further. In 1446 their captains reached the mouth of the Senegal river. In 1472 they entered the Bight of Benin, having reached Elmina the year before. In 1482–83, they got as far as the mouth of the Congo. In 1488 Diaz rounded the Cape of Good Hope at the extreme southern point of Africa. Ten years later Vasco da Gama led three ships right round the Cape of Good Hope, up the eastern coast of Africa as far as Malindi (in modern Kenya). There he found an Arab pilot, Ibn Majid, who took him across the ocean to India.

With this voyage, the Portuguese had passed through the ocean gates of the 'Golden East'. Seamen of other European countries followed, boldly risking long months at sea in small, slow sailing ships and suffering many deaths and disasters, but drawn on always by the powerful hope of loot and profit. After the Portuguese and Spanish there came the French and

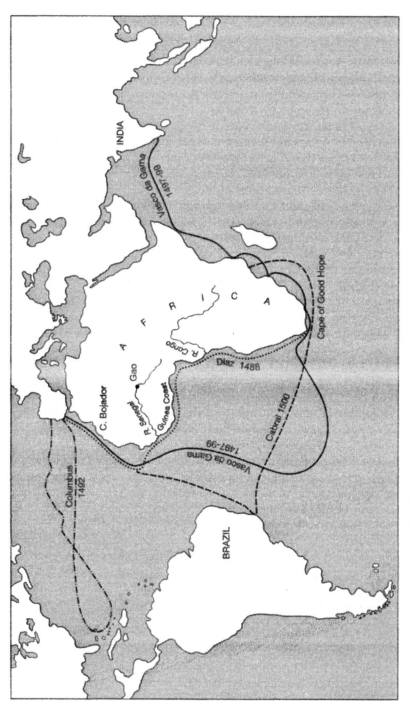

Map 12.3   European voyages of exploration after 1433.

English and then, towards the end of the sixteenth century and later, the Dutch and Danes, the Swedes and Germans of Brandenburg (as the state of Prussia in Germany was then called). All these Europeans fought and quarrelled with each other, disputed their 'rights' to this or that region of the sea and coast, but also added to European knowledge and experience.

Sometimes this work of exploration was violent and destructive, for early European captains often tried their hands at raiding and looting. For the most part, though, West African states were too strong to be attacked with much hope of success by soldiers from the sea. This being so, the raiding and looting soon gave way to peaceful trade and then to friendship.

A fateful partnership

Coastal Africans now found that they could buy metal goods and other useful things from European traders who came right to their beaches. This was highly convenient for these Africans of the coast, who had formerly had to buy such goods through middlemen from the Western Sudan. Europeans, for their part, found that they could sell their goods for gold and ivory and pepper, all items of great value when resold in Europe, but items they had formerly had to buy, through many middlemen, from the traders of North Africa. The records show that Africans and Europeans alike welcomed this new coastal trade. Both sides benefited. They bargained keenly with each other, but they also respected each other. If this partnership could have continued into the future, history would have had a very different tale to tell.

But this mutual benefit became, as the years slid by, increasingly a one-sided and therefore unequal benefit – a benefit that became a curse. The trade developed *away from* the peaceful exchange of raw materials and manufactured goods and *towards* a massive and eventually very destructive kind of trade – the Atlantic slave trade that took African captives for sale in America.

Origins and Growth of the Atlantic Slave Trade

Origins and Growth of the Atlantic Slave Trade

While these political developments were unfolding along the coastal regions, the influence of sea-merchants from Europe continued to grow as European mariners improved their techniques. By the early years of the seventeenth century, ships from several European nations were arriving on the West African coast between Senegal in the east and the great Gulf of Benin in the west. But the Europeans who arrived in these ships had as yet no political or military importance, and whenever they threatened violence they found that the Africans could easily handle it.

Their ships were weak and unreliable, their charts and navigating instruments primitive, their maps (when they had any) often wrong or misleading. To the perils of the ocean and the fevers of the mainland were added other risks. These Europeans were not united. They fought each other fiercely and often. At first the Portuguese had the upper hand over the English and the French. Then the Dutch came into West African waters and took the lead, the Dutch being at that time the foremost trading nation of Europe. In 1637 the Dutch attacked and captured the Portuguese castle at Elmina with the help of local Africans. Five years later the Dutch threw the Portuguese out of the Gold Coast altogether.

European rivalries on the West African coast

Having broken Portuguese control of Europe's trade with West Africa, the Dutch now tried to set up their own control. But other rivals at once came on the scene, notably the English.[1] There followed years of battle and

---

[1] England and Scotland became united in 1603, but the word 'British' came into general use in later times.

ambush between these Europeans. These violent rivalries were watched with keen attention by coastal Africans. The Africans sided now with one European group and now with another, according to their judgement of where their best interests lay.

Yet the sea-merchants kept coming, and gradually worked their way to a peaceful partnership both with each other and with African merchants along the coast. Once again it is easy to see why. Behind these sea-merchants there were powerful political and commercial companies and interests in Europe. These were now getting themselves strongly established in the Caribbean and on the mainland of the Americas. They needed the African trade as part of their system of commerce; therefore they needed peace among themselves. So the coastal trade steadily became more extensive and less violent. Soon it was being carried on peacefully at dozens of regular markets along the seaboard. Of the 41 trading castles that were eventually built by Europeans in West Africa, no fewer than 28 were constructed before 1700.

While the seventeenth century was thus the period of the *establishment* of the European–American trade with West Africa, the eighteenth was the period of its large *expansion*. By the year 1800 there was scarcely a single coastal people without a close interest in this trade. And by that time the influence of the trade had pushed inland to many peoples who lived a long way from the coast.

Yet the Africans, though deeply influenced by the coastal trade, for long held the upper hand. The Europeans were masters on the water, but Africans were masters on the land, and made sure that they remained so. Only late in the eighteenth century, with growing European control of trade along the coast, did this balance of power begin to come down on the European side.

Many people in faraway Europe, now beginning to feel strong enough with their ships and their soldiers to go anywhere they wished and do anything they liked, fell into the mistake of thinking that the African trade was all run by Europeans. But the truth, as the traders on the coast well knew, was quite different.

'There is no small number of men in Europe', a Dutch official at Elmina Castle, William Bosman, wrote home to a friend in 1700, 'who believe that the gold mines are in our power, and that we, like the Spanish in the West Indies, have nothing more to do than to work the mines with our slaves. But you should understand that we have no means of getting to these treasures, nor do I believe that any of our people have ever seen a single one of these mines.'

Even on the Gold Coast (modern Ghana) the sea-merchants landed and settled only with permission from the people of the seaboard. The Europeans might sit strongly in their forts, but they still had to pay rent for the land on which the forts were built. Beyond their walls, they could dominate the country only for the range of their musket-shots. Often these Europeans were attacked in their castles, and sometimes these castles were taken by African armies. In 1693, for instance, the big Danish fort of Christiansborg in Accra was seized by the soldiers of Akwamu, held for a time under the flag of Akwamu,[2] and given back to the Danes only after the latter had paid a large amount of gold.

Throughout this period, in short, the Africans were generally in complete control of their side of the trade. Often they were strong enough to punish European misbehaviour and insist on compensation for damages. They also made use of the Europeans for their own political plans and needs.

Growth of the Atlantic slave trade

Yet there was one thing that the Africans could not control, and this was going to mean a lot. They could decide to some extent what the Europeans wished to *sell* them. But they could not control what the Europeans wished to *buy* from them. And what the Europeans now wished to buy, more and more, and soon with a driving eagerness that overcame all opposition, were slaves.

The slave trade began, as a large and regular *system of trade*, only after about 1625. This was when the Portuguese had become well established in Brazil; the Spanish on other parts of the mainland of South, Central and North America; the English, French, Dutch, Danes and Spanish on the islands of the Caribbean Sea. All these opened more and more mines and plantations. They wanted more and more slaves. They went to Africa to buy or capture them. They bought or captured many millions of them.

Why did they succeed in this? The key to understanding why the slave trade began, and why it grew, lies in the master–servant organization which existed in many states and among many peoples. As in other countries of the world, then or at other times, chiefs and kings regularly turned war-captives and certain classes of law-breakers into slaves. These slaves, as we have seen, were not very different from most other men and women except that they had fewer rights. As often as not, they were just servants who had special duties and work they had to do.

And just as in other countries, then or at other times, these kings were easily persuaded to sell, barter, or simply give away their servants or slaves. So it was easy for European kings, when they found their own supplies of European or American slaves coming to an end, to get some from Africa. In 1562, for instance, the English captain John Hawkins was presented with a lot of war-prisoners, whom he turned into slaves and sold across

---

[2] The Akwamu flag showed an African waving a sword, as a sign of the power of Akwamu.

the Atlantic. He got these Africans in exchange for some military help that he gave to two kings of Sierra Leone. Slave-trading was a cruel aspect of the world of that time. Many rulers and rich merchants had their part in it.

Slavery in Africa, generally, was a much less cruel servitude than the chattel slavery that now developed in the Americas. Yet it seems unlikely that African kings, chiefs and merchants would have stopped selling their servants and war-captives even if they had known the fate to which they were sending these men and women. For these kings, chiefs and merchants were under two very powerful and growing pressures to continue selling men and women.

The Europeans now began to ask for slaves more than anything else, because the European settlers in America needed cheap labour more than they needed gold and ivory. If they could not buy captives at one market along the coast, they simply went on to the next market; if denied by one chief, they applied to his neighbour. Secondly, kings and chiefs now began to feel the need for guns. And only the Europeans, at that time, could provide guns.

Just as iron-pointed spears had proved better than clubs and stones a thousand years earlier, so now the musket became the most powerful weapon. A situation began to arise where chiefs and kings felt safe only when they were sure of a supply of firearms. But these chiefs and kings, living in a non-industrial society, were unable to make firearms for themselves. They had to buy them from abroad. Apart from a few that were brought south across the Sahara, all the firearms had to come by sea. Yet the Europeans insisted on selling their guns in part-exchange for captives. So the oversea slave trade, begun in a small way, soon became a big export to the Americas of captured men and women.

There were many cases where African kings, chiefs or elders, seeing how destructive this slave trade had become to peace and prosperity at home, tried hard to bring it to a halt. We shall look at some of these cases later on. But the pressures were too strong for them. Little by little, the oversea slave trade spread to the lands behind the coast, profiting repeatedly from the disunity among African states.

Firearms

This spreading influence was also linked to changes in ways of government. The rise of professional armies came at about the same time as the arrival of the first firearms. Large quantities of muskets now began to be imported. From England alone, at the height of the eighteenth-century African trade, the gunsmiths of Birmingham were providing more than 100,000 a year.

Here also there were gains as well as losses. By selling these guns, Europeans helped to spread war among Africans, because the buying of guns called for the capture of war-prisoners who could be sold into slavery. But the guns also strengthened Africans against European invasion or attack. The Europeans saw this very clearly. Yet they, on their side, were as powerless to stop the sale of guns to Africans as the Africans were powerless to stop the sale of war-prisoners to Europeans, and for the same reason: they could never get agreement among themselves. The Dutchman, William Bosman, then living in Elmina Castle, explained this in a letter written home in 1700:

> The main military weapons are muskets or carbines, in the use of which these Africans are wonderfully skilful. It is a real pleasure to watch them train their armies. They handle their weapons so cleverly, shooting them off in several ways, one man sitting, another creeping along the ground or lying down, that it is surprising they do not hurt each other.
>
> Perhaps you will wonder how the Africans come to be furnished with these firearms. But you should know that we sell them very great quantities, and in doing this we offer them a knife with which to cut our own throats. But we are forced to do this. For if we [the Dutch] did not do it, they would easily get enough muskets from the English, or from the Danes, or from the Prussians. And even if we governors [of the official European trading corporations] could all agree to stop selling firearms, the private traders of the English or the Dutch would still go on selling them.[3]

The slave trade: consequences in West Africa

It is well to remind ourselves, at this point, that West Africa traded with the European sea-merchants in many goods besides slaves. Gold and ivory were important in the early times of trade, and continued to be in high demand throughout the long period we have studied. There was always some trade in other exports, too, notably in pepper, ostrich feathers, gum and several other products of West Africa. After 1600, however, it was increasingly the European demand for slave labour that dominated the coastal markets and sent its influence far inland. In summing up the consequences of the Atlantic trade, we must direct our attention to this side of the business.

The slave trade was generally a disaster for the peoples of Africa. But it was bad in different ways at different places. It was worst of all for the

---

[3] William Bosman, *A New and Accurate Description of the Coast of Guinea* (London, 4th edn 1967). First published in Dutch in 1704.

victims themselves. Once delivered to the captains of European and American ships, they were stripped, branded, and pushed into airless underdecks, crushed together, often chained by hand and foot. Like this they crossed the Atlantic in harsh weeks of sailing. Perhaps as many as one in every six captives died on the voyage across the ocean. Often the captives rose in brave revolt against their masters.

Back in Africa, the slave trade had other consequences. Many millions of strong young men (and a smaller proportion of women) were forced out of Africa by the slave trade. How many? We do not know. Probably the total number landed alive in the Americas was somewhere between ten and fifteen million people. Many other millions were lost to Africa in raids and wars for captives, as well as in the death of those who perished on the dreadful 'Middle Passage' across the Atlantic.[4]

The long-term consequence of the slave trade, for West Africa, lay in any case not so much in the field of population numbers as in two other fields: the field of *production*, and the field of *politics*.

In the field of production, the slave trade obliged West Africa (like some other parts of Africa) to export its most valuable source of wealth, which was human labour. Year after year, tens of thousands of African farmers and craftsmen were shipped away to work in American plantations, mines and cities. By their labour they created great wealth and profits: but for America and Europe, not for Africa. All that Africa received in exchange was the manufactured goods of Europe.

This exchange of raw material (as we may call human labour in this case) for manufactured goods was an early kind of *colonial exchange*. By it, the slave trade helped to make West Africa into a subject part of the economic system of Europe and America. In other words, the slave trade opened the way for the colonial system that was to follow in the second half of the nineteenth century. The slave trade helped to pull West Africa *back*, and to push Europe and America *forward*.

A few Africans did well out of the slave trade: these were kings and rich merchants. *In the field of politics*, the slave trade brought wars and ruin.

Resistance to the slave trade

On the African side, the slave trade grew out of the old customs of chiefs and kings. These were accustomed to regard all war-prisoners as property that could be sold or exchanged or simply given away. Certain groups of

---

[4] The question of numbers lost to Africa has been much contested. For two different views from specialists in this matter, see P.D. Curtin, *The Atlantic Slave Trade: a Census* (Wisconsin, 1969), and J.E. Inikori (ed.), *Forced Migration: the Impact of the Export Slave Trade* (London, 1982).

people were turned into permanent servants or house-slaves of rulers and rich men. We have seen how the lords of old West Africa took part in the buying and selling of men and women, sending many across the Sahara to North Africa and Arabia both before and during the ocean slave trade, in the same way as the lords of Europe and Asia did.

There were several African efforts to cut down the ocean slave trade, or to stop it altogether. But such efforts largely failed, because the pressure of European and American demand was too great for them. Here are some examples.

The first occurred as early as the sixteenth century. In 1526 a famous king of the Bakongo state of Kongo, near the mouth of the river of that name, wrote an angry letter of protest to the king of Portugal. King Nzinga Mbemba, whose Christian name was Affonso, complained to the Portuguese king, his ally and partner in trade, that the slave trade was doing great hurt to his country. Together with certain Bakongo 'thieves and men of evil conscience', he wrote, Portuguese traders were 'grabbing and selling' his people, even including members of his own family. He wanted nothing from Portugal, he went on, except 'priests and people to teach in our schools, and no other goods but wine and flour for the holy sacrament'. Above all, he demanded that the Portuguese king, who was himself deep in the business of the slave trade, should recall his traders from Kongo, 'because it is our will that in these kingdoms of Kongo there should not be any trade in slaves nor any market for slaves'.

But the advantages and temptations offered by European-made goods, for which the sea-merchants increasingly demanded slaves, were too much for many of King Affonso's chiefs and sub-chiefs. They went on with the trade.

Another example was noted in 1789 by a Swedish traveller in northern Senegal. A year before his visit, wrote this traveller, the *almamy* of the little state of Futa Toro had passed a law, 'very much to his honour', which declared that no slaves were to be taken through Futa Toro for sale abroad. But the *almamy* was up against a powerful trading system which yielded great profits; and this system defeated his good intentions.

Waiting in the Senegal river, as usual, were several French slave ships. Their captains, seeing they could not now hope to buy any slaves in Futa Toro, complained to the *almamy* against his law. They asked him to change his mind and do away with the law. He refused to agree. He followed this refusal by sending back to the agents of the French slave-trading company a number of presents they had given him, adding that 'all the riches of that company would not make him change his mind'. Faced with this refusal, the French captains discussed among themselves what they should do next. Then they found that the inland slave-dealers, also angry at the *almamy*'s new law, had worked out another route for taking captives to the coast. So the French captains weighed anchor and sailed down the coast to this new market; and there they supplied themselves with the captives whom the *almamy* had prevented them from buying in the Senegal river.

There were other such acts of resistance, or attempted resistance. They all failed. And they failed because the slave trade, until soon after 1800, had become a valuable part of the commercial system of the western world, the system to which large regions of Africa now increasingly belonged. Only a change in this system could stop the trade in slaves.

The beginnings of this change occurred in the closing years of the eighteenth century and led, among other things, to the foundation of what were to become the free republics of Sierra Leone and Liberia.

But we should also look at another main consequence of the Atlantic trade. This happened outside Africa, and yet it is, in many ways, a large and very remarkable part of African history. Large populations of African origin were taken to the lands beyond the Atlantic. Their toil, skills and achievements played a big role in building the civilizations of the Americas. Without Africa's contribution, those civilizations could never have become strong or rich.

Africans beyond the seas

By 1800 about half the population of Brazil were Africans, or the descendants of Africans. So were about half the population of Venezuela. So were a smaller but still large part of all the populations of the trans-Atlantic republics, whether in North, Central or South America, or in the Caribbean islands.

It was these men and women of African descent who conquered the wilderness of the Americas, clearing and working countless farms and plantations, founding and opening innumerable mines of iron or precious metals. Harsh and painful as it was, the oversea slave trade (like the not much less harsh and painful movement of millions of hungry or jobless men and women from Europe) laid the foundations of the American republics.

These Africans beyond the seas have their place in the story of Africa, the story of West Africa, for what they attempted and achieved was also a reflection of the strong and independent civilization from which they came. Whenever they could, and from the earliest years of their enslavement across the Atlantic, they broke from their bondage and fought for their freedom. Unable to return home across the seas, they marched away into the South American wilderness and formed new states of their own. Many such islands of liberty were formed. None was more famous or successful than the African kingdom of Palmares, established in north-eastern Brazil in about 1605, which beat off many assaults by Dutch and Portuguese settlers or soldiers and was overthrown by the Portuguese only in 1694, nearly 100 years after its formation. Here in Palmares, thousands of Africans who had escaped from slavery joined together in a new life of their own, elected their own rulers, and governed themselves by the methods remembered from Africa.

Another famous example of African struggles for freedom across the seas was the heroic and successful campaign for liberty and independence that was conducted by the ex-slaves of the French Caribbean colony of St Domingue. In 1789, at the moment of the French Revolution, this French colony in the Caribbean was probably the wealthiest colony in the world. Its tens of thousands of African slave-workers produced enormous quantities of sugar; whole European communities lived off the profits.

Haiti: 'the revolution has no colour'

When news of the French Revolution of 1789 reached St Domingue, these slaves claimed their share in its ideals and benefits. They demanded their freedom. Denied this, they rose in revolt against their masters. In years of hard fighting against large armies sent by France, and afterwards against large armies sent by Britain, these men of St Domingue won their freedom and founded the republic of Haiti. Yet *more than half* these soldiers of freedom had made the 'middle passage' across the Atlantic. More than half, in other words, had been born in Africa, had spent their childhood in Africa, had learned in Africa their respect for freedom; while nearly all the rest were the children or grandchildren of people born in Africa. And they were led by Africans: by men of genius and courage such as Boukman, the unforgettable Toussaint Louverture, and Dessalines.

Raised by Toussaint and his Africans, the banner of freedom across the Atlantic was carried from people to people. Many threw off their bondage. Large numbers of men of African origin fought in the armies that made the United States what they are today. It was a general of African descent, Antonio Maceo, who became a leader in the military struggle for Cuban independence against Spain which began in 1868.

Like other men of vision, Maceo had no time for racism, for the false idea that one race of men is better or worse than any other. Some of the whites of Cuba disagreed with him. They were Spanish settlers who thought that white was going to be better than black even in an independent Cuba.

One day Maceo was approached by a Spanish Cuban who suggested that the regiments of the independence army should be divided into whites and non-whites. Maceo made him a reply which became famous in Cuba. 'If you were not white,' Maceo said to this man, 'I would have you shot on the spot. But I do not wish to be accused of being a racist as you are, and so I let you go. But with this warning. I shall not be so patient another time. The revolution has no colour.'

Expansion of the Atlantic slave trade

The slave trade grew ever larger because of settler demand for cheap labour in the distant lands beyond the Atlantic.

After the Spanish discovery of how to reach the Caribbean, in 1492, Spanish settlers and colonists began the ruin of the native American peoples whom they found. The Spanish intention was not trade, but loot; not peace, but war; not partnership, but enslavement. They fell upon these lands with greed and the fury of destruction. And the American peoples, unlike the Africans, were unable to defend themselves. Being at an earlier stage of social and technical development than the Africans, they fell easy victims to Spanish violence. Along the coast of West Africa, the Portuguese and other Europeans had begun by trying their hands at violence. But they had given that up. The Africans they met were too strong for them.

There was widespread destruction of the 'Indians', the name that was mistakenly given by these raiders to the native-born American peoples whom they found. A Spanish report of 1518, only 26 years after the first voyage of Columbus across the Atlantic, says that when the island of Cuba was discovered it was reckoned to contain more than a million 'Indians', but 'today their number does not exceed 11,000. And judging from what has happened, there will be none of them left in three or four years' time, unless some remedy is applied.'

No remedy was applied, in Cuba or anywhere else; or none that made much difference. Whole populations of enslaved 'Indians', forced to work for Spanish masters in mines and on plantations, withered and died, rebelled and were killed.

Trying desperately to find new sources of free labour, the Spanish rulers began sending out Spanish people under conditions no better than slavery. But they could not find enough of them. Where else to look for slaves? The answer was West Africa. Already the Portuguese and Spanish had imported a few West African captives into their own countries. Now they began to carry West African captives directly to the West Indies and the mainland of the Americas.

In this they faced many problems. They had to seize or buy their African captives and find prisons or shipping for them. They had then to get these men and women across the Atlantic alive. That was a big problem in the foul old sailing ships of those days. Lastly, they had to turn these captives, or those who were still alive after the crossing of the seas, into slaves. But this, too, proved very difficult. For the Africans resisted enslavement by every means they could. They broke out in revolt after revolt, led by heroes whose names we shall never know. They fought to the death. They spread fear and panic among the European settlers. They went into the mountains or deep into the forests and formed free republics of their own. They made history in their fight for freedom.

But European arms and organization, together with the golden profits of this slave trade, proved too strong. In 1515 the Spanish shipped back to Europe their first cargo of Caribbean sugar, then an expensive luxury. And it was in 1518, a grim date in the history of the Atlantic slave trade, that the Spanish carried their first cargo of captives *directly* from West Africa to the West Indies. After that, throughout the sixteenth century, the slave trade grew rapidly.

It continued to grow in later years. As the wealth and size of the American plantation-colonies became ever larger, so also did the demand for slave labour. There developed what was to become known as the *triangular trade*. This was a commercial system which greatly helped to build the industrial and technical progress of western Europe in the eighteenth and nineteenth centuries, and especially the progress of Britain and France.

This new and profitable trading system, started in the late sixteenth century, was called 'triangular' because it had three distinct stages or 'sides'. Each of these 'sides' brought a profit to the merchants and manufacturers of western Europe.

In the first stage or 'side' of this trade, merchants in the big ports of western Europe bought, and shipped to West Africa, goods such as cottons, alcoholic spirits, metalware and firearms. These goods they sold to African chiefs and kings in exchange for slaves. The slaves were prisoners of war or condemned criminals. If they had stayed in West Africa, they would have been domestic or household slaves: African chiefs and kings often exchanged such 'slaves' among themselves. So it was fairly easy for the Europeans to buy captives.

The second 'side' of the triangular trade lay in taking these captives across the Atlantic, usually in chains, and in selling them to plantation-owners in exchange for sugar, tobacco, rum and other products. And the plantation owners turned the captives into slaves.

The third 'side' consisted in taking the American products back to Europe and selling them at very profitable prices.

Through all these years, while the Atlantic slave trade continued to overshadow and poison the life of many peoples, there was none the less a continued political and social development in West Africa. We turn now to this side of things.

Map 13.1 The triangular trade.

Map 13.2 Dahomey and its region in the eighteenth century.

The kingdom of the Fon and the Delta states

The thinly wooded republic of Benin (formerly the kingdom of Dahomey) is part of the open country which divides the dense forests of Nigeria from those of modern Ghana. This is one of the reasons why its history shows many differences from that of its neighbours.

Modern Benin (not, of course, the Nigerian city of the same name) includes the coastland between the frontiers of Nigeria and Togo as well as the inland country for some 650 kilometres to the north. Its frontiers were established by French colonial invaders at the end of the nineteenth century.

In the seventeenth century the position here was very different. There were then two different sets of states. One of these was along the coast itself, the length of seaboard which European traders then called the Slave Coast. It consisted of a string of small city-states. The other lay in the inland country and was composed of a number of more loosely organized states. The most important of these was formed by the Fon people, with their capital at Abomey.

Most of these peoples, whether along the coast or in the interior, have traditions which point to a common origin. By 1600, however, they were long since divided into different groups. Those along the coast now discovered the same chances of trade with sea-merchants as their neighbours in the Niger Delta or along the Gold Coast (modern Ghana). The empty ocean became for them, too, a 'frontier of opportunity'. They took this opportunity with energy and courage. They prospered with the new trade. If they are now long forgotten by the wider world, they became famous in their time.

199

Close to the ocean surf, the best-known of these seaside states were Jakin, Whydah (also called Ouidah or Fida), and Grand Popo. Immediately behind them lay Great Ardrah or Allada, the principal power along this coast for most of the seventeenth century and the one that generally controlled its weaker neighbours. All of these took shape around 1650: at about the time, in other words, that increasing sugar production in the West Indies began to make increasing demands for African labour. Later, other seaside states were formed. These included Badagry and Ajase (Porto Novo).

Ardrah and Whydah: dealers in slaves

These little states used the sea-merchants to their own advantage in the same way as the city-states of the Niger Delta. Their kings fixed prices for the sale of goods, including captives, and sent their agents to bargain with the ships' captains. They made the Europeans pay taxes. In order to trade with Great Ardrah, a European merchant called John Barbot reported towards the end of the eighteenth century, 'Europeans usually give the king the value of fifty slaves in goods, for his permission to carry on trade, as well as paying customs duties in respect of each ship. They also give the king's son the value of two slaves for the privilege of obtaining water for their crews, and the value of four slaves for permission to cut timber.'

At first these kings found that the Europeans quarrelled so violently among themselves that they spoiled the trade. They took steps to stop this. They shared out the trading facilities among the various Europeans, and reduced the amount of violent competition. The results were impressive. 'Whydah', wrote an English visitor, John Atkins, early in the eighteenth century, 'is now the greatest trading place on the coast of Guinea, selling off as many slaves, I believe, as all the rest together. Forty or fifty ships [French, English, Portuguese and Dutch] load their cargoes there every year.'[5]

Then came a new challenge from the inland country. This same visitor explained why. The king of Whydah, Atkins reported, was in the habit of buying captives from his neighbours. 'But if he cannot obtain sufficient numbers of slaves in that way, he marches out with an army, and depopulates the country. He and the neighbouring king of Ardrah commit great depredations inland.'

Now the Fon people of the inland country, who were raided in this way, already had problems of their own. Like Ardrah and its neighbours, they were officially subject to the Yoruba of Oyo. In the fairly open country where they lived, they found themselves at the mercy of cavalry raids by

---

[5] John Atkins, *A Voyage to Guinea, Brasil and the West Indies* (London, 2nd edn 1737), p. 172.

the armies of Oyo who made them pay tribute. So the Fon came together in self-defence. They built a strong state of their own.

The Fon autocracy

They did this by highly dictatorial and therefore harsh methods. The great legend was that the king's power was like a strong pot, and the people were the water in the pot: so long as the pot was not damaged or upset, the water would be safe. This meant that the whole Fon people became directly involved in support of their king. Everyone served the king, because everyone's safety and happiness was thought to depend on the king. Government in this kind of state became organized, unavoidably, on army lines. Chiefs got power not by membership of this or that family, but by courage and success in warfare; and they could be promoted, downgraded or transferred to other duties as the king thought fit. Even women were called into this work of supporting the king by direct service. Regular companies of women soldiers fought for the king, often with success.

By the eighteenth century the king, as 'guardian of all the Fon', had direct power through his own orders, or indirectly through the orders of the ministers whom he appointed, over a large 'state sector' of economic and political life. Every year there was a census or public counting of the people, and also of the principal goods they produced by farming and handicraft industry. Based on the town of Abomey, this strictly autocratic state may be said to have begun its history with King Wegbaja in about 1650. Wegbaja was followed by Akaba in about 1685, and Akaba by Agaja in 1708. Agaja was an outstanding general and a statesman, who reigned for 32 years. Under his rule the state of Abomey or Dahomey became strong enough to capture the coastal states, though still forced to pay tribute to Oyo; and its people formed themselves into a nation.

King Agaja seems to have had two motives in attacking the coast. In the first place, there is evidence that he wanted to call a halt to the slave raids of the coastal states, and even to stop the export of Africans. It is certainly true that the number of Africans sent away from here became much smaller after Agaja's conquest.

Secondly, Agaja wanted to assure himself and his government and traders of better access to the sea-merchants: they were tired of having to pay for their guns and gunpowder at the very high prices demanded by the 'middlemen' traders of the coastal states. These prices the Fon found unusually high after 1712, for in that year the annual tribute exacted by Oyo, then the imperialist overlord of the Fon, had to include 41 cases of guns, each case having to contain 41 weapons. This meant that the king had to provide his overlord of Oyo with a total of 1,681 guns every year, as well as supplying weapons to his own army.

Agaja's warriors marched on Great Ardrah in 1725, and conquered and sacked it. Three years later they pushed south again to the smaller states of Savi and Whydah. In 1732 they took Jakin. After that, and for more than 150 years, this coast was dominated by the kings of Dahomey.

But the Fon hold on the coast was not kept easily. Whydah and its neighbours tried to regain their freedom of action; in this they were sometimes helped and encouraged by European captains and agents. Not until the 1740s did the Fon win complete control. Then Whydah became a Fon colony under the power of officials sent from Abomey, the capital of Dahomey. Of these officials, the most important was the *yevogan*. It was with him that the Europeans had to deal.

European influence was limited to the beach itself, and even there the Europeans were closely supervised by the *yevogan* and his staff. Only by special permission could Europeans visit Abomey. But as time went on, official European agents were generally allowed to go to Abomey and pay their respects at court. By 1793 the English agent[6] at Whydah could report that 'from Whydah to Abomey is perhaps the most beaten track by Europeans of any part of Africa'. Most of these visitors to Abomey thought that the king was an outright dictator. In this they were somewhat mistaken. Though the king's power was undoubtedly very great, he still needed the assent of his counsellors. Even then he could not act without obeying many traditional customs which also limited his power.

The Fon and Oyo

Formed in self-defence against raids from Oyo and raids from the coast, the Fon and their rulers had developed a considerable military strength. But dangers from outside their kingdom did not stop when Agaja seized control of Ardrah and Whydah. Agaja still had to face his overlord, the *alafin* of Oyo, who did not welcome Dahomey's increase of strength and who was asked by the coastal states for help against Agaja.

As a result the *alafin* of Oyo sent his famous cavalry into Dahomey in 1726, soon after Agaja's march to the coast. They completely defeated Agaja's army, and repeated their invasions in 1728, 1729 and 1730. But Dahomey still kept a hold on its coastal positions, though its rulers had to sell captives to Europeans so as to get guns and gunpowder.

All these conditions, but especially the imperialist pressure of Oyo, played a part in reinforcing the military and political growth and power of the Fon state. They likewise strengthened all those customs which were thought of as protecting or helping the king, since the king was the symbol

---

[6] Archibald Dalzel (pronounced *Dee'ul*).

of Fon safety. Royal customs which were believed necessary to the king's welfare had to be maintained at all costs, even when, as for a long time, these customs required the yearly killing at Abomey of a large number of human victims.

Built by Agaja, this strong state was further strengthened by King Tegbesu (1740–74). He concentrated on increasing the power and efficiency of his government. This made him unpopular with European merchants who began to prefer to trade elsewhere. Tegbesu was followed by Kpengla (1774–89) and Agonglo (1789–97). Rivalries for power now appeared, and a civil war broke out between the rival groups. Only with King Gezo (1818–58) did the power of Dahomey recover.

Though controlled by the Fon, some of the old coastal states continued to flourish. By about 1780, Whydah was the main market for the whole lagoon traffic along the shore. Badagry also became active in business.

Westward, other lagoon markets did well at Grand and Little Popo. These had good defensive positions in their creeks and lagoons. They managed for the most part to escape from Dahomey's control. They dealt largely in ivory. Here is an English description of one of them at the end of the eighteenth century:

> The houses are well constructed, and generally two storeys high with stone steps. There is a good market with the most abundant supplies of stock of every kind, and many delicious fruits. The [people] and chiefs are respectful, honest, and desirous for trade. Ivory abounds here in endless quantities, being constantly sent from the inland towns.[7]

The states of the Niger Delta

The history of these small states was not unlike that of the city-states further eastward along the Niger Delta. All the Delta states grew prosperous on the Atlantic trade, not least the trade in African captives. One reason for this lay in their *middleman* position of monopoly. Because they occupied every river-mouth, and were skilful in politics, they obliged the ships from Europe and the Americas to deal with them, and only with them. Another reason for their prosperity lay in the fact that the lands behind the Delta were rich in population.

This density of population helped to feed the trade in captives. As time went by, the trade became ever more highly organized, being carried

---

[7] By Lt. Edward Bold.

on by well-established rules and regulations for more than two centuries. Many of the black people of the Americas descend from parents who were bought from the traders of the Niger Delta.

We may compare this long-standing export of people, this forced emigration to the Americas, with the similar export of people that was going on from Europe at the same time. Just as millions of people were taken out of West Africa, so also were millions of people taken out of Europe in these centuries: Italians, Germans, Irish, Scots, Poles and many others. Few of the latter, it is true, were sent abroad by being captured and sold as slaves; they were none the less forced by hunger and unemployment to leave their homes and seek a new life across the seas. The real difference lay in the actual conditions of life for the Africans and the Europeans who were thus removed from their homelands. These conditions were far worse for the Africans, just as they would remain far worse for most black Americans in later times.

How flourishing this Delta trade was may be seen in many records of the time. An English captain[8] who wrote about Bonny, for long the biggest of the Delta states, described it as 'the wholesale market for slaves, since not fewer than 20,000 are sold here every year. Of these, 16,000 come from one nation, called the Ibos, so that this single nation has exported over the past twenty years, not fewer than 320,000 of its people; while members of the same nation sold at New and Old Calabar, in the same period, probably amounted to 50,000 more.'

The slave trade here, as elsewhere, was horribly brutal but generally well organized. Regular markets were held, governed by strict rules. This same English captain wrote:

> The preparation for these markets generally occupy the Bonny people for some days. Large canoes, capable of carrying 120 persons, are launched and stored for the voyage. The traders add to their trade-goods by obtaining from their friends, the captains of the slave-ships, a considerable quantity of goods on credit . . . Evening is the period chosen for the time of their departure, when they proceed in a body, accompanied by the noise of drums, horns and gongs. They generally come back at the end of the sixth day after their departure, bringing with them 1,500 to 2,000 slaves, who are sold to Europeans the evening after their arrival, and taken on board the ships.

Buying and selling with the European and American captains, again here as elsewhere, was a tricky business. There was much bargaining. The money used was generally composed of trade goods like iron bars, rolls of

---

[8] Captain John Adams, who knew West Africa between 1786 and 1800, and whose book was published in 1822.

cotton or quantities of yams (needed by the slave-ships to feed their captives as well as their crews during the voyage across the Atlantic); cowrie-shells were also an important form of money. Any attempt by the European traders to bully or cheat their African partners was likely to be answered by a boycott. The Africans, operating through associations like Ekpe, simply closed the river to European trade until the Europeans made good the damage they had caused. Here in the Delta the Europeans had no castles and few shore stations. Instead, they lived in old ships, called hulks. These hulks were permanently anchored near the shore of the trading towns.

The complications of this trading system may be seen from the deals that were made. In 1676, for instance, the captain of the English ship *Bonaventure* bought 100 men, women and children, and had them duly branded by his crew with the special mark of the British Royal African Company: *DY* for Duke of York. For these carefully selected captives he paid 5 muskets, 21 iron bars, 72 knives, half a barrel of gunpowder and various lengths of cotton stuff.[9]

Time and patience were needed for such bargains, as an extract from the records of another English ship, the *Albion-Frigate*, which arrived at New Calabar in 1699, shows. First of all, as the customs prescribed, the captain sent messengers ashore to greet the king of New Calabar and ask him to start a deal.

The king agreed, but not with the prices that the English offered. 'He gave us to understand that he expected one bar of iron for each slave more than Edwards [the captain of another English ship] had paid him. He also objected to our metal basins, mugs, beads and other goods, and said they were of little value at the time.' Bargaining continued. The next day 'we had a conference with the king and principal natives of the country, about trade, and this lasted from three o'clock until night. But it had no result. They continued to insist on having thirteen bars of iron for a male, and ten for a female.' The Europeans of the *Albion-Frigate* thought this too expensive. They had supper with the king and went back to their ship. Agreement was reached only after another four days of argument.

Like their fellow-sufferers who were forced to leave Europe by hunger and unemployment, the Africans who were sent abroad faced terrible weeks at sea in foul old ships, got bad food and met shipwreck and frequent death. But unlike the European emigrants, they were often chained during the dreaded 'Middle Passage' from fear that they would revolt against their oppressors. This fear was well justified, for brave or desperate revolts at sea were many. Once the captives were landed across the Atlantic, they were held in lifelong slavery under cruel conditions.

---

[9] This trade was now done in special 'units of exchange' called 'trade ounces'. Each 'ounce' consisted of a certain number of goods of various kinds, according to their cost in Europe – see p. 213 n. 5.

Senegambia after 1700

Senegambia after 1700

A detailed record of the history of these years, which cross the threshold to modern times, would take us outside the scope of this book. The great dramas that were now to unfold in Africa, including West Africa, which is our subject here, derived from the approaching threat of western European imperialism and its instrument of dispossession, which was to become known as colonialism. That story has been told many times, and in whole libraries of books. It marks the prelude to the times in which we now live.

Meanwhile an often bitter rivalry between the various European sea-merchants, and between them and the African peoples and nations of the seaboard, remains an important part of the historical record, and has a drama and purpose of its own. The sea-merchants and their backers in western Europe naturally pursued their own trading interests. They went often, and annually, to the Gold Coast (modern Ghana) because their trade in trying to buy gold, and now captives for export as slaves to the Americas, became ever more valuable. By contrast, they found less to attract them along the westerly seaboard, and generally avoided visits to the coasts of the country that soon became Liberia, and part of Sierra Leone. But something more needs to be said about this.[1]

Part of the problem lay in the fact that safe and easy harbours for sailing ships were hard to find along this westerly coast. Another part was that an important local people, the Kru, were opposed to the slave trade.

---

[1] The old sailing-ship captains had their own names for the West Africa coastline. These included *The Windward Coast*, from about the Gambia river to Cape Palmas (eastern end of modern Liberia), and *The Leeward Coast*, east of Cape Palmas. The main reason for these names was that the prevailing winds in this part of the Atlantic blow from the west or south-west, so that when sailors were on the western sections of the coast they thought of themselves as being to 'windward' (towards the wind), and when they were on the central and eastern sections of the coast they thought of themselves as being to 'leeward' (away from the wind). Some of the *Windward Coast*, chiefly that of modern Liberia, was unfavourable to the safe anchoring of ships, and was little visited until the nineteenth century.

Map 14.1 The coastline of the Ivory Coast, Liberia, Sierra Leone and Senegambia in the seventeenth century.

They dealt actively in ivory for export but refused to deal in slaves. Worse again, from the European point of view, the Kru bought guns, and used these guns to defend themselves against European raids from the sea. Like their neighbours, the Kru built a small state but a strong one.

The political ideas and methods of these states along the western coast should be of interest to all those, especially, who may have imagined that pre-colonial Africans did not know how to govern themselves in peace and prosperity.

Sierra Leone and the Poro association

Some of these early states of Senegambia were monarchies, others were ruled by councils of chiefs. All of them shared with many other states, whether monarchies or not, a 'built-in' capacity to control the power of their rulers. We have seen how this worked, in segmentary societies, by balancing separate loyalties to individual family descent-lines with united loyalty to groups of families; and we have noted that this arrangement of 'checks and balances' on the use or abuse of power was always closely linked to religious beliefs.

Another method of 'checking and balancing' was the use of political associations. Sometimes these have been called 'secret societies'. But they were not secret. Only their ceremonies, meetings and special equipment (such as masks) were secret: otherwise everyone knew about these associations and, indeed, had to know about them. This method was much used by the peoples of Sierra Leone. They had many political associations for regulating the affairs of everyday life. Of these the most important was the Poro, an association which took shape several centuries ago. It was mainly through the Poro that these peoples ruled themselves. They used it to settle a wide variety of daily problems, and to control the power of their chiefs and kings.

The Poro had many branches and, as a method of self-rule, was especially useful to small communities of a few thousand people. Yet it would be a mistake to think that this method of government by political association was only fit for small communities. In many ways the Poro was like the much larger Ogboni association of the Yoruba, and there were times when several million Yoruba paid respect to Ogboni rules.

An essential point about the Poro, as about the Ogboni of the Yoruba or the Ekpe of the Cross River Efik, was that it linked religion with political controls. Every man had to join it if he was going to enjoy the respect of his neighbours. But he was permitted to join it only after going through a period of schooling. This usually took place when a boy was old enough to become a man, and was completed by the ceremony of circumcision. Poro schooling ensured that every man would understand the rules of good behaviour and would be able, according to the measure of his talents or ability, to shoulder the responsibilities of grown-up life.[2] But the Poro did not allow everyone to have a share of power. It gave power into the hands of chiefs and rich men who won it by seniority, or because they could pay the high fees which were needed to enter the senior grades of the Poro. Yet even the 'inner councils' of the Poro could not do as they liked. They had to obey the rules.

They acted in two main ways. At one level the 'inner councils' of senior elders looked after many everyday affairs such as traditional schooling, the control of local trade and market prices, political and military decisions, the administration of justice, and the providing of popular entertainments of dance and music. But they also operated at a higher and religious level. They were expected to look after the shrines of the ancestors, to make sure these shrines were properly used for prayer and ceremony, and generally to give ordinary people the assurance that all was well between them and the world of the spirits.

---

[2] Women had a separate and parallel association, the Sande, with social powers but no political authority.

What should in any case be noted here is that the Poro, like other such associations elsewhere, provided a skilful method, strong and yet flexible, of uniting communities behind common laws and rules; of confronting the problems of everyday life as well as answering the deeper questions of spiritual need; and, as the years passed, of adapting old ways of behaviour to new situations.

This was the complex political scene into which tens of thousands of Africans from other lands, set free in Sierra Leone by the British navy from slave ships, would be required to fit and build a new life for themselves. Out of this mixture of local inhabitants and of new-comers from other parts of Africa there came the settlement of Freetown[3] in Sierra Leone. This colony was the work of settlement during the nineteenth century; but, as its vivid history shows, it was also the work of the peoples already living in Sierra Leone, such as the Mende, Temne, and their neighbours.

Senegambia after 1600

Continuing westward from Sierra Leone, we find the same picture of local African enterprise and varying contact with the sea-merchants. But in Senegambia the contact was more frequent, and the trade more valuable, than along the seaboard of Liberia, of the Ivory Coast, or even of Sierra Leone; and the influence of the sea-merchants was therefore greater.

The British at that time were especially interested in the Gambia river, rightly believing that this could prove a good channel for trade with the inland country. Along the banks of the Gambia they found hardworking people who were in touch with the inland peoples of the old kingdoms of Mali and the empire of the Wolof, and who also had little towns of their own.

An English captain[4] early in the seventeenth century described one of these Gambia towns, which he visited on a trading mission, as being strongly defended by a 3 metre fence. 'Inside the fence', he wrote,

> they have built various rooms which are like little towers. From these they can shoot arrows and throw spears whenever they are attacked. Outside the fence, too, they have a deep trench which is very broad, and outside that again the whole town is encircled by

---

[3] Where the first black settlers arrived from England in 1787, and today the capital of Sierra Leone.
[4] Richard Jobson in 1623.

posts and tree-trunks which are set fast in the ground and joined together, so as to make another fence about five-foot [2 metres] high. Beyond that again they have another fence like this. And the reason, they explained to me, is that they need these in order to defend themselves from the attack of cavalry – from the raiding horsemen, that is, of the inland country.

This captain was impressed by the skills of the Gambians. He has left us a lively description that is useful not only for the Gambians, but also for many other folk along the coast, since it is quite certain that these same skills were practised elsewhere as well. Writing in 1623, he says that he found three main kinds of craftsmen among the Gambians: smiths who made weapons and metal tools; leather workers who made shoes, sandals and harness for horses; and clay workers who made many sorts of pots and also built clay-walled houses. But everyone, he adds, also worked at farming.

The Gambia

The estuary and lower reaches of the River Gambia have a special history of their own, because it was here that Europeans found particularly favourable trading opportunities, and safe anchoring ground for their ships. The first of them to make a regular base in the Gambia after 1600 were agents of the Duke of Courland, the ruler of a small German state on the southern shore of the Baltic Sea in north-eastern Europe. The Germans built a small fort in 1651 on what was later named James Island. After many disputes, in which the French and the Dutch also took a hand, the British Royal African Company seized this fort in 1661 from a Courland garrison reduced to seven men and two women. Twenty years later the French African Company acquired a foothold on the north bank of the Gambia, opposite James Island, at Albreda; and for many years an uneasy peace then reigned between the agents of these rival companies.[5]

---

[5] These companies were the outcome of new mercantile methods in Britain, Holland and France during the seventeenth century. They were corporations of merchants founded with government backing. Most of them went bankrupt in their early years, mainly because they had to deal in barter on the African coast: they had to exchange, that is, so and so many European goods for so and so many African goods. Without a common money between the two sides, the companies found it hard to calculate how to make a profit. Later on, they invented a 'unit of exchange' called the 'trade ounce'. The value of this 'ounce', in terms of goods bought in Europe for the African trade, was usually fixed at double the cost of these goods in gold. This 100 per cent 'mark up' enabled the companies, as well as private merchants operating on their own, to make good profits in spite of losses by shipwreck and other causes.

Map 14.2   The estuary and lower reaches of the River Gambia.

The eighteenth century was filled with wars between the British and the French, fighting each other for supremacy at sea; and most of the forts and trading states of Western Guinea changed hands several times. After the middle of the century the British became the stronger, and were able to base themselves at St Louis in the Senegal river as well as on James Island in the Gambia river. This introduced an early experiment in Crown Colony government on the lines of the British colonies in North America. In 1765 this coast between the Senegal and the Gambia was declared the British *Province of Senegambia*. Its governor lived at St Louis, with a second-in-command on James Island.

Yet this early and foreign attempt at uniting Senegal and The Gambia proved far from stable. In 1778 the French hit back. They seized James Island and pulled down its fort. A year later the British retook James Island, but not St Louis. A peace settlement in 1783 confirmed this division of power, and the Province of Senegambia was abolished. After that there came a period of peace with The Gambia left to its own devices, until the British campaign to end the slave trade became important after 1807.

These European quarrels and changes did not have much importance for the Africans of Senegambia. They continued to trade with the European forts and warehouses, and it did not matter to the Africans if these were French, British, Dutch or Portuguese. Only much later, during the rise of European colonialism in the second half of the nineteenth century, did these coastal bases offer a serious threat to African independence. Then they became the bases for European colonial invasions.

Yet the European trading presence along the seaboard had important results for Senegambians. It enlarged the power of the states near the coast at the expense of the inland states. More importantly, it led to local expansion of the slave trade. It developed here in the same way as elsewhere. Local kings and rich merchants went into partnership with Europeans at the expense of the mass of ordinary folk. If they refused to sell captives from their own peoples, they proved very willing to go to war for captives from neighbouring peoples, or to buy captives from the traders of the Western Sudan. Some kings regretted this when they saw the damage it did to village life. But once the slave trade had begun, it proved very difficult to stop. If one king refused to make captives and sell them, another could always be found who would agree. Kings found it more and more difficult to draw back, because they feared to deprive themselves of guns and gunpowder. These could be bought only from Europeans, but Europeans would sell them only in exchange for captives.

By the end of the eighteenth century the kings of the Gambia river region were exporting more than 3,000 captives every year. Only the Europeans, it was found, would be able to end the evil which they themselves had first created. This was to be among the tasks of the nineteenth century.

The Union of the Golden Stool

Necklace in Ashanti gold used for the insignia and splendour of high court officials. (Werner Forman Archive and British Museum)

The Union of the Golden Stool

But the slave trade, however terrible, was only a part, and even a small part, of the African experience in those years. For while the Fon kings of Dahomey (the modern republic of Benin) were building their power and making ready to push their armies to the coast, other successful peoples were also at work, in the forest lands which now lie within the southern part of modern Ghana. Enterprising communities such as the Akwamu and Denkyira competed for power and trade. But the greatest affair of the seventeenth century, and after, was the work of another Akan people, the Asante (often spelt Ashanti in English). This was to be the formidable Union of the Golden Stool, and its building of the powerful and wealthy Asante empire.

From at least the early sixteenth century, the Asante had shone as ingenious and skilled farmers. In many ways they carried the skills of tropical farming to new heights. Then they turned their organizing skills to political work, and in this they excelled. They enclosed a country larger than the area of modern Ghana within their system of government. They commanded the politics and trade of the central region of West Africa for nearly two centuries.

Origins of the Asante empire

The Asante capital at Kumasi grew into a large and bustling centre of political, commercial, intellectual and religious life. Here gathered men of action and men of thought: learned Muslims; chiefs and soldiers from the forest lands; envoys from many states; Dyula merchants from Bobo, Kong, and Jenne to the west and north; Hausa merchants from Kano, Katsina, and other eastern cities, together with Kanuri from Bornu.

219

Let us look ahead, for a moment, and see what Kumasi was like at the height of Asante power. A good description was written in 1817, when some English officials went there. They were greeted by nearly 5,000 people, most of whom were warriors, and by a great deal of military music. William Bowdich, who was one of the visitors, wrote:

> There was so much smoke from the firing of muskets shot off in welcome that we could see only what was near to us ... We were halted in the midst of a circle of warriors, where English, Dutch and Danish flags waved and flourished all around ... The dress of the captains was a war cap, with gilded rams' horns projecting in front, the sides extended beyond all proportion by immense plumes of eagles' feathers ... [and] they wore a vest of red cloth that was covered with charms in gold and silver, and loose cotton trousers with long boots of a dull red leather that came half-way up their thighs ...
>
> What we had seen on our way [coming from the coast to Kumasi] had made us expect something unusual. But we were still surprised by the extent and display of the scene which burst upon us here. An area of nearly a mile in circumference was crowded with magnificence and novelty. The king, his chiefs and captains, were splendidly dressed, and were surrounded by attendants of every kind. More than a hundred bands broke into music on our arrival. At least a hundred large umbrellas, each of which could shelter thirty persons, were sprung up and down by their bearers with a brilliant effect, being made in scarlet, yellow and the brightest cloths and silks, and crowned on top with [models of] crescents, pelicans, elephants, barrels, arms and swords of gold.[1]

These English visitors of 1817 found the city of Kumasi much better than they had expected. 'Four of the principal streets', Bowdich wrote afterwards, 'are half a mile long, and from fifty to a hundred yards wide. The streets are all named. There is a senior captain in charge of each of them. Every household burns its rubbish every morning at the back of the street, and the people are as clean and careful about the appearance of their houses as they are about their own appearance.'

What is the story of the state that could found and support this imposing city?

At some time before AD 1600, numerous groups of farmers began leaving the Adansi region, where they were then living, and moved some 80 or 100 kilometres to the north. Scholars have suggested two main reasons for this movement, or migration. Firstly, these farming groups wanted to find

---

[1] T.E. Bowdich, *Mission from Cape Coast to Ashantee* (London, 1819).

Map 15.1   The expansion of the Asante empire.[2]

more land in which to cultivate their crops. Secondly, they wanted to win a share in the prosperous gold and kola trade which flourished to the north of them. Of these groups the most enterprising were the Oyoko clan.

They settled not far from a small lake called Bosomtwi in the country known as Amansie. There they cleared farms, gradually took the lead among their neighbours (who spoke Twi as they did), and built a town called Asantemanso. They became active in the business of producing and selling gold and kola to merchants from the north as well as to merchants

---

[2] This map, and much of the record in this chapter, follows the work of Professor Ivor Wilks in his two great books on Asante history. These are *Asante in the Nineteenth Century* (1975) and *Forests of Gold* (1993).

who came from the coast, and were joined by other groups from Adansi. They steadily grew stronger, and called themselves the Asante.

But they still had two big problems. They were subject to the powerful state of Denkyira, to whose ruler, the Denkyirahene (*hene* meaning 'king' in Twi language), they had to pay tax and tribute in goods and slaves. They had serious rivals for land and trade in the Domaa, another Akan people who lived north-west of them. So long as these problems existed, the Asante could be neither very safe nor prosperous. And it was to solve these problems that they began to find ways of acting together. This happened soon after 1650.

At first their acting together was no more than a loose alliance of different groups, Juaben, Kumawa, Nsuta, Bekwai, Mampong and others, each of which had a little state of its own. They stood together when it suited them against their common overlord, the Denkyirahene, or against their rival, Domaa. They generally recognized a common leader, the best known of whom was Obiri Yeboa. But this loose alliance could not solve their problems. They needed to come still closer together so as to have the strength to become independent. This need led them, in about 1695, to an important *act of union*.

This act of union was the work of two famous leaders, Osei Tutu and his friend and adviser, *Okomfo* Anokye (*okomfo* means priest). These two statesmen worked together to combine several neighbouring but separate Akan groups into a single strong union. They are said to have done this in about 1695 after Osei Tutu had been enstooled as ruler of the Asante. *Okomfo* Anokye declared that he had a mission from Nyame, supreme god of the Akan. Nyame, he declared, had ordered him to make the Asante into a great people. To spread this message the new Asante ruler, Osei Tutu, who was working closely with Anokye, called a vast assembly of people. At this gathering *Okomfo* Anokye 'brought down from the sky' a wooden stool that was partly covered in gold, causing this stool to come to rest on Osei Tutu's knees.

Having done this, *Okomfo* Anokye announced that the Golden Stool contained the soul or spirit of the whole Asante people. He told the chiefs and people that their power and health, bravery and welfare, were all symbolized in this Stool; and the chiefs and people accepted this. Osei Tutu then began to make laws for the Asante groups, who were thus welded into a union. Among the first of these laws was one of common citizenship, which forbade anyone to speak about any of the old *separate* history of the now united groups. In this way the Asante acquired a *single* history about their past, and this single history was to act as a powerful means of keeping them united.[3]

---

[3] The old separate histories were often remembered, but in secret.

The origins of the Asante, in short, are firmly linked in popular memory to a deliberate and highly successful act of statesmanship. This act achieved unity among Akan groups who were living side by side but governing themselves separately. When the Golden Stool 'came down from heaven', these groups gave up their separate governments and united under the single rule of Osei Tutu and his counsellors.

The Asante empire

Osei Tutu was enstooled as Asantehene, or king of Asante, in about 1695 after Obiri Yeboa had perished in battle against Domaa. He ruled until his death in about 1717 and was the first great builder of the Asante empire.

He began, as Professor Adu Boahen tells us, by reorganizing the Asante army. He brought in

> the Akwamu military formation consisting of the Van (*Adonten*), the Rear (*Kyidom*), the Left (*Benkum*) and the Right (*Nifa*) wings. Each member state [in the Asante Union] was assigned a place in one of the wings, and each wing was placed under a commander who was at the same time the king of a state. Thus the Mamponghene was made the Krontihene or Commander-in-Chief of the Asante national army, the Esumengyahene and the Ejisuhene became the commanders of the Left and Right wings respectively, while Bekwai and Nsuta [two other states in the Union] were made members of the right and left wings. All the other *Aman* or states adopted this square military formation while they retained their places in one of the wings of the Asante army. If Osei Tutu borrowed this military organisation from the [neighbouring] Akwamu, he and his successors certainly were able to develop it to an unprecedented peak of perfection and efficiency.[4]

Having built up his new forces, Osei Tutu turned first upon Domaa, avenged the earlier Asante defeat under Obiri Yeboa, and then got ready for the big struggle with Denkyira, ruled at that time by a king named Bosianti.

Denkyira was still the biggest power of all the country that lies in the south-western part of modern Ghana. This meant that Denkyira controlled the trade with Elmina Castle; and Elmina at that time was the wealthiest market on the Gold Coast, the main source of European goods including guns, and the possession of the Dutch (who had taken it from the Portuguese in 1637). Needing guns and ammunition and other European goods, the Denkyirahene made much use of the Dutch at Elmina.

---

[4] A. Adu Boahen. *Topics in West African History* (London, 1966), p. 75.

But in order to buy these guns and other goods the Denkyirahene, like other kings trading with the sea-merchants, had to pay for them in gold and in slaves. He accordingly imposed heavy taxes, in gold and in captives, on his subject peoples. Among these subject peoples, as we have seen, were the Asante.

The Asante therefore had another strong reason for wanting to get the better of Denkyira. So long as they were separated from Elmina and other coastal markets by the power of Denkyira, they could never be sure of obtaining regular supplies of guns and other foreign goods. Yet war between Asante and Denkyira did not come at once. To begin with, Denkyirahene Bosianti tried to win Osei Tutu's friendship. Wisely preferring to negotiate rather than to embark on the risks and losses of war, he offered Osei Tutu compensation for past wrongs. He or his sub-chiefs even allowed Osei Tutu to buy guns from the Dutch at Elmina.

But Osei Tutu was not won over. Very strong in his own country, he was set on becoming independent of Denkyira. War broke out in 1699 when a new Denkyirahene, Ntim Gyakari, demanded from the Asante a larger tax than usual. By about 1701 the power of Denkyira was smashed, though at the outset of the war Asante was badly defeated. United as never before, the Asante then carried their war into the dominions of Denkyira. They brought most of these under their overlordship.

They captured much booty. But among the things they captured and brought home to Kumasi there was a piece of paper; and this piece of paper was important. For this was the rent agreement for Elmina Castle. Signed originally by the Dutch with the coastal chiefs of Komenda, this Note, as it was called, had passed into the hands of the Denkyirahene when the chiefs of Komenda had fallen under his control.[5] From this time onwards, the Dutch at Elmina were in direct touch with Asante. The power of Asante, in other words, had reached the coast. This meant that it had also reached the Europeans in their seaside castles. Asante and these Europeans now faced each other directly, as friends or as enemies. Many important developments were to result from this.

Having defeated Denkyira and made most of its chiefs his subjects, Osei Tutu turned his armies against the main ally of Denkyira. This was Akim, which had fought on Denkyira's side against Asante, and was even said to have lost as many as 30,000 soldiers in doing so. Osei Tutu marched against the Akim Kotoku, and made them pay tax to him. But the Akim armies did not give in easily. There had to be a second war against them.

This second war against Akim is said by the traditions to have been led by Osei Tutu, who was then killed by an Akim marksman while

---

[5] But the Ghana historian, K.Y. Daaku, has argued that the Denkyira never possessed the Elmina Note. He believes that the defeat of Denkyira simply caused the Dutch to go all out for good relations with Asante.

crossing the Pra river in 1731. But modern research in Ghana suggests that Osei Tutu really died in 1717; that the second war against Akim occurred in 1719; and that the name of the Asantehene who was killed on the Pra river was deliberately left out of the traditional records. These state, in any case, that the next Asantehene was Opoku Ware. He was probably enstooled, meaning enthroned, in about 1720. He reigned for 30 years. Under this strong and very successful leader, the achievements of Osei Tutu and *Okomfo* Anokye were made firm and carried further.

Expansion and reform

Opoku Ware's first big problem was a hostile alliance of the warriors of Denkyira, Sefwi and Akwapim, who all joined Akim in trying to crush the rising power of Asante. The allies failed in two harsh wars, during one of which an Akim army even took Kumasi and searched for gold in the royal graves.

But the Union of the Golden Stool did not break down. Opoku Ware defeated the allies, and also brought the neighbouring states of Tekyiman, Banda, Gyaaman and Gonja on the Black Volta river under Asante rule. In 1744–45 he sent his armies into Dagomba, far to the north, and established Asante authority there as well, thus reinforcing his control of the trade routes to the Middle Niger. By the end of his reign, 'Asante was occupying an area much larger than modern Ghana'.[6]

Opoku Ware was followed by Kwasi Obodom, who reigned from about 1750 until 1764, when the royal stool was occupied by another outstanding ruler, Osei Kwadwo. King Osei Kwadwo strengthened the empire by military victories. More important, he introduced a number of political reforms designed to bring Asante government into line with the tasks and responsibilities of imperial conquest. These reforms consisted mainly of changes in the king's bureaucracy or civil service. They are important in the history of Asante. They are also a clear example of the way in which the growth of strong kingdoms led to an extension in the personal power of kings.

Up to Osei Kwadwo's time, men were appointed to positions of political power on the basis of *ascription*: that is, by inheriting this or that position of authority because they were members of leading descent-lines (descent, in this case, through mothers and not fathers). Now the empire had grown so large that new positions of authority were needed if the central government was going to be able to control its many distant provinces, as well as its many trading and military activities.

---

[6] Boahen, *Topics in West African History*, p. 76.

As in other strong kingdoms, Osei Kwadwo began to appoint chiefs on a new basis, that of *achievement*. He made it possible for men to become leaders not only because of their birth but also because of their devotion to the Asantehene, their courage in battle, or their skill in diplomacy and trade. In this way a new group of governors or commissioners came into existence, owing their promotion to merit and not to birth.

These political reforms, designed to strengthen the king's own power by increasing the number of officials who owed their appointment to royal favour and not to family inheritance, were carried further under Kings Osei Kwame (1777–1801) and Osei Bonsu (1801–24). Humble men could now win great positions in the service of the state. One such was Agyei, a salt-carrier in his youth, who rose under Osei Bonsu to be minister for foreign affairs. Another was Opoku Ferefere, who became the same king's representative in the empire's financial affairs.

These changes were accompanied by the adoption of new methods of ensuring peace inside the empire and the security of the king's power. This was done by raising a special force of police-troops, the Ankobia. They were always commanded by appointed officials and kept available in Kumasi, the capital, so as to be ready to deal with any revolt. Once again we may see how the growth in the personal power of kings led to the establishment of long-service troops who could defend the king and the 'king's men' (the new group of officials appointed by merit) from rebellion by hereditary chiefs (those who owed their positions to their birth).

These reforms were successful, for they reflected a tough political realism. They did not prevent many revolts by conquered provinces such as Gyaaman and Banda, whose peoples continued to desire their former independence.[7] But they gave the Asante king and his government a large number of fully reliable officials in every part of the empire. With these officials the king kept in touch, week by week and sometimes day by day, through a system of foot-messengers linking Kumasi to the outlying centres. Knowing what was going on, even in distant places, the Asante king could take preventive action in good time, and for this preventive action he had plenty of military strength. What weakened the Asante, later on, and brought the eventual downfall of this big empire, was the repeated clash with British invaders from the coast.

Yet for more than 100 years the Asante dominated most of the country of modern Ghana, some of the inland country of the Ivory Coast, and parts of modern Togo. Here they succeeded in building another large and unified system of government and trade such as had existed earlier in the Western Sudan – under Ancient Ghana, Mali, Songhay, Kanem-Bornu – or under Benin and Oyo in the east.

---

[7] Gyaaman, for example, rebelled against Asante in 1752, 1764, 1799 and 1818, while Banda did the same in 1764 and 1818.

All important rulers in West Africa recognized the strength and dignity of the Asantehene. Ambassadors went back and forth between them. Muslim clerks and teachers accompanied the Dyula and Hausa traders down the routes from Kano, Kong, Jenne and other states and cities of the Sudan. They were welcomed in Kumasi and other centres of the empire, and were invited into the service of the Asantehene and his government. In the nineteenth century, if not earlier, Muslim clerks were regularly employed to keep the records of the central government, and to conduct its official correspondence with foreign governments. Trade continually expanded. There were constant exchanges of ideas and information between Asante and other African states.

Asante, Fante and Britain

Southward along the coast of modern Ghana, the power of the Asantehene was well known to the Europeans in their castles, and, through them, to the courts of European kings and the boardrooms of European and American banks and trading companies. But here in the south there were some contrary developments.

The Dutch and British in Ghana now became an important factor in African plans and policies. Denkyira, and then Asante, had made a trading partnership with the Dutch at Elmina and at one or two other forts. But the Asante and the Dutch were not the only partners in this business. There were also the Fante and the British.

Like the early chiefs of the Asante, those of the Fante, whose territory lay along the coast between Elmina and Accra, now came together in an alliance for their common good. Living near the sea, the Fante chiefs made a similar trading partnership with the British at Cape Coast and other castles. So there arose a second 'set of partners': the Fante made use of the British, just as the Asante had made use of the Dutch. This soon brought Asante and the Fante chiefs into conflict. In 1806, after years of growing hostility, war started between them. It led to the defeat of the Fante army at Abora.

Abora was not far from the ocean shore. Pressing on after their victory, the Asante armies came right down to the water's edge. Their advance guard occupied Kormantin and demanded the surrender of Fort Amsterdam, then held by their friends the Dutch, who at once gave in. The Asante generals next turned their attention to Anomabu, where the remnants of their Fante opponents had taken refuge under the walls of a British fort garrisoned by five officers and twenty men. These decided to help their Fante allies. The result was a battle for the fort itself.

227

In this way Asante and Britain came into conflict for the first time. Later on, as British imperialism steadily took shape, hostilities like these were to break out time after time. But in 1806 peace was quickly made.

The fort held out against determined Asante efforts to storm its gun-defended walls, and both sides were glad to leave it at that. The British were far too weak to consider war against Asante, while the Asantehene, for his part, wanted only that the British, like other Europeans, should recognize his authority over this part of the Gold Coast shore. He was perfectly successful in obtaining this recognition. His armies again entered the coastal country in 1811 and 1814, destroyed the military alliance of the Fante, placed the Fante chiefs under Asante governors, and subdued Akim and Akwapim further to the east. As for the Europeans on the coast, by now consisting only of the British and the Dutch, they hastened to make their peace with the Asantehene. Not long afterwards, the Dutch left the coast altogether. By about 1820 the power of Asante was supreme.

Gonja, Kong, Bonduku

The story of the northern part of the modern republic of the Ivory Coast is in many ways like that of the northern part of modern Ghana. Each had become linked with the expansion of inland trade since the expansion of the empire of Mali after about AD 1325.

We have seen how Dyula and other traders pushed their activities south towards the forest country, and how, after 1550, warrior groups from the north founded Gonja in northern Ghana. Much the same thing happened in the open country of the Ivory Coast. There is no doubt that strong trading centres existed in this country long before the founding of Gonja, notably at Kong and Bonduku. These trading centres gradually developed into self-governing towns which built themselves up into small states.

In the seventeenth century these little states became more highly organized. Gonja, established before 1600 in the northern part of modern Ghana, later expanded under a strong chief called Jakpa. Commander of a force of armoured cavalry, Jakpa came south from the region of Jenne, where he and his warriors had long been active in one way or another, and reached Gonja in about 1629.

Kong, in the Ivory Coast, remained an important state until the French colonial invasion of the last years of the nineteenth century. Bonduku, another key point on the trade route with the forest lands, had a some-what different history. It was much influenced by its powerful neighbour, the Asante empire, and was placed under an Asante governor in the middle of the eighteenth century.

Two warrior queens

The Baulé and Anyi of the southern Ivory Coast also belong to the history of the Akan. After the death of Opoku Ware in about 1750, there rose a dispute as to who should have the power. Sections of the Asante decided to leave home and seek fresh lands to the west. Some were commanded by a courageous woman called Awura Poku. She and her followers went away and settled in the country to the east of the River Bandama, which flows from the forestland of the modern republic of the Ivory Coast down to the ocean at Grand Lahou. The people whom they found in possession of the land they gradually pushed out, the Senufu to the north and the Guru to the west, although we may be sure that they also took wives and husbands from among these and other Ivory Coast peoples. These successive migrations from the Akan homeland formed the Baulé and Anyi during the eighteenth century.

Queen Poku died in about 1760 and was buried in her capital town of Warebo, which is near Bouaké. Her niece, Akwa Boni, followed her as queen of this Akan group, who now called themselves the Baulé. Under Akwa Boni, the Baulé took over the gold-bearing lands to the west of the Bandama region. Queen Akwa Boni died in about 1790. After that the unity of the Baulé was lost, because of quarrels between the heads of important families, and they never succeeded in creating the same close unity as their Akan relatives in the empire of Asante. Yet they continued to rule much of the southern Ivory Coast country until French colonial invasion at the end of the nineteenth century.

After Many Disasters

Overleaf

Drawing made in about 1750 of an old trading castle on the west coast. (Fotomas Index)

After Many Disasters

A history book, unlike history itself, has to have a conclusion, and in this case our conclusion comes at the end of the nineteenth century, when, at Berlin in 1885, half a dozen powerful European nations, having pushed aside quarrels among themselves, eventually decided to share out Africa without going to war against each other – but not, of course, without going to war against Africans. This 'share-out' process was indeed long and far from peaceful, but the European powers concerned were able to avoid going to war against one another until the inter-European massacres of the Great War, as it became known, which began in 1914. Meanwhile Africa was being divided up into many 'colonies', meaning territories ruled directly and dictatorially by European governments, along frontiers fixed between the European powers.

Thus began what history has called the colonial period, which endured for many decades through the end of the nineteenth century and much of the twentieth. A great and deep disaster for the peoples of Africa, the colonial period deprived them not only of their political freedom and right to think for themselves, thus bringing to a stop the onward flow of Africa's own history, but also, in large measure, undermining their sense of confidence and self-respect.

This colonial period of direct, non-African rule was thus a process of imperialist dispossession. It was a prolonged process often muddled and always incomplete, as may be seen in our chapter about the Union of the Golden Stool. Ashanti lost its independence during the colonial period, but did not lose its sense of existence. Like other old political realities, it went into eclipse but began to re-emerge when, late in the twentieth century, the colonial period came to an end.

All this was costly in terms of life and well-being. The Africans lost their independence. But they did not lose it easily. In this ragged process of imperialist invasion and dispossession, the European powers had to fight hard for the territories they carved from Africa and enclosed in their overseas empires.

Much about these colonial invasions belonged to an age that is already far away. As I have written elsewhere, 'Of the initial fleet of some 600 vessels' which carried the French invasion force across the Mediterranean Sea in 1830,

> a force of some 38,000 men and 4,000 horses with all their stores and arms, only six small ships were under steam; all the rest relied on sail. Its commanders were among the best that France could produce; yet most of them were graduates of military academies presided over by the Emperor Napoleon, and one or two of them had served in the campaigns of Napoleon which had ended in 1815.[1]

Like other wars in the imperialist dispossession of Africa, this one was painful for the invaders as well as for the invaded.

When the colonial period at last was over, and the Europeans had withdrawn, African peoples had to decide how best to build their new governments and settle their affairs. For the most part, under a variety of pressures and for a range of different reasons, they turned their backs on their own long history of pre-colonial self-government. They decided to modernize their countries on European lines. The past successes of pre-colonial independence, such as the development of the Union of the Golden Stool and other such developments, had been consigned to what the European rulers, in the thinking of the colonial period, had condemned as a useless and barbaric time that could have no value for the modern world.

There were reasons for agreeing with this. Africa needed to modernize itself in line with all the technical and scientific advances of the industrialized world. But when in due course it also became obvious, by the 1990s, if not before, that the work of 'modernizing Africa' on European lines was producing neither health nor wealth but repeated violence and confusion, there were African thinkers who began to remember what their grandfathers and great-grandfathers had said at the beginning of the colonial period.

Two modernizing thinkers

One of the foremost of these thinkers was a Gold Coast (Ghana) leader called Joseph Ephraim Casely Hayford (1866–1930). He argued in his books and other writings that the colonial powers – Britain in the case of the

---

[1] B. Davidson, *The People's Cause* (1981).

Gold Coast – had failed to introduce the effective and equitable government that modern times demanded.

This failure, Casely Hayford went on to say, was not primarily Africa's responsibility. It derived, chiefly, from the European colonial refusal to understand and adapt 'Africa's ancient and honourable traditions and institutions of statecraft'. Britain, as the colonial power in question, 'had tended to upset local institutions' evolved through Africa's indigenous history; and, instead of attempting to rebuild and modernize these old institutions, 'the British had abetted their disintegration by assuming they were dealing with a savage people'.[2]

Another of the old Gold Coast political thinkers who maintained the same truths as Casely Hayford was John Mensah Sarbah (1864–1910). Like Casely Hayford, Mensah Sarbah had carefully watched the distant but successful efforts of the Japanese to modernize their system of government, during and after the 1860s, in order to meet the threat to Japan of Western invasion. He compared these Japanese reforming efforts with ideas then at work in the Gold Coast as well, noting that the Japanese were successful but that the new colonialism, in Africa, 'ruthlessly crushed' the reforming plans of the Africans. This ruthless crushing was psychological as much as physical: Africans started to doubt whether they could modernize themselves.

In the many troubles of the 1990s, after the formal end of the colonial period, new African thinkers have looked back on their forebears and perceived the same truths. Foremost among these is a distinguished Nigerian, Professor Adebayo Adedeji. He has recalled and reapplied to current African problems the arguments of Casely Hayford and his friends many years ago. 'So great and pervasive has been the down-thrusting of colonial rule', Adedeji maintained to a widening audience in 1992, 'that many Africans and most non-Africans have persistently denigrated the pre-colonial historical achievements of the continent: its arts, customs, beliefs, system of government and art of governance'. The consequence of this, Adedeji continued, 'has been that when the opportunity came to cast aside the yoke of colonialism, no effort was made to reassert Africa's self-determination by replacing the foreign institutions, and systems of government, with rejuvenated and modernised indigenous African systems' such as could master the problems of the modern world.[3]

This was a verdict that Adedeji and his colleagues drew from the study of West African history: only Africa's solutions, it was repeatedly said, would be able to get the better of Africa's problems.

---

[2] I have drawn here on Professor R.W. July's statement of the case, still in many ways the best, in his *Origins of Modern African Thought* (1968), p. 438.
[3] Adebayo Adedeji, writing in the *Bulletin* of the African Centre for Development and Strategic Studies, Ijebu-Ode, Nigeria, 1992.

Human resources, African responses

But what have been these African solutions, and how should they be applied in Africa today? These two questions have increasingly dominated all serious African (and some non-African) debate since the great social crisis in West African public life – indeed, of public life in all regions of the continent during the past years – has brought widening poverty and confusion at least since the 1970s. And, following this debate especially since about 1985, there has been a steady piling-up of evidence bearing on these questions among dedicated African thinkers and their colleagues outside Africa.[4]

The consensus of these expert inquiries and discussions has been repeatedly supported by the manifest outcome of the miseries which have derived from the post-colonial structures of centralized government. The essential key to successful reconstruction in Africa today, these thinkers have shown, has to depend on Africa's repossession of Africa's own history after all the decades of foreign rule: meaning, above all, the modernization and renewal of Africa's indigenous traditions of peaceful and productive self-development. And this, in turn, has to depend on the application of democratic forms of social and economic participation wherever people have become free to rule themselves in community.

The freedoms for self-government won by the nationalists of half a century ago were supposed and intended to introduce the ethos and the attitudes of a genuine democracy. But what happened in practice, as the record of this half-century shows, was that the colonial dictatorships were followed not by new forms of African democracy but by new forms of African dictatorship: by what soon became stigmatized as a 'neo-colonialism' in which real governing power remained in non-African hands. The brave flags of freedom said one thing; reality said quite another.

Unleashed by the anarchic influences of greed and crime, military or quasi-military autocracies installed by this or that 'strong man' and his clients have bitten deep into Africa's customs and capacities for honest and effective self-government. As a Nigerian political scientist, Professor Dele Olowu, described this degradation in an analysis of 1989, 'Institutions that were established to promote participation, such as parliaments, political parties, local governments and independent print media, have been legislated out of existence, or transformed into institutions which are clearly dominated by their executives.'[5]

---

[4] See a copious bibliography, and especially Mamadou Dia, *Africa's Management in the 1990s and Beyond* (World Bank, Washington, 1995).
[5] Olowu, writing in the *Newsletter* of the African Association of Political Science, Lagos, April 1989.

236

Meanwhile the rigidly centralist, and therefore bureaucratic and inherently dictatorial, policy and practice of the post-colonial state continued to stand unyieldingly by its denial that anything constructive could be learned from the long and rich record of Africa's own history. But with the deepening social and political crisis of the 1980s and after there came a reaction against this blind approach to the continent's experience. What was now argued was that pre-colonial history, with all its failures and upsets, still contained an indispensable source of inspiration and civility, as well as a power of self-correction and moral strength; and that these remain capable of great acts of creative restitution. To that end, independent and therefore objective African scholars, with no few colleagues outside Africa, have called for African-sponsored and African-applied programmes of reform and new initiative.[6]

As the old millennium moves to its final years, it can be seen that the creative powers of Africa's social history are gradually reasserting their scope and capacity for democratic renewal. Despite the destitutions of the slave trade and its corresponding racism over decades and even centuries, and then the disastrous century-long dispossessions of the colonial period, Africa and its peoples have begun to reclaim their birthright.

---

[6] Again, a copious bibliography is available. See, for example, the proposals put forward by the United Nations Economic Commission for Africa in 1989, and since then supported by a wide range of specialist organizations and individuals, published as *Transformation and Recovery*. For a penetratingly clear review of these and other materials and proposals, see a brilliantly inclusive survey and analysis by the British economist Michael Barratt Brown, *Africa's Choices* (Penguin Books, London and Baltimore, 1995, and Westview Press, Boulder, Colo., 1996).

Appendix: Table of
Comparative Dates

BC	West Africa			Elsewhere
	WESTERN REGION	CENTRAL REGION	EASTERN REGION	
4000	The Old Stone Age family of languages used in West Africa begins to split up into the 400 or more different languages which are now spoken there			Early farming in Egypt. New Stone Age comes to an end with spreading use of copper for many purposes
3500	New Stone Age farming and cattle raising in the Sahara, at this time green and fertile. Old Stone Age (without farming) continues in the forest lands			Early states in Egypt
3200	The Sahara and neighbouring lands are still green and fertile			Unification of two states of Upper and Lower Egypt. Beginning of the civilization of Pharaonic Egypt
2500	Sahara begins gradually to dry up			Building of the pyramids
2000	Gradual movement of farming peoples out of the Sahara, where water is now growing scarce			Great period of Egyptian history

BC	West Africa			Elsewhere
	WESTERN REGION	CENTRAL REGION	EASTERN REGION	
1800–1700				Asians, called Hyksos, invade Egypt. They introduce use of horses and chariots.
1575				New Egyptian empire under Pharaohs of 18th dynasty.
1000	Carts and chariots drawn by donkeys or horses begin to be used for crossing the Sahara between North and West Africa			Rise of Berber civilization in North Africa
814				Traditional date of foundation of Carthage by Phoenicians in Tunisia
800				Rise of civilization of Kush on Middle Nile. Soon Kush invades Egypt and holds most of it for a century.
500	Farming begins to develop in the forest lands			
300	Iron-working begins to appear in West Africa south of the Sahara. The Nok Culture. Trade continues between North and West Africa across the Sahara			Greek kings (the Ptolemies) in Egypt
				Wars between Rome and Carthage. Rome wins and destroys Carthage

	West Africa			Elsewhere
BC	WESTERN REGION	CENTRAL REGION	EASTERN REGION	
105	More African peoples learn how to make iron			Romans defeat King Jugurtha of the Berber kingdom of Numidia. Much of Tunisia and Algeria are brought within the new Roman empire
100	Trans-Saharan trade now using increasing numbers of camels instead of horses and donkeys			Iron-working begins to appear in central South Africa
AD 300	Continued spread of iron-working through West Africa			Many fine and prosperous cities flourish in Roman North Africa
550				Emergence of Christian kingdoms in Nubia on Middle Nile
622				The Prophet Muhammad enters Medina. The first year of Islam.
750	Ancient Ghana grows important	Origins of Gao	Sao culture (L. Chad)	Muslim conquests in North Africa and Spain far advanced
800	Ghana commands the international trade in gold and salt. Becomes a powerful empire	Islam begins to appear in West Africa through Muslim Berber traders from the Sahara	Traditional date for founding of early state of Kanem (about 850)	Egypt becomes a great centre of Muslim civilization

	West Africa			Elsewhere
AD	WESTERN REGION	CENTRAL REGION	EASTERN REGION	
1000	Ghana at height of its power	King of Gao accepts Islam (about 1010)	Kanem expands. Founding of early Hausa and Yoruba states	Fatimid caliphate in Egypt (969–1171)
1054	Almoravid Berbers capture Audaghost from Ghana	Early Songhay state of Gao. Its rulers are the Dia line of kings.		Almoravids set up new Muslim states in Morocco and Spain (1061–1147)
1076	Ghana begins to collapse under Almoravid attacks.			Arts and early sciences flourish in Muslim Spain and North Africa
1086			King of Kanem (Hume) accepts Islam	
1200	Time of confusion leads to end of Ancient Ghana		Early state of Benin under Ogiso rulers	Almohads set up new Muslim state in North Africa and Spain (1147–1289)
1230	Sundiata becomes king of small Mandinka state of Kangaba: defeats his enemy Sumanguru: founds early state of Mali, begins to conquer neighbouring lands			Ayyubids rule Egypt (1171–1250) Fall of Christian kingdoms in Nubia
1255	*Mansa* Uli (*d.* 1270) continues to hold empire of Mali	Growing commercial power of Gao	Rise of first Kanem-Bornu empire to east and west of Lake Chad	Mamluk soldier-kings rule Egypt (1250–1517)

AD	West Africa			Elsewhere
	WESTERN REGION	CENTRAL REGION	EASTERN REGION	
1300	Wolof states founded in Senegal	Early states in forest country	Yoruba states under spiritual leadership of Ife	Christians reconquer most of Spain. There remains only the small Muslim kingdom of Granada (1232–1492)
1312	*Mansa* Musa comes to throne of Mali. Dies in 1337 after expanding Mali far across both western and central regions of West Africa. Takes Gao into Mali empire in 1325			
1335	Mali continues at height of its power	At Gao, *Dia* line of kings followed by first of a new line, called the *Sunni* kings		English and French fight feudal wars against each other
1375	Mali begins to decline	*Sunni* Suleiman-Mar of Gao wins back independence from Mali. Gao begins to grow in power	Bulala dominate Kanem east of Lake Chad. Kanem rulers temporarily much weakened	First detailed map of West Africa is drawn by Cresques of Majorca
1400		Songhay of Gao raid Niani, capital of Mali. Bono-Manso and Mossi states in existence	Hausa and Yoruba states grow stronger and wealthier. Nupe and Jukun founded at this time	Kilwa on East African coast (Tanzania) becomes rich and powerful; dominates gold trade with Arabia and Far East

AD	West Africa			Elsewhere
	WESTERN REGION	**CENTRAL REGION**	**EASTERN REGION**	
1415		Timbuktu and Jenne are centres of Muslim scholarship		Portuguese, raiding overseas for first time, capture Ceuta, a port in north-western Morocco
1434	Portuguese begin sailing down Atlantic coast of West Africa. They are soon followed by other Europeans is small numbers.		Benin is now a big empire. Islam reaches Zaria (1456)	Egypt ruled by strong Mamluk Sultan Baybars (1422–37)
1464	Mali continues to decline	*Sunni* Ali comes to throne of Gao and begins to build the Songhay empire	Muhammad Rumfa of Kano (1465–99)	Empire of the Monomotapa (Zimbabwe)
1472		Songhay capture Jenne (1473)	Portuguese reach Bight of Benin. Christian missionaries soon follow them	Portuguese and Spanish attacks on Morocco, which is much weakened by them
1482	Much European trading on the coast of Senegambia	Portuguese build Elmina Castle on Gold Coast		Portuguese make contact with Bakongo kingdom near mouth of River Congo (1483)
1492		*Sunni* Ali dies		Columbus reaches Caribbean

AD	West Africa			Elsewhere
	WESTERN REGION	CENTRAL REGION	EASTERN REGION	
1493		*Askia* Muhammad becomes ruler of Songhay	Al-Maghili of Tuat at Kano and Katsina: writes *The Duties of Kings* for King Muhammad Rumfa of Kano	First Tudor king of England, Henry VII (1485–1509)
1507		Big expansion of trade between interior and coastline. Jenne becomes very prosperous	*Mai* Idris Katarkamabi becomes ruler of Bornu. Wins battle of Garni-Kiyala and regains control of Kanem	Spanish conquests in Caribbean and Central America
1517		Mahmud Kati of Timbuktu starts writing *Tarikh al-Fattash* at this time	Kebbi gains independence from Songhay empire. Attacks Gobir and Katsina	Ottoman Turks conquer Egypt and move west along the coast of North Africa
1528		*Askia* Muhammad followed by *Askia* Musa in Songhay		
1534	Mali asks help from Portugal			
1550	Trading partnerships between European sea-merchants and African coastal states become established firmly in this period	The state of Gonja founded by Mandinka warriors at this time		Religious wars in Germany cause terrible destruction
1553	In Senegal, Cayor revolts against Jolof (1556), becomes independent	*Askia* Dawud rules Songhay empire (1549–82)	English visit Benin for first time	English fight Spanish at sea in these years

AD	West Africa WESTERN REGION	CENTRAL REGION	EASTERN REGION	Elsewhere
1559	Tenguella Koli establishes new line of kings in Takrur (Futa Toro). They were called the Denianke	Gold trade expands		Portuguese invasion of kingdom of Ndongo (Angola) in wars which last many years
1575			Hausa states revolt against Songhay	Portuguese invasion of Morocco smashed by Mulay the Victorious, who becomes king (1578)
1580		Songhay and Morocco clash at Taghaza	*Mai* Idris Alooma becomes ruler of Kanem-Bornu and establishes new empire by the time of his death in 1617	Spanish Armada fails to invade England (1588)
1591	Mali empire in last stages of decay	Songhay empire begins to collapse under Moroccan invasion (battle of Tondibi, 1591)		Judar leads a Moroccan army across the Sahara and defeats Songhay
		Ruin of Songhay empire as Moroccans occupy the cities and local peoples rebel against Songhay lords		Peoples of western Angola defend themselves against Portuguese invasion; are not defeated until middle of 17th century

	West Africa			Elsewhere
AD	WESTERN REGION	CENTRAL REGION	EASTERN REGION	
1600	Wolof states in Senegal active in trade with sea-merchants	Gonja fights Dagomba. Timbuktu ruled by Moroccan pashas	Kanem-Bornu under Idris Alooma is most powerful state in this region	Dutch become strongest European sea-power. European powers now form their early chartered companies for trading with Africa and other distant countries
1650	Wolof states compete for trade with sea-merchants; many wars between them	Early Bambara state of Segu. Rise of Denkyira. Rise of Fon state in Dahomey under King Wegbaja, who reigns until 1685	Rise of Oyo. Oyo empire extends over most Yoruba states and Dahomey. Rise of new city-states in Niger Delta	Dutch make small settlement at Cape of Good Hope (1652): origins of South Africa. British fight the Dutch for sea supremacy (1653–54 and 1665–67). British fight the Spanish and the French for supremacy at sea (1655 onwards).
1659	French found St Louis in Senegal			
1661	English rebuild Fort James on Gambia river	Asante states begin to combine		Reign of Louis XIV of Fance
1677– 1681		Expansion of Akwamu under Ansa Sasraku	Kanem-Bornu enters period of confusion which leads to its gradual decline	
1705		Asante a strong power under Osei Tutu	Tuareg and Jukun raid North Nigeria (1670–1703)	War of Spanish Succession (1702–13)

AD	West Africa WESTERN REGION	CENTRAL REGION	EASTERN REGION	Elsewhere
1713	Europeans expand trade with Wolof and Takrur	Founding of Bambara state of Segu under Mamari Kulibali (1712–55)		With Treaty of Utrecht (1713) between Britain and France, British become the biggest buyers and carriers of slaves from Africa.
1725	Foundation of imamate of Futa Jallon	Fon take control of city-states on Dahomey coast. End of Akwamu empire (1730)		Europeans in West Indies now making tremendous profits out of sugar grown by African slaves
1750	Spread of Muslim revival across Western Sudan	Asante predominates in central Guinea. Emergence of Baulé and Anyi states in Ivory Coast	Muhammad Teirab is Sultan of Darfur (1752–87)	Britain enters her *industrial revolution* with invention of important machines: 1733 Kay invents mechanical weaving shuttle; 1738 Paul invents mechanical spinning roller; 1768 Hargreaves develops the 'spinning jenny', by which one worker can operate many spindles together; 1776 Watt invents his mechanical pump; 1803 Trevithick builds a steam locomotive to run on iron rails
1753		Foundation of Bambara state of Kaarta	Niger Delta states at height of their trading expansion	
1765	Formation of British colony of Senegambia (ended in 1783)			

| AD | West Africa | | | Elsewhere |
	WESTERN REGION	CENTRAL REGION	EASTERN REGION	
1775	Foundation of imamate of Futa Toro: end of Denianke line of rulers (1776)	Asante empire becomes very powerful	Decline of Benin. Oyo still powerful	Britain's North American colonies fight for their independence. They win
1789				French Revolution
1791	Foundation of Freetown			Toussaint declares independence of Haiti
1796		Mungo Park reaches Segu		
1798				French under Napoleon invade Egypt
1804	Church Missionary Society in Sierra Leone. Methodists and others soon follow		Fulani conquest of Hausa kingdoms (1804–11)	British and French at war: European coalition against the French emperor, Napoleon, who is finally defeated in 1815
1806	Dakar independent under Diop family (1810). Later (1837) French take Dakar	Britain clashes with Asante, but peace is at once restored. Asante continues to dominate the greater part of W. Africa and neighbouring grassland countries	*Mai* Ahmad reigns in Kanem-Bornu (1793–1810). Collapse of Oyo empire	Rise of Zulu empire in Natal (South Africa): King Shaka begins reign in 1816
1830	French open colonial invasion of Algeria			
	Other European colonial invasions begin and continue after 1860s			

Index